"…all that I could possibly need into one book,
a wonderful, stress-reduccing resource…"
Amie McKinney, Bride

"The most comprehensive wedding resource in Vermont."
Vermont Life Explorer

"It's a bride's bible to preparing and organizing their dream wedding!"
Danielle George, Bride

"This is the 'must have' for anyone looking to plan a successful wedding."
Ian J. Bradley, Sales & Catering Professional

"This book is the leader in wedding publications. It is far more comprehensive
than others—filled with great information…!"
Riki Bowen, Wedding Wizard

"Great place to organize your happy event.
The Ultimate Checklist was my guide and kept me on schedule."
Janet Brown, Bride

"…great publication…the resource book just continues to get better!"
R. Oosman, Bates Mansion at Brook Farm

"Vermont's premier wedding planner…"
Vermont Magazine

"It was so great to have everything I need at my fingertips.
Elizabeth Dwinell

"All in one book, it's great!"
Donna Goodman

"…the book covered everything, even down to the weather!"
Rachel, Bride

Photo courtesy of Portrait Gallery

2010 EDITION

The Book for All Brides
Vermont Wedding Resource Guide

Your Complete Planner and Detailed Guide
to Vermont's Finest Wedding & Event
Related Businesses and Services

WEDDING
Resource Publishing

www.theBookforAllBrides.com

THE BOOK FOR ALL BRIDES
THE VERMONT WEDDING RESOURCE GUIDE

Cover Design and Layout by Michel Newkirk

Front and Back Cover
Location
Echo Lake Inn
Photography by
Saint Phalle Photography

The Book for All Brides
The Vermont Wedding Resource Guide.

ISBN 978-0-9819992-3-4

ADVERTISING
If you are interested in your company being represented in this book, please contact us at 802-749-4843, info@vermontweddingbook.com or the address above.

Vermont Map

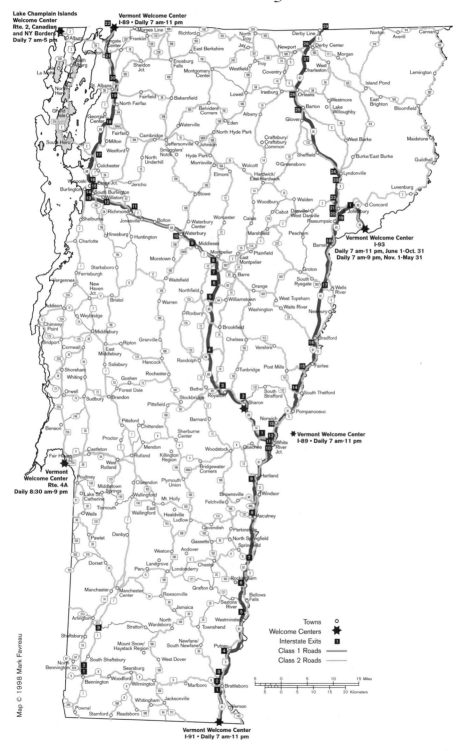

Lake Champlain Islands
Welcome Center
Rte. 2, Canadian
and NY Borders
Daily 7 am-5 pm

Vermont Welcome Center
I-89 • Daily 7 am-11 pm

Vermont Welcome Center
I-93
Daily 7 am-11 pm, June 1-Oct. 31
Daily 7 am-9 pm, Nov. 1-May 31

Vermont Welcome Center
I-89 • Daily 7 am-11 pm

Vermont
Welcome Center
Rte. 4A
Daily 8:30 am-9 pm

Vermont Welcome Center
I-91 • Daily 7 am-11 pm

Towns   ○
Welcome Centers   ★
Interstate Exits   ▮
Class 1 Roads   ▬▬▬
Class 2 Roads   ───

5   0   5   10   15 Miles

5   0   5   10   15   20 Kilometers

Map © 1998 Mark Favreau

Acknowledgements

Many thanks to Michel Newkirk, Robin Lindsay and Tammy Allard, without their help this book would not have been possible. Their many hours of hard work, patience and understanding are greatly appreciated. It is a pleasure to work with such good people.

Special thanks to my family for always being there to listen, especially Kevin for his love, guidance and never ending support.

To Our Advertisers

Thank you to all the professionals who participate in our book. It is their services that make Vermont a top destination wedding location, and the *Vermont Wedding Resource Guide* a great success! Year after year their creativeness, thoughtfulness, hard work and attention to detail ensure your wedding day will be unforgettable and just as you have always dreamed!

How to Use this Book

Whether you are the bride, the groom, the mother or the wedding coordinator, this book will help you follow time-honored traditions. The book will help you to incorporate your own personal touch into the wedding, save you time, money, misunderstandings and help minimize unnecessary frustrations.

The layout of this book allows you to use it as your wedding workbook and appointments calendar. The worksheets and blank pages will help you organize and record every detail of your wedding. Keep it with you at all times, jotting down ideas and referring to it as questions come up.

Choosing wedding services is important, that is why our Guide gives you full-page detailed information on hundreds of services. Remember, most service providers in the book regularly travel to wedding site locations throughout the state, so contact a variety of them to choose the one that is just right for you.

Many service providers now have online packages or will send you their wedding package by mail. It is always best to have a few to compare and then choose the one that fits you best.

This book is also a complete planner that will walk you through each stage of your wedding. Our checklists have received rave reviews from numerous couples and the Ultimate Checklist will keep you on track!

We wish you the best in planning your big day!

From the Publisher

Welcome to the Book for All Brides – Vermont Wedding Resource Guide, where our goal is to help you plan your dream wedding as effortlessly as possible and to introduce you to all of the wonderful wedding professionals in Vermont. If you are like most brides, this is the first major event in your life that involves the planning and coordination of so many different details and decisions. Whether you are a bride with the vision and budget for a formal, elegant celebration, an environmentally conscious "green" bride or a bride looking for a casual, low-key celebration with close family and friends, we hope that you find our book is right for you. "A friend in print," designed to answer all your questions, even before you know what questions to ask.

Planning a wedding or event can be very stressful. We hope you find the resources and professionals in the following pages helpful in minimizing your stress. Use the Ultimate Checklist and Budget Worksheets in the back of this book to help you put the whole process into perspective. Each chapter contains helpful checklists to ensure that you cover all of the details, to help you organize your thoughts, fulfill your dreams and keep you within your budget, however big or small that may be.

As you flip through our book, we want you to know that there are many talented and creative professionals behind every page. Take some time to explore their pages here and then get to know them better through their websites, and by contacting them directly. You will find that these great people have a willingness to share their knowledge, experiences and passion for what they do – bringing great visions to life.

We hope this book helps you to enjoy the planning of your wedding as much as your wedding day itself. We wish you all the best and many years of future happiness.

⁓ Susan Scacchi

Other Uses for this Book

The popularity of the **Vermont Wedding Resource Guide** and the responses we received from past surveys in the book indicated that many people use the guide for purposes other than weddings. Whether you find yourself planning a special party, Vermont vacation, fundraiser or family gathering there is no doubt this guide will be helpful to you.

Birthday, Holiday or Company Parties

Will you need a cake, a party site, musicians, or a caterer? Find them in their appropriate sections. The guide will tell how far in advance you will need to reserve a site.

Vermont Vacations

The guide highlights many romantic hideaways throughout the state's Green Mountains and other nice-to-know tidbits while touring the state.

Fundraising

If it is a black tie event, you can use practically the entire book—just cross out bride and groom! The budget planning section is helpful for all fund raising events that use similar services.

Family Gatherings

50th wedding anniversaries, reunions… Where is everyone going to stay? Who's picking up Great Aunt Milly?

Just Remember

As you flip through the guide, recognize that the services provided are there to help you with their specialty—a specialty with many uses other than weddings.

Best of Luck with all of your other events!

Contents

Photo courtesy of Portrait Gallery

Something Blue

Take a look in the back of the book at our

Bride's Blue Pages

A directory of wedding professionals
throughout Vermont.

Travel is more than just A to B.
Travel should launch life's greatest journey.

Whether it's the rehearsal dinner, wedding ceremony,
reception, honeymoon suite or brunch,
let the Hilton Burlington make your special day
the perfect beginning to your happily ever after.

60 Battery Street, Burlington, Vermont 05401
1-802-658-6500   burlington.hilton.com

Hilton
Burlington

Travel should take you places®

A CHARMING RUSTIC LOCATION FOR WEDDINGS & SPECIAL EVENTS.

We offer the finest cuisine, a charming setting for receptions and ceremonies, the perfect place to create the memory of a lifetime.

Our chef, Roland Gaujac, a graduate of the Grenoble Hotelry School in France, would be delighted to have you as our guest and will provide the perfect menu for your wedding celebration.

Excellently situated, the Old Lantern is only 15 miles from Burlington and only 20 miles from Middlebury. We can accommodate both small and large parties, up to 300 guests. Please visit us at www.oldlantern.com or call 802.425.2120 for more information.

The Old Lantern

3260 Greenbush Road, Charlotte, VT 05445

To the Story of the Equinox
A NEW CHAPTER IS ADDED.

© Fisher Photography

Nestled amongst the tranquil backdrop of Manchester Village, Vermont, the Equinox has stood as a landmark of warm and gracious hospitality for well over 200 years. Today it stands more appealing than ever as a wedding destination, thanks to a recent $20 million restoration. A stunning new great room, sophisticated, updated rooms and suites, two new restaurants and an eclectic array of activities including our award-winning spa all serve to make your guests as welcomed as ever. The selection of wedding venues is practically limitless, accommodating parties of most every size. From stately ballrooms to outdoor pavilions to intimate garden weddings, if you can imagine your dream day, we can create it.

RESERVATIONS 800.362.4740 | EQUINOXRESORT.COM

EQUINOX

A LUXURY COLLECTION
GOLF RESORT & SPA

Vermont

Celebrate your wedding at a beautiful Vermont country inn
that is exclusively yours for the weekend.

Personalized service with our in-house wedding coordinator

Quintessential Vermont country setting

Fully custom-designed weddings up to 150

Picturesque venues for rehearsal dinner, ceremony & reception

30 individually appointed rooms, including six suites,
offering you & your guests the finest accommodations

Dedicated to serving the freshest local food possible

You will be amazed at how easy we can make it...
and how much you will enjoy your special day.

The Old Tavern
AT GRAFTON, VERMONT

800-843-1801   OldTavern.com
92 Main Street, Grafton, VT 05146

Avigliano

A truly unique and unforgettable setting for your wedding.

Traditional, casual or black tie…we will be there to surround your guests with our family hospitality…a mix of elegance and warm familiarity.

Avigliano
at Honora
Winery & Vineyard

www.honorawinery.com

Honora Winery & Vineyard
1950 Collins Rd, West Halifax, VT 05358
(802) 368-2930

YOUR FIRST STOP FOR YOUR NEXT EVENT.

Weddings, Tents & Events is dedicated to providing customized quality service that encompasses the needs of each client. With over twenty years in the rental business we make the perfect wedding look easy. From the engagement party to the wedding day, we help you along the way.

Plan a visit to our showroom, where one of our event coordinators will happily assist you throughout your planning process. In addition we specialize in providing all your rental needs including – crystal, china, linens, as well as tables, chairs, lighting, and more!

WEDDINGS, TENTS & EVENTS
155 CARROLL ROAD
WAITSFIELD, VT 05673
TOLL FREE: 888.898.3839   VERMONT: 802.496.3545
WWW.WEDDINGSTENTSEVENTS.COM

Personal wedding planning services & World class chef driven menu's at Spruce Camp.

Stowe
MOUNTAIN RESORT

781 Mountain Rd. Stowe VT 802.253.3666 Stowe.com

OKEMO VALLEY

Your place in Vermont

SEE ALL THAT WE HAVE TO OFFER YOU.

Hawk Inn & Mountain Resort

Echo Lake Inn

Castle Hill Resort & Spa

...FOR THE PERFECT WEDDING!

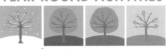
Your place for...

something old

something new

Okemo Valley provides a choice of wedding venues, unique shopping experiences for your guests, outdoor adventures for the explorers in your group, and exceptional dining.

Okemo Valley - Your Place in Vermont for a Dream Wedding!

yourplaceinvermont.com   **toll free: 1-866-216-8722**

Photo: Saint Phalle Photography

Photo: Ellen O'Connor Photography

rrie Fisher Photography

Photo: Michael Riddell Photography

Mountain Top Inn

Photo: Curran Photography

amily, Friends &

Breathtaking Natural Beauty....

THE
**MOUNTAIN TOP
INN & RESORT**

New England
Inns & Resorts
Association
SINCE 1907

Members of Vermont
Wedding Association

Just a short drive from Killington.

Photo: Bertram Studios

Photo courtesy of Barrie Fisher Photographers

Plan your wedding, guest accommodations, and activities with these FREE resources:

~Vermont Country Inns and B&Bs Brochure
~Vermont Vacation Guide (Summer/Fall Edition)
~Vermont Winter Vacation Guide
~Official Vermont Road Map & Guide to VT Attractio
~Vermont Ski Resort Map & Maple Syrup Guide

Request one, or a hundred - Free Shipping!
Contact the Vermont Chamber of Commerce:
802-223-3443 or info@vtchamber.com

www.vtchamber.com

Vermont Hospitality Council
A Division of the Vermont Chamber of Commerce

www.VisitVT.com

BLOOD'S
CATERING &
PARTY RENTALS INC

"When you want your event done to Perfection"

www.bloodscatering.com • 802.295.5393
1147 Hartford Avenue • White River Jct., VT 05001
Michael Blood – 802.295.5393 ext.103 – mike@bloodsseafood.com

*Serving Vermont and New Hampshire for over 60 years.
Providing catering and party rental services for your wedding.*

CATERING – *Including but not limited to:*

◆ Consultation with our professional staff about all your catering needs for the rehearsal dinner, wedding reception and Sunday brunch.

◆ A *free* consultation at your home or reception site for measuring and layout is available.

◆ Off-premise catering under our beautiful white wedding or party tents

◆ Rehearsal Dinners, Elegant Wedding Buffets, Plated Dinners or Stations

◆ Fully Licensed Alcohol Catering Services

◆ Specialty Hors d'oeuvre Parties, Intimate Dinners, Luncheons, Dinner Parties, Clambakes, and Barbecues – featuring over 100 menu selections

RENTALS

◆ Beautiful White Wedding Tents with cathedral "French Window" Side-walls

◆ Chairs – Garden, Elegant White Wooden Padded Chairs, Plastic Folding Chairs in White and Brown

◆ Tables – Round and Banquet in Cocktail and Dining Heights

◆ Parquet Dance Floors, Staging, Tent Flooring

◆ Elegant Linens with Complete China, Flatware and Glassware

◆ Complete Event Generator Power Services

◆ Specialty Lighting for Evening Receptions

◆ Portable Tent Heaters, Grills and Ovens

◆ Catering Service Equipment

*Blood's offers computer assisted drawings for you to see
your wedding layout before the day of the event.*

*Call the event planning experts at Blood's today to schedule
your consultation and watch your dreams become a reality.*

*Don't trust your special day to just any company...
Trust the experts at Blood's.*

**Visit our website at www.bloodscatering.com to view our selections
or visit our showroom – the largest of its kind in the Upper Valley.**

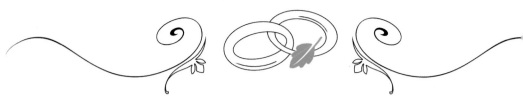

elegantly
green wedding
s h o w c a s e

Date: *February 14, 2010*

Time: *1-5 pm*

Place: *Hyatt Harborside*

Boston, Ma

Exclusive eco-conscious wedding showcase for New England engaged couples.
This is no Bridal Expo. How are we differer

'Green' gift bags for the 1st 100 registered guests.

Special offers and giveaways from vendors.

Purchase items from designated exhibitors.

Informal modeling show instead of a runway show.

Educational Seminars- learn how to green your wedding.

Site tours with the Hyatt. Hotel staff will be available to show you around the property.

Register to win a sweetheart getaway at the Hyatt Harborside.
Stay at the Hyatt the night before you fly out for your honeymoon or for a romantic geta

- One night deluxe harborview accommodations in one of our newly redecorated guest rooms
- Welcome amenity to include couple's choice of either wine & cheese,
  or champagne &chocolate dipped strawberries
- Complimentary breakfast for two in Harborside Grill
- Complimentary Valet Parking for one vehicle
- Complimentary shuttle service to and from the airline terminal

* You must be registered for the event and be present to win. See website for more details.

Admission is $15 advance or $25 at the door.

www.elegantlygreenweddingshowcase.com

*The Ideal location
to Celebrate Your
Weekend Wedding
in Vermont!*

*It's Everything
You've Always
Wished For...*

...And Mor

Echo Lake Inn

*Historic Victorian Inn on Scenic Route 100
5 miles from Ludlow*

800.356.6844   *www.echolakeinn.com*   802.228.8602

Professional DJs Specializing in Elegant, Superbly Orchestrated Weddings since 1995.

LOVE
BEGINS IN
VERMONT

Exchange vows in a field of wild flowers. Travel down a country lane in a horse-drawn carriage. Dance by candlelight in a 19th century barn. Vermont offers the ideal wedding destination to start your next chapter here.

Visit **YourVermontWedding.com** to find out how the Vermont Association of Wedding Professionals can help you plan every step of your celebration.

Vermont ASSOCIATION
Wedding Professiona

Destination Weddings & Custom Events

Elegant Victorian Country Inn
Country Gardens with Gazebo
Restored Carriage Barn
Full Service Tavern & Extensive Wine List
Unique and Charming Atmosphere

Experience Elegance and Style

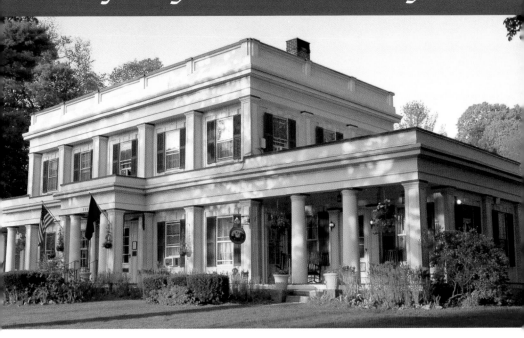

Savor
every minute of your unforgettable day.

Relax as our wedding professionals guide your entire celebration; from your dream reception to pampering spa appointments, a relaxed rehearsal dinner, and wonderful accommodations.

As a proud Partner in Education with New England Culinary Institute, our chefs invite you and your guests to experience the exceptional taste of local Vermont flavors.

AAA
Four Diamond
Award

70 Essex Way, Essex, VT 05452
Stop by or Call 800-727-4295
www.VtCulinaryResort.com

THE *Essex*
VERMONT'S CULINARY RESORT & SPA™

**NEW ENGLAND
CULINARY INSTITUTE®**
Partners in Education

An idyllic Vermont Mountain Setting

As Memorable as Your Special Day

Daria Bishop Photography

Natalie Stultz Photography

Photo: Natalie Stultz Photography

Simply extraordinary. From our location, waterside amidst 5,000 acres of Vermont's most spectacular scenery, to Vermont Fresh Network cuisine and uncompromising service for your every need. The Ponds at Bolton Valley combines the energy and perfection of nature with impeccable attention to detail. Contact us at 877.9bolton or visit thepondsvt.com.

thepondsvt.com | 877.9bolton

THE PONDS

at Bolton Valley

UNIQUELY VERMONT

Create your perfect day on the Lake.

May through October, our grand wraparound porch and rolling lawns
are the perfect location for your wedding ceremony and reception.

grandislelakehouse.com 802.372.5024

GRAND *Isle* LAKE HOUSE

Photo courtesy of Jeff Schneiderman Photography

This is why...

©2008 Spencer Leonard Photography

they get married in Vermont!

Katie and Noah got married at Windekind Farm
in Huntington, Vermont on August 9, 2008

VERMONT WEDDING ASSOCIATION

vermontweddingassociation.com

Vermont Elegance

A special wedding keepsake for your guests.

Dannie & Zach
SEPTEMBER 26, 2009

Visit us at VermontArtStore.com

Photo courtesy of Sunny Valley Creations

Your Engagement

Congratulations! What an exciting time for you and your fiancé. Your engagement will be filled with excitement and anticipation of what is to come. Be sure to enjoy every moment including planning for the big day. You will always remember your engagement as well as the wedding day, so make it special for you both.

Length of Engagement

The engagement is a period of time that allows the bride and groom to mentally adjust to spending a life together. There is no specific length of time you have to be engaged before getting married. For a more traditional wedding, the longer the engagement the better, so you have ample time to make the many necessary arrangements. Whether your ceremony to celebrate life's greatest commitment is big or small, enjoy your period of engagement. It is a very special time for growing closer together and planning your future.

Announcing Your Engagement

After you have discussed your marriage and adopted a shared vision for your big day, it is time to let people know about your good news.

The usual order of announcement is, if you have children, to inform them first. If you don't have children, your parents should be first (traditionally the bride's parents first). It is important to inform both sets of parents as close in time as possible—you don't want one family to feel left out. Then you can announce it to the rest of your family and close relatives. Next, tell your close friends who will participate in or attend your wedding. Once you make your personal announcements you may choose to make a formal one.

Your family members and close friends should hear about your upcoming wedding directly from you, either by personal visit, phone call, or letter, and not learn second hand via the grapevine or from the newspaper.

Traditionally, the groom's family calls the bride's family to welcome her to the family.

Formal Announcements

There are several ways to make a formal wedding announcement. Many people choose to have an engagement party and others may simply choose to have a newspaper announcement.

The engagement party is a perfect time for your family to announce your engagement to their colleagues and relatives. It is also a good time to let all your co-workers and friends in on the big news. Frequently the bride's parents, or other close relatives (or even friends) will hold an engagement party for the couple to honor their union. If you organize the party yourself, you may consider not announcing the purpose until your guests are present. Whoever hosts the party, it is best to make personal phone calls as an invitation so that guests do not feel they need to bring gifts.

Newspaper announcements are an easy and formal way to let your community know about your union. If you choose to make a formal newspaper announcement, call the newspaper right away. Many newspapers have guidelines and a fee for announcements and can take months before they have space for it. You should place announcements in the couple's area of residence newspaper and the hometown newspapers of the bride and groom's parents.

Important Details to Remember

If you decide to put your wedding date in your announcement, make sure that you have already confirmed your location and ceremony site. You may be surprised to learn that many places are booked months, even a year in advance, and you don't want to make unnecessary last minute changes.

Warning! You have announced to the world a date on which you will not be home. Ask someone to stay at your home during the wedding festivities.

Sample Newspaper Announcement

Mr. and Mrs. Smith of Burlington (hometown) announce the engagement of their daughter, Joanne Marie, to Mr. John Jones, son of Mr. and Mrs. Jones of Los Angeles, California. A September wedding is planned.

For the couple hosting their own wedding

Jill Palmer, Manager for ABC Company, is to be married in September to John Corwell, CEO of EFG Company, Ms. Palmer is the daughter of Mr. and Mrs. Nathan P. Palmer of Naples. Mr. Corwell is the son of Mr. and Mrs. Joseph Corwell of Bridgeport.

If parents are divorced you may add "and" between the two parents names with their current full name and titles.

Your Wedding

Where to Start: Your Budget

It is hard to accept that the most romantic day of a couple's life should fit within a budget, but that is reality. Just because there is a limit on how much you can spend on your wedding, doesn't mean it won't be fabulous! Weddings are about love and sharing, qualities that can be demonstrated in inexpensive ways. Once you get all the money issues out of the way, you can concentrate on all the fun activities such as picking out food, testing cakes and trying on dresses!

Unknown and hidden wedding expenses can get out of hand, which is the reason for a budget (and this guide book). It is important that you be realistic about what you can afford and what you want to spend. You can have a beautiful wedding and be cautious with your money.

Budgets are different for every couple. Many couples pay for their own wedding, while others get support from their families. Either way, work this out first so you do not have any surprises when the bills come in. Debt and ill feelings about money dampen a romantic start to married life. Knowing your budget also allows you to be direct and up-front with the wedding services that you call. This will not only give them the price range to work within, but will allow them to give you their best service. Together you can come up with a plan that will make you smile from ear to ear (good practice for the photos!).

The budget section in this book will give you an idea of what amount is typically spent on specific items and who traditionally pays for them. But as you will be continually reminded, this is your wedding; choose what works for you.

Begin Your Wedding Plans

A wedding publicly expresses your love for each other by the bond of marriage. With your partner, discuss openly the type of wedding you both want. Be sensitive to each other's concerns and wishes; together you can plan a wonderful wedding. Remember that your wedding is a reflection of you—it should not be formed to fit someone else's standardized mold—which is the beauty and joy of being your own wedding planner.

Have a Clear Vision

The best time for you and your fiancé to sit down and talk about your wedding visions is right after your engagement. Clarifying your expectations is very important. It is an essential starting point for planning your wedding. It is amazing what you will learn about your partner during this process. You should come to agreement about the wedding style and how to include each individual's favorite things. Perhaps one of you may love music and feels that this is the top priority, while the other insists that the food is the premiere issue. Resolve these issues early, especially if they impact the budget. The fewer last-minute decisions that have to be made, the more relaxing and stress free the wedding will be. Be willing to compromise on issues that really aren't all that important, and give lots of compliments to each other at this time. (And that's good advice for all your married years.)

Now that you have a general understanding about what your wedding will be like—the type of service, music, and time of day—you are ready to create your wedding outline. <u>Write out a detailed outline!</u> Continuously check back with your outline as you put details together, and make certain the plans fit your budget.

Be sure your families, and the services that you hire to help plan your wedding, understand your wedding vision. This way everyone involved can picture the type of wedding you want to reflect your future together.

Having Your Own Style

Many couples have a basic understanding of what their wedding style will be, especially those brides that have known forever what their weddings will be like. It can be enormous fun to plan a gathering and have it radiate with your own personal touches. It is not often you get this opportunity, so make the most of it.

If you are unsure of the wedding style you want, a little research will help. One of my favorite places to look at various styles is *Martha Stewart Weddings*. It visually displays up-to-date styles and it is an easy and inexpensive way to get great ideas. Many other bridal magazines have great ideas as well.

A wedding consultant can also be a tremendous help. They have an endless supply of ideas, books and pictures of a variety of wedding styles. They can work with you on your outline and help you fill in all the missing pieces.

The services that you choose to work with can also help you determine your wedding style. If they have been in the wedding business a long time, they've seen many appealing styles. For example, the bakery will have pictures of cakes and the bridal shop will help you find the perfect dress. Remember, stick to your budget, it can be very easy to get carried away.

Important Questions to Answer

What Kind of Wedding Do You Want?

It is very important that you and your fiancé talk about the type of wedding you want before you get your families involved. The wedding should be a reflection of your relationship and your individual styles. Do you want a traditional, casual, black tie formal, garden setting or nature themed wedding? Do you want to get married in the summer, winter, spring or fall? Do you have a particular color scheme? Will it be a large group of people or a small gathering of close friends and family members? Think through all of these questions carefully before you start to put your plans together.

How Involved Do You Want Your Families To Be?

Every family situation is different. Discuss with your fiancé how much family involvement you want. If they are going to play a key role, ask them to help you plan the type of wedding you have already decided on. They probably will have some of their own suggestions; be understanding of their wishes, but do not compromise on something that is important to you or your fiancé.

Most families have their share of strained or difficult relations. Your wedding is not the time for choosing sides or trying to make amends. Treat everyone courteously (and seat them apart if necessary), but do not compromise your wedding day.

Who Will Pay For the Wedding?

More frequently today, brides and grooms are paying for their own weddings. If your family wants to help you financially, it may be easier to give them specific ways to help. Whether it is a specific amount of money or a specific item, make sure to give them guidance so you are not in an uncomfortable situation later.

Whether your family is financially helping with the wedding or not, parents want to share in your excitement. Keep them informed of your plans, especially if they live far away.

Does Your Budget Match Your Vision?

Weddings are great fun, but they can also be costly. According to numerous statistics, the average wedding cost in Vermont usually falls within the range of $20,000 to $35,000. But remember, this is an average. You set the priorities and must decide how much you can (and want) to spend.

No matter what your budget, you can make your wedding special and something you will remember forever. The services listed in this book will help you determine costs and help you work within your budget.

Will the Ceremony Encompass a Specific Religion or a Mix of Religions?

Traditionally, weddings have a religious undertone. Even if religion is not significant to the marrying couple, you should resolve this matter with parents before the wedding plans are cemented. Religious protocol, if pertinent, can be established by working with an officiate of the relevant religions. If the religious figure you contact is insistent on controlling your wedding in a manner incongruous with your wishes, you may want to approach another. All priests (rabbis, ministers) are not the same, nor do they conduct marriage ceremonies in the exact same manner. Find an officiant that complements you and your spiritual needs.

Any Special Family Traditions?

Are there any family traditions that you can include in your ceremony to give it that special touch? Ask members of your family—better to find out before rather than after. Or even better yet, create a family tradition!

Is the Bride Changing Her Name?

It is the bride's prerogative whether to change her name to the groom's family name or not, and she should not be pressured by either family. If the bride is changing her name, get all the necessary forms together (insurance, driver's license, bank accounts, social security, passport, credit cards) so that everything can be changed as soon as possible after the ceremony.

Is Anyone Feeling Overburdened with Wedding Preparations?

Ask to be certain no one is feeling overwhelmed or burned-out by wedding preparations. You may want to take time out together, maybe a weekend away, when wedding discussions and decisions become overwhelming.

How Will You Resolve Conflicts Regarding the Wedding?

When planning for your wedding, open and honest communication is crucial. Listen to each other's needs and concerns while you plan for your big day. You are probably already very busy with your work, home and other obligations without the difficulties of planning a wedding. If you come to an impasse in planning, realize that you can get advice from a mutual friend, wedding planner, or someone who has traveled this road before.

Things to Remember

You and your fiancé are marrying each other, not your parents, not your friends or siblings. Include them, it's very special for them too, but remember that this is your day.

℘

You both need to play an active role in the planning. Even if certain aspects of the wedding don't matter much to you, realize that your partner cares and wants your approval and support.

℘

It is your wedding—plan it to fit your needs and desires. Everyone has some opinion of what you should do, if it matches yours, great, if not…

℘

During the planning stage of your wedding, you may get stressed, but remember you are blessed with each other and your wedding day will be the beginning of a wonderful life together.

℘

Planning your wedding will take time, lots of appointments and visits. Plan ahead for site visits and times to make calls. If you work on a small piece at a time you won't feel so overwhelmed by the entire process.

℘

Everyone wants the wedding to be perfect, but remember this is not Fantasy Island and Tattoo is nowhere around. Things may go wrong. Don't get consumed about the little things. Even if there are a few slip ups on big things, it's not a catastrophe and the show will go on. If you are having a great time, everyone else will too. If you cry over the wine stain on your sleeve, guests will remember that too. Happiness is a choice, so is a fun wedding.

℘

A marriage is about love. Constantly display a relaxed and loving attitude throughout your wedding and everyone will remember it as a beautiful day.

How to Plan Your Big Day

Delegating Duties

Now that you see all the tasks inherent in presiding over a successful wedding, and you have begun contacting some businesses, you might be asking, "How are we going to pull this off?" The two most important steps to planning a successful wedding or event are to first: delegate, delegate, delegate as much as possible and second: check up, check up, check up.

One of the best ways to delegate is to hire a consultant. Planning a wedding is a lot of work, and it really helps to have a professional on your side. A consultant makes sure everything falls into place. You can have them do as much or as little as you want. They will help you decide what is best for your wedding.

If you choose not to hire a consultant, then make sure you delegate many of the duties. Just think of yourself as the coach of a baseball team; the team does most of the work but you are guiding the entire process. You and your key players will be following the same game plan if you all have a copy of this book.

As this book previously advised, create a list of things for each person to do, meet with that person (or call them if they are not near), ask for their assistance and make sure they feel comfortable doing what you are asking of them.

The easiest way to make sure all your bases are covered is to use this book's Ultimate Check List. Next to each item (and the ones you add) put a person's name who will be responsible for overseeing that item the day of the wedding. When your Check List is complete you can give everyone their own list of things to do.

A Planning Test

Let us share a little secret to use when planning events to make sure everything is in place. Once you have completed all the arrangements, or think you have, run "the test" described below.

The Test

Put yourself in the shoes of each person who has a different role, then in your mind, run through everything they have to do from start to finish. Every person, item, and activity should link. This will let you know if there is a missing link.

Example: A Guest at the Ceremony

Guests will arrive at the church at 10:45 a.m.; they will park their car in the parking lot behind the church; they will enter the front of the building; they will be ushered to their seat; they will watch the ceremony; be handed birdseed packages on the way out the door; they will throw the birdseed at the couple; they will then go to the reception site and park in the lot next to the building.

Questions

Is there ample parking at the reception site? Do ushers know where special guests are sitting? Is there a special side of the room for the groom and bride? Who is passing out the birdseed? Does the church allow birdseed? Does everyone know how to get to the reception? Who brings the flowers from the ceremony site to the reception?

Complete the Test

As you can see, there is a lot to think about. You will need to run through the entire event several times. Every time you foresee a possible glitch, write yourself a note and then call the person in charge of that area to be sure he or she has addressed your concern.

Perform a Test For Every Group

Do a test run-through for each of these groups: The guests at the ceremony, guests at the reception, bride through the whole day, groom through the whole day, entire reception outline, entire ceremony outline, attendants, father of the bride, relatives, your service providers and so on...

Make Sure You Use

The Ultimate Checklist, **Your Budget** and **Your Worksheets** starting on page 275.

Photo courtesy of Emma Dodge Hanson Photography

All About Vermont

Vermont Weather and Sunsets

As the old saying goes, "If you don't like the weather, wait a minute." Regardless of the season it is difficult to forecast the weather in Vermont. You have no control over the weather; don't let it control you either, just prepare for it.

If you choose an outside wedding make sure you plan for all types of weather. It's imperative that you reserve a tent far in advance. (See the category labeled "Decorations and Rental Items.") If yours is a winter wedding, your guests may want to come in a day early in case of airline delays.

The weather information below is from the Weather Channel for Burlington, Vermont:

Average Temperatures											
Jan	Feb	Mar	Apr	May	Jun	Jul	Aug	Sep	Oct	Nov	Dec
18°	20°	31°	44°	56°	66°	71°	68°	59°	48°	37°	25°

Summer temperatures reach high 70's to mid 80's. Days are typically sunny and comfortable, ideal for outdoor activity, with light clothing for days, sweaters or light jackets for evenings. The Autumn and Spring months have highs in the mid 50's with a variety of casual dress suitable. Below freezing temperatures are the rule during the Winter season. Coats, heavy jackets, gloves and warm, dry boots are recommended through mid March.

Sunrises and Sunsets

Sunrise and sunset times are different for each location and for the day of the year. Below are approximate eastern standard times.

Sunrise	Jan	Feb	Mar	Apr	May	Jun	Jul	Aug	Sep	Oct	Nov	Dec
Between	7:15	6:32	5:41	4:48	4:14	4:11	4:12	4:40	5:16	5:51	6:31	7:09
(a.m.)	7:29	7:11	6:30	5:34	4:43	4:11	4:36	5:11	5:47	6:25	7:06	7:29
Sunset	Jan	Feb	Mar	Apr	May	Jun	Jul	Aug	Sep	Oct	Nov	Dec
Between	4:24	5:02	5:41	6:21	6:58	7:31	7:23	6:36	5:39	4:48	4:16	4:14
(p.m.)	4:57	5:40	6:18	6:54	7:27	7:42	7:41	7:18	6:29	5:33	4:42	4:21

Vermont Marriage Requirements

Do we need a marriage license? Do we need blood tests?

Before your ceremony, you must purchase a Vermont marriage license. It must be given to the officiant before your marriage is performed. While your license may be purchased up to two months before your ceremony, it "becomes void 60 days from date of issue if the proposed marriage is not solemnized." You do not need a blood test.

Where do we get a marriage license and how much does it cost?

If both bride and groom are Vermont residents, you may go to the town clerk in either of your towns of residence. If just one of you is a resident, you must buy the license in that town. It costs $45.00.

What if we are not Vermont residents?

First, decide where in Vermont you wish to be married. Out-of-state residents must buy their license in the county where they plan to marry. Any town clerk in that county can issue the license.

Who can get married in Vermont?

A man and a woman who are each at least 18 years old can marry in Vermont. Other information regarding under the age of 18 and other restrictions, please contact the Vermont Department of Health at 800-439-5008 (toll free in Vermont only) or 802-863-7275.

What information must we provide to get a marriage license in Vermont?

You must know your legal town of residence, and your place and date of birth. You will also need to know your parents' names, including your mother's maiden name, and the states where your parents were born. (A certified copy of your birth certificate can supply most of this information.) Vermont law requires that at least one of you sign in the presence of the town clerk, certifying that all facts are correct. However, most town clerks prefer to see both of you in person before issuing your license to marry, as the law requires that they satisfy themselves that you are both free to marry under Vermont laws. They may legally ask to see documented proof of your statements (birth certificates, divorce decrees, etc.). You will also be asked to provide information about your race, the highest grade you completed in school, the number of times you have been married, and how your previous marriage(s), if any, ended. This information does not become part of the marriage certificate.

What if either of us has been married before?

If you are a widow or widower, you are free to marry. You will be asked the date your spouse died. If you are divorced, you may remarry after the date on which your previous marriage is dissolved.

Can a marriage license be issued through the mail? Can we be married by proxy?

No. A marriage license cannot be issued through the mail, and you cannot be married by proxy.

Is there a waiting period?

No.

Where can we get married?

A Vermont license is valid only for a marriage performed in Vermont. If you are a Vermont resident or are marrying a Vermont resident, you can get married anywhere in Vermont. If you are not a Vermont resident, you must be married in the county where your license is issued.

Who can marry us? Do we need witnesses?

A judge, supreme court justice, assistant judge, justice of the peace, or an ordained or licensed minister, rabbi or priest residing in Vermont can perform your ceremony. A priest, rabbi, or minister from another state can perform your ceremony if he or she first obtains a special authorization from the probate court in the district where the marriage will take place. Vermont law does not require witnesses. If you are planning a religious ceremony, check with your church or synagogue to see if religious tenets require witnesses for your marriage.

What do we do with the license? What happens to it after the ceremony?

By law, you must deliver the license to the person who will conduct your wedding ceremony before the marriage can be performed. After the ceremony, the person who performs the ceremony (officiant) will complete the sections concerning the date, place and officiant information, and sign your license. It must then be returned by the officiant to the town clerk's office where it was issued within 10 days, so that your ceremony may be officially registered. It is not a complete legal document, useful for passports, Social Security, etc., until it has been recorded in the town clerk's office where it was issued.

How do we get a copy of our marriage certificate?

When you buy your license, you can arrange with the town clerk to mail you a certified copy of your certificate as soon as your marriage is recorded. The cost is $55.00 ($45 for the license and $10 for the certified copy). Or two weeks or more after the ceremony, you can request, in person or in writing, a copy from the town clerk's office where you bought your license for a $10.00 fee. Or six or more weeks after your ceremony, you may request, in person or in writing, a certified copy from the Vermont Department of Health, Vital Records Unit. Either way, the fee is $10.00, and you will receive a copy of the original certificate, embossed with the town or state seal and signed and dated by the appropriate official. This is accepted for all legal purposes.

Justice of the Peace
Vermont Secretary of State Office
802-828-2363 or www.sec.state.vt.us
or
Vital Records for Your Local Town Clerk's Office
800-439-5008 (toll free in VT only) or 802-863-7275

Civil Union Requirements

A civil union is a legal relationship that provides same-sex couples in Vermont all the benefits, protections and responsibilities under law as are granted to spouses in a marriage.

Who can form a civil union?

Both parties to a civil union must be of the same sex and therefore ineligible for marriage. Both parties must be at least 18 years of age, of sound mind, and not already in a marriage or another civil union. Vermont also does not allow a civil union between most close relatives. You cannot enter a civil union with a parent, grandparent, sister, brother, child, grandchild, niece, nephew, aunt or uncle. Anyone under guardianship must have the guardian sign an affidavit consenting to the union. You do not have to be Vermont residents to form a civil union in Vermont.

Do we need a license? Do we need blood tests?

You will need a license, but you do not need blood tests, and there is no waiting period.

Where do we get a civil union license and how much does it cost?

Licenses are issued by Vermont town clerks. If both parties are Vermont residents, you may go to the town clerk in either of your towns of residence. If just one of you resides in a Vermont town, you must buy the license in that town. The license costs $45.00, and is valid for 60 days from the date it is issued. During that time period, you must have the union certified by an authorized person, otherwise, the license is void.

What if we are not Vermont residents?

If neither party is a Vermont resident, you may get the license from any town clerk in the state.

What information must we provide to get a civil union license?

Besides basic information about yourselves (names, towns of residence, places and dates of birth), you must also provide your parents' names, including your mothers' maiden names, and their places of birth. (A certified copy of your birth certificate can supply most of this information.)

Vermont law requires that at least one of you sign the license in the presence of the town clerk, certifying that all the information you provided is correct. However, most town clerks prefer to see both of you in person before issuing your license. The law requires that town clerks satisfy themselves that you are both free to form a civil union under Vermont laws.

Therefore, they may ask to see legally documented proof of your statements (birth certificates, divorce decrees, death certificates, etc.). You will also be asked to provide information about your race, the highest grade you completed in school, and the number of previous marriages or civil unions and how they ended. This information is confidential and does not become part of the civil union certificate.

What if either of us has been married or in a civil union before?

If your husband, wife, or civil union partner has died, you are free to form a civil union. The clerk will ask the date your spouse or civil union partner died. If you are divorced, you may form a civil union after the date on which your previous marriage or civil union was legally dissolved.

Can a license be issued through the mail? Can we form a civil union by proxy?

No. A civil union license cannot be issued through the mail, and you cannot form a civil union by proxy.

Where can we have our civil union certified?

With a valid Vermont license, your civil union can be certified anywhere in Vermont, but only in Vermont.

Who can certify our civil union? Do we need witnesses?

A supreme court justice, a superior court judge, a district judge, a judge of probate, an assistant judge, a justice of the peace or an ordained or licensed member of the clergy residing in Vermont can certify your civil union. A clergy person residing in an adjoining state or country can certify your civil union if his or her church, temple, mosque, or other religious organization lies wholly or partly in Vermont. A clergy member residing in some other state or in Canada can certify your civil union if he or she first obtains a special authorization from the probate court in the district where the certification will take place. Vermont law does not require witnesses, but, if you are planning a religious ceremony, check to see if the religion's tenets require witnesses.

What do we do with the license before and after the ceremony?

By law, you must deliver the license to the person who will certify your union (officiant). After the ceremony, the officiant will complete the sections concerning the date, place and officiant information, and sign your license. At that point, the license becomes a civil union certificate. The officiant must return the certificate to the town clerk's office where it was issued within 10 days of the certification, so that your union can be officially registered. The certificate is not a complete legal document until it has been recorded in the town clerk's office where it was issued.

How do we get a copy of our civil union certificate?

When you buy your license, you can arrange with the town clerk to mail you a certified copy of your certificate as soon as it is recorded. The cost is $55.00 ($45 for the license and $10 for the certified copy).

Two weeks or more after the certification, you can request, in person or in writing, a copy from the town clerk's office where you bought your license. Or six or more weeks after the certification, you may request, in person or in writing, a certified copy from the Vermont Department of Health, Vital Records Unit. Either way, the fee is $10.00, and you will receive a copy of the original certificate, embossed with the town or state seal and signed and dated by the appropriate official. This is accepted in Vermont for all legal purposes as proof of a valid civil union.

Information provided by Vital Records. Call 1-800-439-5008 (toll free in VT only) or 802-863-7275 to locate town clerk's office close to your civil union location.

Photo courtesy of Echo Lake Inn

Vermont Guest Considerations

Entertaining Guests

Vermont weddings provide an extra attraction for out-of-town guests. Your guests will witness two special people getting married in a state that is known throughout the world for its charm and beauty. Make a list of all the fun things to do and see in the area or include local brochures with specific activities. It is easier to provide your guests with things to do than to continually entertain them while you get ready for the big day.

Plan specific outings or wedding events with your guests making them feel welcome without tying up your whole schedule. They understand that you have a lot to accomplish. Do what you can to see them, but don't give yourself a guilty conscience if you can't cater to their every moment.

Plan Ahead for Accommodations

Anywhere you plan a wedding, you need to consider accommodations for guests. Vermont has a wonderful selection of B&B's, inns, resorts and hotels, as you will see in the Banquet and Reception Sites and Guest Accomodations sections of this book. Send your guests a list containing a range of prices and places to stay. Consider sending out the accommodations list far before your invitations go out. Many Vermont towns, especially during peak seasons, are booked six to eight months in advance.

It might make sense for you to reserve a block of rooms and allocate them for guests who you want to stay together and also who may not have realized the necessity of making far-in-advance reservations.

Adding a Vacation

Guests may take a vacation in conjunction with your wedding. They could be in town the entire week before or after your wedding. It would be helpful if you gave them lodging suggestions and a list of things to do so that their vacation does not become your responsibility. Call the Chamber of Commerce in the area that you are planning to wed and ask for the list of upcoming events. Your guests will be impressed and appreciative when you send this information.

A Few Things to Do in Vermont

Fishing, biking, festivals, hiking, boating, antiquing, sight seeing, kayaking, canoeing, water-skiing, snowshoeing, sailing, skiing, cross-country skiing, shopping, sleigh rides—you name it, Vermont probably has it. Pick an area that has those activities which are important to you and your guests.

Vermont Chambers of Commerce

Addison County
2 Court Street
Middlebury, VT 05753
Phone: 802-388-7951
www.midvermont.com

Barton Area
P.O. Box 403
Barton, VT 05822
Phone: 802-525-1137
www.centerofthekingdom.com

Bennington Area
100 Veterans Memorial Dr.
Bennington, VT 05201
Phone: 800-229-0252
www.bennington.com

Brandon Area
P.O. Box 267
Brandon, VT 05733
Phone: 802-247-6401
www.brandon.org

Brattleboro Area
180 Main Street
Brattleboro, VT 05301
Phone: 802-254-4565
www.brattleborochamber.org

Burke Area
P.O. Box 347
East Burke, VT 05832
Phone: 802-626-4124
www.burkevermont.org

Central Vermont
P.O. Box 336
Barre, VT 05641
Phone: 802-229-5711
www.central-vt.com

Dorset
P.O. Box 121
Dorset, VT 05251
Phone: 802-867-2450
www.dorsetvt.com

Fair Haven Area
P.O. Box 158
Fair Haven, VT 05743
Phone: 802-265-3855
www.fairhavenchambervt.com

Franklin County Regional
2 North Main Street,
Suite 101
St. Albans, VT 05478
Phone: 802-524-2444
www.stalbanschamber.com

Great Falls Regional
17 Depot Street
Bellows Falls, VT 05101
Phone: 802-463-4280
info@gfrcc.org
www.gfrcc.org

Hardwick
P.O. Box 111
Hardwick, VT 05843
Phone: 802-472-5906
www.hardwickvtarea.com

Jay Peak Area Association
P.O. Box 177
Troy, VT 05868
Phone: 802-988-2259
www.jaypeakvermont.org

Killington
P.O. Box 114
Killington, VT 05751
Phone: 802-773-4181
www.killingtonchamber.com

Lake Champlain Islands
P.O. Box 213
North Hero, VT 05474
Phone: 802-372-8400
www.champlainislands.com

Lake Champlain Regional
60 Main Street, Suite 100
Burlington, VT 05401
Phone: 802-863-3489
www.vermont.org

Lamoille Valley
P.O. Box 445
Morrisville, VT 05661
Phone: 802-888-7607
www.stowesmugglers.com

Londonderry
P.O. Box 58
Londonderry, VT 05148
Phone: 802-824-8178
www.londonderryvt.com

Lower Cohase Regional
P.O. Box 209
Bradford, VT 05033
Phone: 802-222-5631
www.cohase.org

Lyndon Area
P.O. Box 886
Lyndon, VT 05851
Phone: 802-626-9696
www.lyndonvermont.com

Vermont Chambers of Commerce

Mad River Valley
4061 Main Street
P.O. Box 173
Waitsfield, VT 05673
Phone: 802-496-3409
www.madrivervalley.com

**Manchester &
The Mountains**
5046 Main Street, Suite 1
Manchester Ctr., VT 05255
Phone: 802-362-2100
www.manchestervermont.net

Mount Snow Valley
P.O. Box 3
Wilmington, VT 05363
Phone: 802-464-8092
www.visitvermont.com

Northeast Kingdom
51 Depot Square, Suite 3
St. Johnsbury, VT 05819
Phone: 802-748-3678
www.nekchamber.com

Okemo Valley
P.O. Box 233
Ludlow, VT 05149
Phone: 802-228-5830
www.okemovalleyvt.org

**Quechee Gorge Visitor
Center**
P.O. Box 106
Quechee, VT 05059
Phone: 802-295-6852
www.hartfordvtchamber.com

Poultney Area
P.O. Box 151
Poultney, VT 05764
Phone: 802-287-2010
www.poultneyvt.net

Randolph Area
P.O. Box 9
31 VT Route 66
Randolph, VT 05060
Phone: 802-728-9027
www.randolphvt.com

Rutland Region
256 North Main Street
Rutland, VT 05701
Phone: 802-773-2747
www.rutlandvermont.com

Springfield Regional
14 Clinton Street, Suite 6
Springfield, VT 05156
Phone: 802-885-2779
www.springfieldvt.com

Smugglers' Notch Area
P.O. Box 369
Jeffersonville, VT 05464
Phone: 802-644-2239

Stowe Area Association
P.O. Box 1320
Stowe, VT 05672
Phone: 802-253-7321
www.gostowe.com

Sugarbush/VT Weddings
P.O. Box 173
Waitsfield, VT 05673
Phone: 802-496-3409
www.vermontweddings.com

Swanton
P.O. Box 237
Swanton, VT 05488
Phone: 802-868-7200
www.swantonchamber.com

Vermont Chamber
P.O. Box 37
Berlin, VT 05601
Phone: 802-223-3443
www.vtchamber.com

Vermont's North Country
246 The Causeway
Newport, VT 05855
Phone: 802-334-7782
www.vtnorthcountry.org

**Upper Valley
Bi-State Regional**
P.O. Box 697
White River Jct., VT 05001
Phone: 802-295-6200
www.uppervalleychamber.com

**White River Junction and
Quechee Area**
100 Railroad Row
White River Junction,
VT 05001
Phone: 802-295-7900
www.quechee.com

Windsor/Mt. Ascutney
P.O. Box 41
Windsor, VT 05089
Phone: 802-674-5910
www.windsorvt.com

Woodstock
P.O. Box 486
Woodstock, VT 05091
Phone: 802-457-3555
www.woodstockvt.com

Plan your wedding, guest accommodations, and activities
with these FREE resources:

~Vermont Country Inns and B&Bs Brochure
~Vermont Vacation Guide (Summer/Fall Edition)
~Vermont Winter Vacation Guide
~Official Vermont Road Map & Guide to VT Attractions
~Vermont Ski Resort Map & Maple Syrup Guide

Request one, or a hundred - Free Shipping!
Contact the Vermont Chamber of Commerce:
802-223-3443 or info@vtchamber.com

www.vtchamber.com

Vermont Hospitality Council
A Division of the Vermont Chamber of Commerce

www.VisitVT.com

Landwehrle Photography ©2006

Vermont Convention Bureau
A Division of The Lake Champlain Regional Chamber of Commerce
60 Main Street, Suite 100, Burlington, VT 05401
Phone: (802) 860-0606 • Toll Free: (877) 264-3503 • Fax: (802) 863-1538

Vermont Weddings

You already know you love Vermont

Invite your friends and family to embrace your ceremony
as you envision it in Vermont!

Our membership spans the state with wedding and civil union
venues from historic bed and breakfasts, to beautiful resorts,
to boats, picturesque fields, mountain vistas and waterfront properties.

For all your function and guest accommodations needs,
please contact the Vermont Convention Bureau at

annie@vermont.org

23

MAD RIVER VALLEY, VERMONT

Mad River Valley Chamber of Commerce
Mad River Valley Association of Wedding Professionals
info@vermontwedding.com
1-800-828-4748

*Wedding professionals in Vermont's Historic Mad River Valley work
together in a collaboration to make your day seamless and beautiful.*

Visit our comprehensive site of area professionals:

Wedding Sites & Facilities
Honeymoon Spots
Caterers and Cake Bakers
Florists
Music & Entertainment
Rehearsal Dinner Locations
Rental Necessities
Spas & Salons
Transportation Options
Legalities, Wedding Officials & Planners
Personal Celebration Notebook & Checklist

And for your Guests:

Activities
Events
Lodging & Free Reservation Concierge Service
Planned Outings
Shopping

Contact us via phone or website to order your complimentary
Wedding Planner, a companion piece to
www.VermontWeddings.com

Photo taken at Honora Winery & Vineyard by Jag Studios

Reception Sites Map

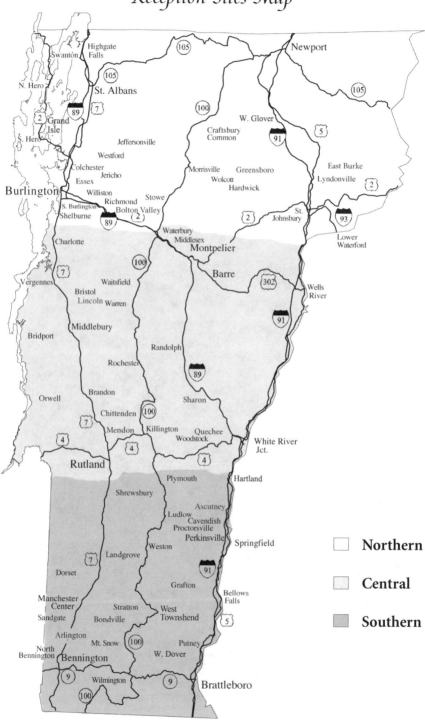

Northern
Central
Southern

How to Plan Your Reception

Researching Reception Sites

Choosing a location for your reception is one of the first items on your list. The waiting list for some of the most popular wedding reception sites can be two years or more. Even renting an elegant tent for an outdoor wedding can require lengthy advance notice. Don't delay. Once you start your wedding plans, start arranging for your reception site! During your site research, ask what their available dates are; if none of their dates work for you, even if they are otherwise perfect, you'll have to move on. This underscores the importance of early planning.

The variety of reception sites is amazing, ranging from casual to very elegant. Work within your budget to find the site that is right for you. You'll save a lot of time when researching reception sites if you confirm when they are available and get an idea of their setting before you set out on a visit. Be sure to call ahead and set up a time they can meet with you. Thoroughly reviewing a site takes a lot of time from you and the proprietor. It would be sad if you drove a long distance to see a place and the proprietors were too busy. It is essential that you visit the location you are considering for your reception site. This is a decision you don't want someone else to make for you.

Choosing a Site

Choosing a location has everything to do with the size, style and type of wedding you want. Therefore, have a fairly clear image of the wedding you want before making site commitments. Vermont has a wonderful selection of wedding reception sites. Many businesses listed in this chapter have years of experience working on a variety of wedding styles.

After you have visited a site and determined that it is what you want, ask the proprietors for references from other weddings. Envision hundreds of your closest friends and relatives attending your wedding there. If the picture feels good, if they have treated you well, if the references check out, and if you have gone over all the questions in this chapter, you are ready to sign an agreement.

When you are looking over a contract, read everything. Make sure the services you requested are listed, if they aren't, discuss it. Keep a copy of all the signed contracts.

Questions to Ask

These questions will help you determine if the reception site is right for you. Many wedding sites can also handle your reception needs, including the meal, drinks, linens, servers, etc. If you decide to do an off-site reception, such as in a park or a personal home, you will need to work with rental companies, decorating businesses and catering services.

On-Site Reception Questions

- ❏ Is our date available?
- ❏ How many people can your location accommodate? Seated and standing?
- ❏ What are your fees and how does your payment plan work?
- ❏ Can we set up a site visit?
- ❏ Do you have a wedding coordinator on staff?
- ❏ What is your decorating style? Your ambiance?
- ❏ What amenities are included with your reception location?
- ❏ What menus are available?
- ❏ What is the price range for your meals? Does that include tax and tips?
- ❏ Are there any extra charges?
- ❏ Is there a dance floor?
- ❏ How long do we have the room for?
- ❏ Can we extend it the day of our event if necessary?
- ❏ Do you have rooms available for guests?
- ❏ Are there any restrictions?
- ❏ Are there additional items we need to consider?

Off-Site Reception Location

- ❏ Is our date available?
- ❏ How many people can your location accommodate? Seated and standing?
- ❏ What are your fees and how does your payment plan work?
- ❏ Can we set up a site visit?
- ❏ Do you have a wedding coordinator on staff?

- ❏ What amenities are included with your reception location?
- ❏ Are there any extra charges?
- ❏ Is there a dance floor?
- ❏ How long do we have the space for?
- ❏ Can we extend it the day of our event if necessary?
- ❏ Do you have rooms available for guests?
- ❏ What are the liquor requirements?
- ❏ Where are the electric outlets?
- ❏ Is overhead coverage available in case of rain?
- ❏ May we set up a tent?
- ❏ Are there any restrictions?
- ❏ Are there additional items we need to consider?
- ❏ Are the rest room facilities adequate?
- ❏ Who is responsible for trash and clean up?
- ❏ Do you have a list of providers that have worked this site before?

Reception Check List

The list below are the items you will need to consider for a reception (on or off site). Put a check next to the ones that are taken care of by the reception site. It is important to know if there is an extra charge for any of the items listed or if it is part of the package. If you are doing an off-site wedding, then your caterer will handle a lot of the list. You will need to call a rental service to have them help you with the rest.

- ❏ Tables
- ❏ Chairs and chair covers
- ❏ Table linens
- ❏ Napkins (linens only)
- ❏ Flatware
- ❏ China
- ❏ Glassware (do not use plastic)
- ❏ Dance floor and musician area
- ❏ Electrical outlets for D.J. or band
- ❏ Rest room
- ❏ Coat room
- ❏ Centerpieces
- ❏ Head table
- ❏ Cake table
- ❏ Cake cutting
- ❏ Cake serving
- ❏ Gift table
- ❏ Bar set up
- ❏ Bartender

- ❏ Hors d'oeuvres
- ❏ Main meal (buffet or sit down)
- ❏ Coffee and tea
- ❏ Wedding cake
- ❏ Gifts for guests
- ❏ Beverage and food servers
- ❏ Flowers
- ❏ Decorations
- ❏ Bathroom baskets (mints, hair spray, comb, etc)
- ❏ Table cards
- ❏ Guest book and pen
- ❏ Parking
- ❏ Tent
- ❏ Place for bride and groom to change for "going away"
- ❏ Other
- ❏ Other
- ❏ Other
- ❏ Other

ye olde England Inne

433 Mountain Road
Stowe, Vermont 05672
Phone: 802-253-7064
Fax: 802-253-8944
Email: englandinn@aol.com
Website:
www.stoweromance.com

Every wedding, rehearsal dinner and honeymoon is unique! Call Lyn or Chris to discuss your dream plans, so we can make them come true.

The Romance of England, The Beauty of Vermont

A luxurious award winning full service country Inne, in the English Tudor tradition, located in a commanding position in beautiful Stowe.

Immerse yourself in the comfort of a bygone era whilst enjoying the amenities of an intimate and upscale resort.

Wedding ceremonies, receptions, rehearsal dinners, cocktail parties, Sunday brunches & bridal lunches.

- We provide comprehensive catering services both on and off property.
- Indoor and outdoor locations for up to 140 guests. Includes the Famous Boathouse deck. A spectacular post & beam structure with removable walls offering substantial savings on tent rentals.
- A renown team of dedicated hospitality/catering professionals whose fastidious attention to detail is legendary.
- National award winning culinary team.
- On site wedding coordinator.
- Close to Churches in Historical Stowe.
- Vintage Bentley & Rolls Royce cars available.
- Full service salon service available for Bridal party nearby.

Pricing
Your event will be customized to reflect your taste, style, & budget.

Inn Facilities
Thirty rooms, super luxurious suites, and cottages each feature comprehensive services and amenities. Four poster beds, fireplaces, & Jacuzzis. Fully air conditioned, heated pool, outdoor hot tub, two dining rooms, and an authentic English pub. Enormous wine cellar, 150 ales, 100 Malt Scotches, & Rare Vintage Ports.

Our Goal
To exceed your expectations in all aspects of our services.
References willingly provided.

The Arlington Inn

#3904 Historic Rt 7A
Arlington, Vermont 05250
800-443-9442
www.arlingtoninn.com

Experience Elegance & Style

The Arlington Inn is among the most gracious Village Estates in Vermont. The Village of Arlington is nestled in a lovely valley midway between Bennington and Manchester.

The Inn is perfectly suited for weddings, rehearsals and other special events. Your guests will be simply delighted as they gather for an intimate indoor affair or perhaps a larger event hosted in our restored carriage barn or country gardens with gazebo and water-falled pond.

Each location offers it's own unique and charming atmosphere, only to be enhanced by excellent cuisine and professional courteous service.

Special Features:

- *1848 Elegant Victorian Country Inn*
- *17 Guest Rooms, Fireplaces, Jacuzzi's*
- *Country Gardens with Gazebo*
- *Inclusive Wedding Packages*
- *Restored Carriage Barn*
- *Full Service Tavern & Extensive Wine List*
- *Full Service Catering*
- *In House Coordinator*

Capacity: Main Dining Room seats 40, Private Dining Room 12 and the Garden Solarium 24. Our Carriage Barn can accommodate 40–80 guests and larger events of 100+ are tented affairs in our gardens and on the patios. Events are booked 4–18 months in advance.

Catering: Full service catering by our Chef/Owner, who offers 30 years of professional experience in banquets, special events and gourmet dining. Please call or e-mail Stay@Arlingtoninn.com for sample menus and our inclusive packages.

Overnight Accommodations: The Inn offers 17 luxurious rooms, each individually decorated and offering a queen or king bed, many with fireplaces, jacuzzi's private porch or patio. For larger events guests would take the entire 17 rooms and be able to enjoy having the Inn and property to themselves.

Paul & I could not have dreamed of a more perfect wedding! The Arlington Inn was a magnificent back drop to a weekend of fun. All the attention to detail made it a truly magical weekend. —NICOLE & PAUL

We look forward to your visit or call!

A Vineyard Wedding in Vermont

Blending Tuscan influences with New England traditions, Avigliano at Honora Winery & Vineyard offers a modern setting for your wedding.

The Setting

A large circular fireplace built with local cut stone forms the centerpiece of a building in the round. Custom mahogany bars are installed into the east and west wings of the building. The French doors provide a panoramic view of our vineyards and grounds here in the southern Green Mountains.

Gazebos, trellises and stone patios dot the landscape offering variety in settings for ceremonies and photographs. New England stonewalls cordon off vineyards and open fields.

The Pavilion

Inside our event center, stands a state-of-the-art commercial kitchen. Recognized by local caterers as the best-equipped facility in the region, our kitchen has capacity to support a multi-course meal for 200 guests. Meeting the ADA laws, people of all ages and abilities can enjoy their private festival in our building. Our parking area accommodates our guests who travel either by personal car or tour bus.

Avigliano is cradled by a working winery and vineyard where local grapes become Vermont-made wines. With a nod to our agricultural roots, Avigliano has access to the freshest local fruits and vegetables, local meat and poultry. Additionally, horse-drawn carriages are available to transport our guests to another age.

Special Features & Amenities

- *Exclusive event on property for the day*
- *Use of space for wedding rehearsal 1-2 days prior*
- *Choice of ceremony locations: 3 white gazebos or a cut stone patio*
- *Wedding day coordination of vendors & deliveries*
- *Seating and escorting guests*
- *Executing provided timeline from ceremony to last dance*
- *200 person capacity*
- *Modern Commercial Kitchen for your caterer*
- *Valet Parking, Bus access*
- *Horse drawn carriage(s)*

For more information or to schedule an appointment to view our property please contact Lorraine Muha, (802) 368-2930 or lorraine@honorawinery.com

www.honorawinery.com

Honora Winery & Vineyard
1950 Collins Rd., West Halifax, VT 05358 (802) 368-2930

33

THE BARN AT BOYDEN FARM

What used to be a hay loft for over 14,000 bales of hay has been lovingly restored. Complete with sparkling chandeliers, tables & chairs to seat up to 200 guests, a caterers pantry, full restrooms, dressing rooms and dance floor. All this and more is ready and waiting for your spectacular wedding event.

Imagine standing hand in hand with the most important person in your life as you are surrounded by the beauty of the Lamoille River Valley and Vermont farm land at its best. Make your wedding day extra special and unforgettable for yourself, the one you love and your family.
Celebrate at Boyden Farm.

Boyden Events, LLC
www.boydenfarm.com
44 VT Route 104, Cambridge, VT 05444
802 644 6363/802 598 5509

4800 Basin Harbor Rd,
Vergennes, VT 05491
Phone: 802-475-2311
888-339-8074
Fax: 802-475-6546
Email:
weddings@basinharbor.com

BASIN HARBOR CLUB
On Lake Champlain, Vermont

© Curran Photography

The perfect lakeside resort for your wedding weekend

Start your weekend with a Lobster Bake rehearsal dinner on the North Dock. Wake to a Vermont Buffet Breakfast. Play 18 holes of golf or get sunkissed on our cruiseboat, the EScape. Stroll to the Wedding Arch. Exchange your vows. Take photos with backdrops of the Adirondacks and our spectacular flower gardens. Join your guests on the Lodge Lawn for lakeside cocktails and hors d'oeuvres. Step inside for candlelight dining and dancing. Party with the night owls at the Red Mill where you will find late night entertainment. Give good-bye kisses at your farewell brunch or late breakfast. Don't stop now... come back in a year for your complimentary anniversary stay.

The Traditions Package includes an open bar for one hour, including beer, wine and house cocktails, stationary and passed hors d'oeuvres and canapés, celebratory champagne toast, soup, salad and entrée selection, either buffet or served. Dinner is followed by chocolate-covered strawberries, traditional wedding cake, coffee, tea and decaffeinated coffee. Price per person starts at $85.00 plus tax and service.

Facility Features
Ceremony capacity — Indoor: 200   Outdoor: 350
Reception capacity — Indoor: 250   Outdoor: 350
Wheelchair accessibility

Special Features and Amenities

- Lakefront Site
- On-site Wedding Planner
- Ceremony site with beautiful wooden arch and marble terrace
- Massage, in-house hair, makeup and nail services, child care and concierge services

- Recreation including hayrides, bonfires, heated outdoor pool, 18 hole PGA golf course, sailing, boating and tennis
- 15,000 square feet of magnificent gardens

Accommodations
Total capacity: 350 guests
Guest rooms: 36   Suites: 12   Cottages: 74

Congratulations!

Blueberry Hill Inn

1307 Goshen Ripton Road, Goshen, VT 05733
800-448-0707
www.blueberryhillinn.com
Email: Info@blueberryhillinn.com

An Ideal Site for
Your Vermont Destination Wedding

Located in the Green Mountain National Forest just minutes away from Brandon Vermont. The Blueberry Hill Inn is the ideal site for your celebration as the Inn and surrounding area becomes your home for the weekend. No ten p.m. curfew here, no moving along for the next wedding, just relax or party hard; the choice is yours.

The garden and grounds make an excellent backdrop for an outdoor wedding — imagine getting married in the open field, having a cocktail gathering in the apple orchard and an evening under the stars in your reception tent; the possibilities are endless. Our wedding coordinator will assist you every step of the way, helping to create the wedding of your dreams. Chef Tim will tailor a feast to your requirements and — our staff will provide you, your family and guests with personal attention and exceptional service.

Please contact us for more information or to schedule a tour of our inn and grounds.

The Ponds at Bolton Valley
The Perfect Vermont Setting for a Perfect Day

The Ponds at Bolton Valley is the ideal wedding venue in any season. Situated among trees and ponds in the heart of a natural sanctuary, the ambiance of The Ponds is unrivaled. The Ponds is in complete harmony with its magnificent setting. The great room, complete with stone fireplace, vaulted ceilings and views across the pond is the perfect setting for the perfect day.

There's always plenty to do at the resort; the Bolton adventure center, off-road driving school, hiking, biking, fishing, swimming and nearby golf during the warmer months and skiing/snowboarding, Nordic skiing and snowshoeing on 5,000 acres of the state's most heralded backcountry terrain during the winter season. Nearby Burlington and Montpelier, Lake Champlain and the surrounding area house Vermont's most popular attractions and scenery. The Ponds at Bolton Valley, the perfect Vermont location for you and your guests, in all seasons. Contact us at 877.9BOLTON; ThePondsVT.com

The
Brandon Inn

20 Park Street, Brandon, VT 05733 • Tel: 800-639-8685/802-247-5766
Fax 802-247-5768 • Email: brandoninn@hotmail.com
Wi Fi www.historicbrandoninn.com • Sarah and Louis Pattis, Owners

"An Historic Inn in a Charming New England Setting."

Wedding Packages: Customized to suit your needs. The choices are endless; from cocktails poolside, evening rehearsal barbecues on the patio, ceremonies beside the river or in the pier mirrored ballroom, sumptuous buffets, and elegant sit down dinners. Please call for our wedding brochure for details on our many meal options or look up the wedding packages featured on our website.

Capacity Information: Several connecting dining rooms allow full view of bride and groom for over 200 guests. The back lawns are secluded and allow an even greater capacity for an outdoor wedding. For small or intimate gatherings, our garden room is perfect. We have 39 individually decorated guest rooms, including two whirlpool tub suites and several family-style rooms. All guest rooms and public areas have wireless Internet access. Special rates for wedding guests may be arranged.

Catering: The chef innkeeper continues to win awards for his food ever since he acquired the inn 21 years ago. Eye appealing attention to detail & top quality fresh ingredients are standard fare. All catering is done on premises.

"We can't imagine a nicer reception or lovelier place in which to have staged it. The ambience was exactly what we had envisioned. Everyone commented on how nice everything looked and particular mention was made to the friendly efficiency of the staff. Of course I can't say enough about the food. It was truly outstanding both in taste and presentation."

(888) burkevt
Danielle Moffatt
Wedding Coordinator
Burke Mountain
Operating Company
dmoffatt@skiburke.com
(802) 626-7394
www.skiburke.com

Your wedding.
The single most important event of your life and one that you will remember long after the last photograph is taken.
And whether your dream celebration is an informal, outdoor exchanging of vows or a lavishly elegant candlelit affair, no one knows how to make that dream a reality better than the wedding professionals at Burke Mountain.
The setting, amenities and service here at Burke will make your wedding truly unique, truly memorable.
Our mountain setting is the perfect backdrop for your photos.
Our chefs will provide a dream menu for your rehearsal dinner and reception.

We are happy to assist in every detail of your wedding.

Call toll free at 888-BURKEVT

BURLINGTON
COUNTRY
CLUB

568 South Prospect Street, Burlington VT, 05401
(802)864-4683 • Fax (802)860-0457
www.burlingtoncountryclub.org
Contact: Kimberly Hein • email: Kim.Hein@BurlingtonCountryClub.org

Burlington Country Club is conveniently located between Interstate 89 and Route 7, just minutes away from many top hotels. Although the club is a private facility, one does not need to be member-affiliated in order to rent space to host receptions or other special occasions. Our ballroom and terrace offer panoramic views of the Green Mountains, creating an ambiance unlike any other in the Burlington area.

At Burlington Country Club we begin with an experienced staff, add your creativity and vision to our expertise, and then deliver an event that will make you the toast of your guests. Whether you're already able to see your special day in your mind's eye or you're looking for ideas, we can help and will deliver the best day of your life. Let us do the work and you enjoy your guests. For a comprehensive menu designed especially for you, please call or e-mail Kimberly today.

Post Office Box 525
Ludlow, Vermont 05149
Telephone: 802-226-7361
Fax: 802-226-7301
www.CastleHillResort.com
Email: sales@thecastle-vt.com
Contact: Lisa Cormier

Michael DeMartino Photography

Regal Elegance in Vermont

On a forested hill, overlooking Okemo Mountain sits a remarkable mansion.
Built in the English Country House style, this exquisite building sets
the standard for luxury…

Castle Hill Resort is perfectly suited for a wedding or special party with a formal entry hall, library and terrace. Castle Hill can accommodate up to 100 guests inside and 250 guests in our function tent; both locations have their own unique romantic and elegant atmospheres. You will receive impeccable service and gourmet food and the presentation that can only come with fine dining. The best of everything is available, no need to rent anything.

Castle Hill has ten luxurious private bedroom suites for overnight accommodations, with private baths, fireplaces or whirlpool tubs, plus all the modern conveniences. With our guest's comfort is always foremost in our minds, we have thought of every detail, including a new full service *Aveda* spa.

This incredible 100-year old castle is an architectural gem. With its' elaborate drawn plaster ceilings, paneled reception rooms and remarkable bedroom suites, your guests will more than enjoy their surroundings on your special day. Our professional social consultant on staff will make sure that every detail of your event is perfect.

To receive our beautiful information package call us at 802-226-7361.

MEMBER OF SMALL LUXURY HOTELS

Photo by Mike Melillo

Common Ground Center

473 Tatro Road, Starksboro, Vermont 05487

802-453-2592 or 800-430-2667

Email: info@cgcvt.org • Website: www.cgcvt.org

Come and celebrate your wedding or special event at Common Ground Center in Starksboro, Vermont. We are located in a beautiful mountain valley on 700 acres of lush green meadows, forests with a meandering stream, a two-acre pond, miles of marked hiking trails and two Har-Tru tennis courts. We have donated an easement to the Vermont Land Trust for 560 acres of the property to be kept forever wild.

We are close to both Middlebury and Burlington. We are 6 hours from NYC, 4 hours from Boston and 2.5 hours from Montreal.

Facility: Common Ground Center is a rental facility and a family camp. Our facility was built using sustainable building practices. We have a large dining hall, lovely screened porch, a renovated Hay Barn (great for ceremonies and meetings) and the Creekside Barn (with a small indoor basketball court).

Accommodations: We are able to accommodate up to 120 overnight guests; housing up to 83 guests in our rustic cabins nestled in our Maple Grove. We also offer tenting in a scenic setting; platforms are available.

Catering: Our in-house chef can create your menu for your special day from hors d'oeuvres to wedding cake. We use fresh local organic products whenever available.

Call us today and arrange for a tour of our wonderful facilities.
See the possibilities for yourselves.

Cooper Hill Inn
...A Place for All Seasons

117 Cooper Hill Road
P.O. Box 146
East Dover, VT 05341

www.CooperHillInn.com

Charles & Lee Wheeler
802.348.6333
800.783.3229

Cyndi Freenman Photography

"Cooper Hill Inn has one of the most spectacular Mountain Panoramas in all New England" according to the Boston Globe. To the East Mount Manadnock in New Hampshire dominates the horizon while to the north you can see Ascutney and Cardigan up near Lebanon. To the South you will pick out Wachusett in Massachusetts and to the west is our own Mount Snow.

We have 10 beautiful acres and trails that lead into the Green Mountain National Forest. One of the unique attractions at Cooper Hill is watching the moon rise on one side of the Inn while watching the sunset on the other.

Most of our weddings and civil unions are held in a tent in front of the Inn. We have comfortably accommodated weddings with 220 guests. Often the romance extends beyond the wedding couple and guests go walking in the moonlight. Some brides choose to get married in the meadow with the view all around while others prefer the intimacy of the rock garden which is alive with flowers throughout the summer months. Whether its 220 outside or a smaller affair inside, the Inn belongs to you for the weekend and all our efforts are focused on your event.

We do not have any packages at Cooper Hill because every wedding is unique and every wedding is treated that way. We like to sit down with a bride and groom to talk about what they would like at their wedding while sharing what we have learned in hosting many such affairs here at the Inn.

We are also the caterers and love to talk about food. Again, our focus is on what you would like at your reception. We have a full liquor license and can structure the bar to suit your needs. We can handle all the details for you or put you in touch with local vendors.

Please give us a call or visit our website for more information.

Johnson, Vermont • 802.635.9078 • info@dreamingmountain.com

www.DreamingMountain.com

A place of enchantment, Dreaming Mountain is a private 372 acre estate, an idyllic setting for your wedding rehearsal, ceremony and reception, as well as family reunions and other social functions.

Panoramic vistas of the Green Mountains, artisan stonewalls, ornamental flower gardens, fruit orchards, three spring fed swimming ponds connected by small waterfalls await you.

Providing a perfect getaway Dreaming Mountain's paradise-like atmosphere is built on eco-operating principles of sustainability and environmentally sound practices. Our extensive landscape, flower and organic vegetable gardens offer you the opportunity to orchestrate your own unique wedding — including a green wedding if you choose, by utilizing seasonal flowers and vegetables abundant on the property.

Please call us to discover how Dreaming Mountain can make your special event even more memorable. Our spectacular setting provides the perfect background, and offers unparalleled photographic opportunities in the Lamoille Valley.

www.DreamingMountain.com

802.635.9078

Portrait Gallery

⊚echo®

LAKE AQUARIUM
AND SCIENCE CENTER
LEAHY CENTER
FOR LAKE CHAMPLAIN

BURLINGTON WATERFRONT
TOLL FREE 1-877-324-6386
EVENTS@ECHOVERMONT.ORG
ECHOVERMONT.ORG

Only ECHO provides this unique and memorable experience for your wedding day.

Capacity

With our lakefront location, breathtaking views of the Adirondacks, 3 floors filled with sparkling aquariums, and elegant indoor and outdoor spaces for ceremonies, dining, and dancing, you'll find ECHO to be the most unique and memorable location around. ECHO's innovative and elegant architecture can seat up to 242 for a plated dinner or up to 228 for a buffet. If you'd like a dance floor these accommodations drop to 170 for a plated dinner or 156 for a buffet. Up to 750 can be accommodated for a standing cocktail reception.

Location

Located on the Burlington Waterfront just 3.71 miles from the Burlington International Airport, one block from several premiere hotels, and walking distance from the Church Street Marketplace, ECHO is a premier lake aquarium and science center where the traditional reception is mixed in with the benefits of your own private tourist attraction.

Special Features

You and your guests will also feel good knowing your event's actually helping the environment and community. ECHO is LEED certified, which means it's designed to minimize water and energy consumption. Additionally, we encourage all our event partners to follow environmentally friendly practices. So, by hosting your event at ECHO you are actually reducing the impact your event has on the environment as well as helping provide our nonprofit with critically needed financial support to continue our mission, to educate and delight guests about the Ecology, Culture, History, and Opportunities for stewardship of the Lake Champlain Basin.

Please contact Private Event Sales for more information and come explore ECHO as a location for your wedding and reception!

Vermont ASSOCIATION OF
Wedding Professionals
MEMBER

Echo Lake Inn

P.O. Box 154 • Ludlow, VT 05149
802-228-8602 • 800-356-6844 • FAX: 802-228-3075
EMAIL: echolkinn@aol.com
WEB: www.echolakeinn.com

Capacity
- Exterior (lawn with tent)—225 sit-down
- Interior — 120 standing or 75 sit-down
  — 75 standing or 55 sit-down

Price Range   Customized wedding packages and menus available.

Catering   Full service in-house catering.

Types of Events
- Wedding
- Elegant Buffets
- Full Service Dinners
- Cocktails and hors d'oeuvres
- Rehearsal Dinners

Availability and Terms
Our banquet facilities are available year round.
Please contact us for specific deposit information.

Description of Services
Seating: Outdoor/Indoor/Veranda
Bar Facilities: Two Bars/Lounges
Parking: 50 Car Capacity

Special Services
We are located across the street from a historic church (1860's) that is perfect
for wedding services. Nestled at the edge of our woods is an old wishing well,
a perfect spot for a romantic ceremony.

A Sophisticated Country Inn
Located in Vermont's beautiful central lakes region, the Echo Lake Inn with 24
rooms and 6 condos was built in 1840 as a Victorian summer hotel. Today it
remains one of the few authentic country inns operating in Vermont. Every year
the Echo Lake Inn hosts many weddings and other important events. Chef Kevin
and his staff were recently featured in *Gourmet* and *Bon Appetit* magazines for
their excellent food and the quality of service that they provided. The warm,
sophisticated hospitality of the Echo Lake Inn awaits you on your special day!

Edson Hill Manor

1500 EDSON HILL ROAD
STOWE, VERMONT 05672
TELEPHONE: 802-253-7371
TOLL FREE: 800-621-0284
FAX: 802-253-6580
WEBSITE: www.edsonhillmanor.com
Contact Person: Billy O'Neil

Named One of the Six Best Inns in North America for Dining
— COUNTRY INNS MAGAZINE

Our Outstanding Property

Picturesque rolling Vermont countryside will be the setting for your most memorable day. Our terraces and lawns can accommodate up to 300 people and we have 25 guest rooms available. Secluded, private and romantic are the words that describe Edson Hill Manor.

Our Menus and Packages

The inn's nationally acclaimed dining room features innovative American cuisine. Buffets are from $30.00 per person plus tax and service. Luncheons are priced individually. We are happy to provide you with one of our wedding portfolios upon request.

Wedding Services

We offer outstanding wedding services: food, flowers, carriage rides, sleigh rides, as well as assistance with photographers and entertainment. Nationally acclaimed dining room and management with more than 30 years experience coordinating weddings and receptions. Our staff is happy to discuss all details of your wedding to assure a perfect day.

Accommodations and Activities

Each of our 25 guest rooms are wonderful and unique, some with fireplaces and canopy beds. The Inn is located in an estate-like setting, with beautiful fields and woods to explore. The property includes a riding stable and cross-country ski center, offering wonderful activities without leaving the premises.

"Edson Hill Manor… commands one of the most beautiful views in Vermont."
—BON APPETIT

*"If I could return to only one inn… it would be Edson Hill Manor…
I can think of nothing more appealing than… lingering over one of the inn's
matchless meals as the moon rises over the mountains."*
—SAN FRANCISCO EXAMINER

47

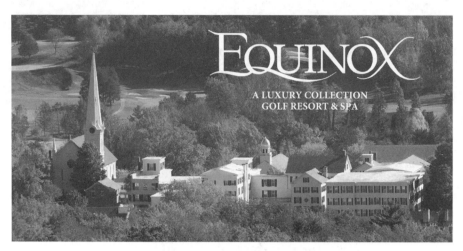

3567 Main Street, Route 7A, Manchester, VT 05254
800-362-4740 • www.equinoxresort.com

The Equinox, a Luxury Collection Resort & Spa, Vermont, one of New England's most luxurious leisure destinations, offers the perfect timeless setting for unforgettable wedding celebrations. A variety of stunning venue options, complete with gorgeous outdoor gardens nestled in the shadow of the beautiful Green Mountains, allow bride and groom to exchange vows among Southern Vermont's idyllic countryside.

Ceremonies and receptions can be held in a variety of photogenic venues including the crystal-chandeliered Colonnade, authentic Pond Pavilion, lush Lincoln Gardens, elegant Rockwell Ballroom, or the charming 1811 House and its Terraced Gardens. These stately indoor and outdoor venues, totaling a combined 18,500 square feet of event space, can accommodate more than 300 guests.

A dedicated wedding concierge at The Equinox helps brides plan every detail of their day; whether it's a formal affair, a relaxed celebration with family and friends or an intimate gathering. With special touches like a horse-drawn carriage, unique menu concepts from the superb in-house culinary team and guidance on every phase of the special event, the resort's wedding planners and concierge assist in designing the perfect white-glove wedding – from venue selection to honeymoon departure.

The Equinox is the perfect all-season destination where bride and groom and wedding guests alike can create memories to last a lifetime. The 195-room Equinox includes the main hotel, the all-suites Charles Orvis Inn, the quaint 1811 House as well as townhouses enabling varied accommodation options for any wedding party. The Equinox offers an array of distinctive amenities and activities from Orvis Fly Fishing, 18-hole championship golf, Land Rover Experience Driving School and the British School of Falconry.

THE Essex
VERMONT'S CULINARY RESORT & SPA™

70 Essex Way
Essex (Burlington), VT 05452

Toll free: 800-727-4295
Phone: 802-878-1100

Web: www.VtCulinaryResort.com
Email: info@VtCulinaryResort.com

It's your special day. We'll make it truly unforgettable.

A superb Vermont wedding is yours to have at The Essex Resort & Spa. Our beautiful resort, set on 18 acres, serves as the perfect backdrop for your most important day. Our standing as a Partner In Education with New England Culinary Institute ensures that no other Vermont wedding reception site can offer our deluxe accommodations and services, the unmatched catering provided by our award-winning chefs, and the attention to detail of our seasoned staff.

CAPACITY
The Essex offers more than 8,300 square feet of indoor and outdoor flexible space, including **The East Lawn, The Atrium, The Ballroom**, and our trio of **Salons**, accommodating up to 300 people.

AMENITIES
As the Burlington area's only AAA Four Diamond hotel, The Essex is a true destination Resort, offering a full-service Spa, Salon & Fitness Center, cooking classes at Cook Academy, tennis, golf, and award-winning restaurant options, all of which perfectly complement our classic accommodations.

SPA AT THE ESSEX
Spa at The Essex is the ideal sanctuary for brides-to-be. From makeup consultations to veil fittings, our professional staff caters to your every need. You are invited to enjoy pampering like you've never experienced before. Take advantage of our private relaxation lounge for a mini-getaway with the wedding party. A soothing massage, a refreshing manicure, perhaps a full body relaxation ritual—there's no limit to the rejuvenation you can experience.

The Essex is the premier choice for your perfect Vermont wedding.

NEW ENGLAND
CULINARY INSTITUTE®
Partners in Education

Vermont's premier eco-friendly wedding & special event site

Forget-Me-Not Farm

FORGET-ME-NOT FARM IS AN 80 ACRE WORKING HORSE FARM

NESTLED IN THE HILLS OF TINMOUTH VERMONT.

WE PRIDE OURSELVES ON THE SUSTAINABILITY OF OUR FARM

AND THE RENEWABLE RESOURCES WE UTILIZE.

—————— OUR $5,000.00 BLISS PACKAGE INCLUDES: ——————

(Call for personalized pricing options.)

- Site use from noon Friday to noon Sunday.
- Ceremony and reception sites.
- Use of our naturally lit 70' x 200' arena, (reducing rental costs and transport impact). Power is available in arena.
- Two hundred fifty chairs, twenty-five round tables, and five banquet tables.
- All trash and recycling cleanup.
- Ample parking.
- Famous outdoor solar hot water showers. Shower under the sky or stars with hot water heated by the sun!

- Farmhouse with three guest rooms with queen beds, one room with twin beds, two full baths, a large gathering room and living room. Fully equipped kitchen with lovely south view of the farm. *Use of the farmhouse is limited to the house guests only.*

FOR MORE INFORMATION:

MELODY SQUIER, 802.235.2718
12 McNAMARA ROAD, TOWN OF TINMOUTH
MIDDLETOWN SPRINGS, VERMONT 05757
msquier@forgetmenotfarmvt.com
http://weddings.forgetmenotfarmvt.com

50

GRAND *Isle* LAKE HOUSE

Located on East Shore Road North, Grand Isle,
on the Shores of Lake Champlain in Northwestern Vermont

Susan Bumbeck: Director of Special Events
Beverly Watson & Russell Holmes: Owner/Operators
Sheryl Eddy: Executive Chef

SEASON: MAY TO OCTOBER

Telephone: 802-372-5024 • Fax: 802-372-3713
P.O. Box 1144, Burlington, Vermont 05402
Email: info@GrandIsleLakeHouse.com • www.GrandIsleLakeHouse.com

The Grand Isle Lake House offers an unparalleled setting for weddings, social and business affairs. Originally built as Island Villa Hotel in 1903 and later operated as Camp Mary Crest for Girls, this historic building offers turn of the century charm with spectacular views of Vermont's Green Mountains and Lake Champlain.

The 55-acre piece of property and buildings that comprise the Grand Isle Lake House were donated as a generous gift to the Preservation Trust of Vermont in 1997. The Lake House represents a partnership between the Preservation Trust and the owners of Isabel's Catering.

The grounds are ideal for wedding receptions, civil unions, rehearsal dinners, family reunions, anniversaries and other social functions, easily accommodating large tents for up to 250 people. The main building offers sweeping views from the grand wrap around porch. The dining room and East Porch can seat up to 150. Our experienced catering director and chefs will work with you to create the prefect menu for your special event. Thirteen comfortable rooms are available for your family and guests overnight.

"Thank you for all of your incredible hard work and attention to detail in making our wedding everything we imagined and dreamed of. We completely enjoyed ourselves in the celebration with family and friends because we knew we could trust all of the details to your care."

BURLINGTON, VT

Hampton Inn & Event Center
Burlington, VT • I-89, Exit 16
Sales Office: 802-654-7646
Email: victoria.walsh@hilton.com
www.burlingtonvt.hamptoninn.com

THE PERFECT DAY...
THE PERFECT TIME...
THE PERFECT PLACE...

Karen Pike Photography

Professional service and attention to detail create joyous wedding celebrations at the Hampton Inn. Be prepared to relax and enjoy your day along with your friends and family as our cheerful, dedicated staff makes your day all that you have dreamed it would be.

The Champlain Ballroom, with brass chandeliers and windows looking out to a lovely garden gazebo provides the ideal backdrop and stage for your wedding. Outstanding cuisine and superior service play their part in a day dedicated to you and your guests. Nothing is overlooked. The hallmark of a wedding at the Hampton Inn is the personal attention you will receive from the day of your initial inquiry right through to your first dance. No question will go unanswered, because everything is important and no detail is too small.

Your guests will remember the fabulous food, the beautiful décor and the outstanding service long after your wedding day, and you will hear many times over that yours was one of the best weddings they have attended. You will remember the personal attention that made all of the happy memories possible.

Weddings at the Hampton Inn...
personal...happy...memorable...beautiful.

• Wedding packages include toast, buffet or seated meal, floral centerpieces, wedding cake, guestroom accommodations for the bride and groom, all taxes and gratuities. You are also welcome to use your own vendors and have us provide the toast and meal only or ask us to cater an event at your location of choice.

• Ask about incentives for Friday or Sunday wedding dates.

• We will also coordinate special overnight room rates for your friends and family.

52

inn & mountain resort

Route 100, Plymouth, Vermont 05056
Telephone: 802-672-2101 or
800-685-HAWK • Fax: 802-672-4338
Website: www.hawkresort.com
Email: ja@hawkresort.com

Mountain Lake Resort located on 1,200 acres in the heart of Vermont. Accommodations in our 50 room Inn or a Mountain Villa. The River Tavern restaurant serves breakfast, lunch and dinner. Complete recreation center with tennis courts, fly-fishing, kayaking, canoeing, water trampoline, hiking, mountain biking, swimming pools, archery, segways, horseback riding, cross-country skiing, snowshoeing, ice skating, sledding, etc…

Capacity
Up to 200 people in our tent located in a beautiful meadow between a mountain and a river.
Indoors: 75 people

Price Range
Customized menus and packages for each wedding.

Types of Functions
Receptions, Bridal Luncheons, Rehearsal Dinners, Welcome BBQ's, etc…

Catering & Beverage Service
Full Service indoor and outdoor catering. Menu's created for each wedding, offering exquisite cuisine and an award winning wine list.

Special Features & Amenities
- On Site Wedding Planner
- Dance Floor, Tables, Chairs, Linen, China, etc. is included
- Bon Fires with Smores
- Extensive Recreation Facility's
- Indoor & Outdoor Heated Swimming Pools
- Full Service Salon and Spa
- Ceremony on-site
- Menu Tastings
- Complimentary Luxury Room for the Bridal Couple

Hilton
Burlington

60 Battery Street, Burlington, VT 05401

Please contact our Wedding Professional
Katie McAllister at
katie.mcallister@hilton.com.
(802) 859-5044 • Fax: (802) 863-7818
www.burlington.hilton.com

Create the perfect event at the Hilton Burlington Hotel

What better way to begin your journey of a lifetime together than with a picture-perfect wedding at the Hilton Burlington! Celebrate your love with your family and friends at our attractive and convenient waterfront locale. With 16,000 square feet of flexible event space, well-appointed guestrooms, custom-designed food and beverage menus and a professional staff waiting to cater to your needs, the Hilton Burlington offers a full complement of wedding-planning services. Whether your needs include the engagement party, bridesmaids lunch, ceremony, rehearsal dinner, reception, post-wedding brunch or overnight accommodations, we offer creative and easygoing planning. Our Catering team will work with you to create memories that will last forever.

Distinctive Catering Our wedding services are as convenient and attractive as our location. Our focus on personalized service will help you create the special touches that will make your event uniquely yours. From our outside Garden Terrace to our Adirondack Ballroom, we offer one-of-a-kind event spaces that can accommodate from 10 to 350 guests and that will provide the perfect background for your celebration. Our wedding packages offer a wide array of pricing options to fit any budget and our Catering team is happy to customize menus to your taste.

Convenience and Location The convenience of planning and hosting your event at our attractive city center location promises to create memories that your family and friends will cherish for years to come. We are located two blocks from the shores of Lake Champlain and are steps away from the Burlington Town Center and the Church Street Marketplace.

Accommodations Our 258 deluxe guestrooms offer fabulous views of Lake Champlain, the Adirondack Mountains and the city skyline. Special discounted room rates can be made available for your family and friends. We offer complimentary access to our heated indoor swimming pool, whirlpool and fitness center as well as airport shuttle service to and from the Burlington International Airport.

*Discover the fresh and contemporary comfort of the Hilton Burlington –
expertly melding modern indulgence with local flair.*

1768
H H **Hubbell**
1768 **Homestead**
AT COLGATE PARK

1768 Hubbell Homestead
At Colgate Park
1357 West Road
Bennington, VT 05201
www.colgatepark.com
colgatepark@myfairpoint.net

Overlooking the Vermont Green Mountains and the Historic Bennington Battle Monument, 1768 Hubbell Homestead at Colgate Park provides a perfect venue for your wedding. Beautiful views and grounds, a one-of-a-kind Tent with accommodations on-site, the historic homestead property can host your special wedding day event.

From sumptuous catered gourmet breakfasts to evening dinners and cocktail receptions to wedding day feasts, event supervision services and breathtaking Vermont scenery, Colgate Park is the place for the ultimate destination wedding.

1868 North Route 116, Bristol, VT 05443
Phone: 802-453-2432 Toll Free: 888-424-2432
www.innatbaldwincreek.com · Linda@innatbaldwincreek.com
Wedding Coordinator: Linda Harmon

Chef-Owner Doug Mack's Celebrated Farm-fresh Cuisine
Flawless Details in a Picture-Perfect Setting
Historic Red Barn for Weddings and Civil Unions

Conveniently situated in the Champlain Valley, just twenty minutes north of Middlebury and thirty minutes south of Burlington, this 1797 historic inn and acclaimed restaurant are located on twenty-five picturesque acres bordering Baldwin Creek.

Facilities:

The Inn hosts carefree receptions for up to 200 guests, catered under a stunning peaked tent. Adjacent to the tent is our Red Barn, circa 1830, that provides a delightful venue for socializing, music and dancing. The barn also accommodates up to 75 guests for smaller rehearsals and receptions. For parties under 45, we recommend one of the Inn's four dining rooms. On-site ceremonies are held on the South Lawn or in the Red Barn. We offer five overnight guestrooms with full breakfast. Nearby bed and breakfasts, inns, and hotels offer additional lodging for large gatherings. Shuttle buses to and from the Inn are easily arranged.

Innovative Cuisine:

Our food is renowned, expertly prepared for the past twenty-five years by professional chef/co-owner Douglas Mack. Wedding menus are designed with a seasonal focus on locally raised, farm-fresh foods. A personal tasting meeting, scheduled during the planning stages, helps fine-tune your menu selections.

Arrangements:

Co-owner and wedding coordinator Linda Harmon schedules only one event per day to insure that each is personalized and hosted with exacting care. The cost is determined by your menu selection and bar arrangements. Price per person includes food, wedding cake, full service beverage, skilled catering staff, tent rental, and coordination and facility fee.

Call or email us to request an information packet or
to arrange for a meeting.

Inn at Lareau Farm
Home of American Flatbread

48 Lareau Road
Waitsfield, Vermont 05673
802-496-4949 or 800-833-0766
Lisabeth Magoun • Innkeeper
Email: play@lareaufarminn.com
Web: www.lareaufarminn.com
www.americanflatbread.com

Our Inn
The Inn at Lareau Farm is a picturesque Vermont farmhouse nestled in on a beautiful meadow beside the Mad River. We offer twelve charming rooms in assorted sizes to suit all your guests' needs. Our inn, set on 60 acres with its' wraparound porches, large airy dining room, meadow pavilion, organic gardens and plenty of space to play is sure to delight your guests. Located in the heart of the Mad River Valley with easy access to many valley wide amenities, the Lareau Farm is the first choice to host your celebration!

At the Pavilion
Our 40 x 80 pavilion can comfortably hold 120-150 guests for dinner or up to 200 for a cocktail party. Additional tents may be rented for larger celebrations. It has a small bandstand, twinkling lighting, wood stove, two patio heaters, removable tent sides and spacious bathrooms. Also included is our wood fired stone kitchen with oven, wok and grill, fire circle, ceremony site, seating and tables for 100 guests. Pavilion pricing for a wedding is $2,500 [based upon 100 guests] Ask about other celebration pricing.

Catering
Lareau Farm offers minimal catering of American Flatbread rehearsal dinners and scrumptious bon voyage brunches. Please inquire about pricing. We welcome proven reliable off premise caterers for larger events and may help you with your selection.

We are the home to American Flatbread Company, where local foods rule. Ask about our traveling wood fired oven, restaurants or whole sale flatbread bakery. We are proud members of the Vermont Fresh Network and Vermont Businesses for Social Responsibilities.

The INN AT
MOUNTAIN VIEW FARM

Box 355, Darling Hill Road, East Burke, Vermont 05832
800-572-4509 • 802-626-9924 • Fax: 802-626-3625
Email: innmtnview@kingcon.com • Web: www.innmtnview.com

Awarded one of "30 Great Inns" by Travel Leisure
Spectacular pastoral views and historic farm estate on 440 acres provide
an idyllic backdrop for your wedding or special event.
"One of the most breathtaking hilltop views in Vermont" —Vermont Life.

Facilities

Our expansive front lawn accommodates 200 people or more under a peaked white heated tent with majestic views of Burke Mountain. The restored Morgan Barn provides a rustic facility for a party of 170 guests. For your indoor celebration, business conference or family reunion, our Willoughby Room with fireplace accommodates 50 people.

Wedding Services

The Inn offers many lovely settings for your wedding ceremony. Whether you wish a romantic garden wedding with a harpist, a canopied ceremony on a breathtaking hilltop, or arrival in a horse drawn carriage, we make it happen for you.

For food service, engage our experienced, local resident caterer. We can recommend distinctive purveyors of flowers, wedding cakes, photography, music, spa services, and horse drawn carriages.

Accommodations & Activities

Our charming inn with 14 guest rooms and luxury suites provides privacy and relaxation for your family and close friends.

Our farm estate is laced with miles of walking, mountain biking and cross-country ski trails, known as the Kingdom Trails. Arrangements can be made for on-site massage and beauty services. Nearby St. Johnsbury Country Club offers superb 18 hole golf.

Service at the Inn is gracious and our staff is friendly and efficient. We will be happy to show you our facilities and assist with details. Please phone for an appointment.

"Our guests were overwhelmed with the beauty of your Inn and
the professionalism of your staff."

The Inn At
QUAIL RUN

The Inn At Quail Run

106 Smith Road • Wilmington, VT 05363
www.theinnatquailrun.com

A special place to celebrate the wedding of your dreams

The Inn is located on 15 wooded acres with views of both Deerfield Valley and Haystack Mountain and only 3.5 miles from the Mt. Snow ski resort. Enjoy the natural beauty of the surrounding countryside and create the day you have dreamed of all your life.

You and your family can enjoy the entire Inn with 10 bedrooms with 10 private baths or just use 6 bedrooms with 6 private baths. Our goal is to make your wedding day and entire stay unforgettable.

The Inn features a grand living room, dining room, game room with billiard table, large commercial kitchen and outdoor pool, all for your private use. In addition to the guest rooms at the Inn, the Owner's Quarters and Cottage offer an additional seven bedrooms.

It's the perfect getaway for you and your guests for your wedding day or weekend wedding!

Come celebrate your wedding day with us.
Please call or email Meiling at (732) 877-8009 or meiling@m3realty.com to discuss our many offerings and to learn how the staff at The Inn at Quail Run will help make your dreams a reality.

Barrie Fisher

The Inn AT THE
ROUND
BARN FARM

1661 East Warren Road
Waitsfield, Vermont 05673
802-496-2276
www.theroundbarn.com
e-mail: info@theroundbarn.com
Anne Marie & Tim L. Piper
Innkeepers/Owners

Experience the Magic of the Round Barn Farm

We invite you to make our magical setting part of your memories for a lifetime. This historic landmark offers 245 acres of meadows, manicured gardens and ponds offering the perfect backdrop for your celebration. We love hosting weddings and it shows!

At the Round Barn Farm we have not only one of Vermont's last remaining historic Round Barns, but we also have our own catering company and a luxurious 12 guestroom Inn.

Our Historic Round Barn — Accommodating parties from 75 – 200 guests, our barn is a fully heated, beautifully restored 3 level facility offering the ideal Vermont barn setting. From the pastels of spring & summer, the gold's of autumn to the rich jewel tones of winter, our barn is the perfect complement to any color scheme or style of wedding.

Cooking from the Heart — The Round Barn Farm is also the home of our renowned catering company. Freshly prepared, locally grown, creative and beautifully presented food is our passion. Our full service event planning staff is friendly, creative, experienced and caring, dedicated to making your event a wonderful lifetime memory for you, your family and friends.

Inn at the Round Barn — Our award winning Inn offers 12 impeccably designed guestrooms. Our warm and friendly staff is dedicated to making your stay relaxed and enjoyable. Because we are in a resort area with over 1,500 beds within 15 minutes of our Inn, the Sugarbush/Mad River Valley can accommodate all of your friend's and family's lodging needs.

Our staff will help to organize spring, summer & fall activities such as golf outings, hiking, fishing & biking. In the winter months, sleigh rides and moonlight-guided snowshoe dinner tours may be arranged. Our desire is to offer you and your guests the complete Vermont destination wedding experience.

Please call us at (802) 496-2276 or contact us at www.theroundbarn.com

Vermont ASSOCIATION OF
Wedding Professionals
MEMBER

Happily Ever After Should Begin at The Top

**The Inn
of the
Six Mountains
at Killington**

2617 Killington Road
Killington, VT 05751
phone 800-228-4676 or 802-422-4302
www.sixmountains.com
sixmountains@hotmail.com

Contact: Brian Halligan

A Perfect Mountain Wedding in Vermont

You're ready for one of the most important days of your life, and you want it to be beautiful. Surrounded by the lush Green Mountains, The Inn of the Six Mountains exudes a charm and rustic elegance for a memorable occasion. We provide everything from professional planning and lovely décor, to sumptuous cuisine and a warm atmosphere for a wedding in Killington, Vermont that you and your guests will always remember. Whether it's an intimate gathering, or a gala event, your wedding will be perfect with us.

Why book your wedding at The Inn of the Six Mountains?

- *A professional and courteous wedding planner is available for you during every step of your wedding, from the engagement dinner, to the departing breakfast.*
- *Our gorgeous outdoor facilities are the perfect backdrop for an outdoor wedding in Vermont (available in season).*
- *We offer an elegant ballroom for 120 guests, as well as other options for a tasteful reception.*
- *The bride and groom receive one night's complimentary lodging with receptions of 100 people or more.*
- *Chef Steve Walker will customize the wedding menu to suit your tastes and budget, with a tasting available prior to final menu selections.*
- *Custom-colored linens and other specialty items are available.*
- *We offer comfortable accommodations with luxurious touches for your wedding guests.*

"Our wedding day was everything we envisioned and more. The setting was elegant, the food was exquisite and your staff was caring and gracious… Thank you for filling this special day with so many fond memories"
—Suzanne & Arden Lathrop

61

Jeudevine Falls

**2259 Craftsbury Road
Hardwick, Vermont 05843
(802) 472-5486
www.weddingfalls.com
www.waterfallswedding.com**

*Just 2-1/4 miles from the jct. of VT
Route 14 North & VT Route 15*

Why Have Your Special Day at an Ordinary Place?

GET MARRIED IN HEAVEN AND HAVE THE RECEPTION OF A LIFETIME AT JEUDEVINE FALLS

Your special day. You found the perfect dress, the perfect rings, and the perfect flowers. Most importantly, you found each other. May we suggest the perfect place? Tree branches spread over you and the music of the rushing waterfall, a soft breeze and native songbirds fills the air. You stand together in a gazebo that looks like it may have grown there as your guests wait for the two of you to be united as one.

Jeudevine Falls in Hardwick, Vermont offers all of this and more. The pride and love we feel for this place shows through in every little detail. We invite you to share your ceremony with those who matter most to you at the falls. We are happy to advise you on lodging for out of town guests, caterers or anything else to help make your special day, your perfect day.

Our search for a beautiful, romantic and fun outdoor location for our recent Wedding ended when we discovered Jeudevine Falls. With its beautifully constructed Gazebo, breathtaking waterfalls and meticulously maintained grounds and gardens we found just what we had been looking for. Bob Edebohls, the owner had just installed a large wedding tent along with a great dance floor. He was also great at helping us with our final details and preparations. We would highly recommend this site for any couple looking for a unique Wedding location…

Thanks again Bob!
Sincerely,
Jim and Ann Severance

228 East Mountain Road
Killington, VT 05751

1.888.64.GRAND
www.killington.com
email: weddings@killington.com

Trust Killington with your most precious memories.

- An award-winning, full-service in-house catering team.

- An on-site sales coordinator, who will help guide you every step of the way starting with your first visit to Killington, to the champagne toast.

- Customized wedding packages and menus to ensure your day is perfect.

- A seating capacity of up to 400 people with spectacular settings and decorating options to suit your taste.

- A complimentary hotel suite for the bridal couple.

- Accommodations including hotel rooms and suites at the Killington Grand Resort Hotel and fully equipped one to four-bedroom condominiums at Killington Lodging.

- The Killington Grand Spa which pampers you with a complete menu of body, skin and nail treatments.

- Relaxing recreation for you and your guests with an on-site 18-hole championship golf course, driving range, tennis, hiking, mountain biking, an Adventure Center with 2 Alpine Slides, climbing wall, and gondola rides to Killington Peak.

- Winter wedding fun with skiing, snowboarding, snowmobiling and snowshoe tours.

The Landgrove Inn

132 Landgrove Road
Landgrove, VT 05148
Phone: (802) 824-6673 or (800) 669-8466
Fax: (802) 824-6790
Email: vtinn@sover.net
www.landgroveinn.com

Even in Vermont there are few locations that equal the idyllic, mountain valley in which The Landgrove Inn still proudly resides.

The original 1810 farmhouse, barn, and add-ons have together operated as a full-service Inn since 1959. Surrounded by mountains, meadows, rivers, and ponds, down a tree-canopied lane, if a bucolic country setting is what you've been searching for – search no more.

What we have to offer you:
- A stunning locale.
- A tented meadow with gardens and views.
- Classic, colonial churches minutes away for your indoor ceremony.
- Outdoor ceremony venues by a winding river or picturesque pond.
- Complete food and beverage service.
- Pool, tennis, biking, hiking, antiques and retail shopping activities nearby for your guests.
- 18 uniquely-decorated rooms with flexible sleeping arrangements.
- Horse-drawn carriage or sleigh rides through the Inn's 35 private acres.
- The peace and quiet of the country.

Capacity and Reservations:
We can comfortably accommodate an indoor ceremony and dining for 65 people in our rustic Rafter Lounge and sprawling Dining Room, or 150 people in our tented meadow outdoors until the end of September.

Your Wedding Package:
We will work closely with you to custom design your special day – *your* way. We have numerous wedding resources available for you to choose from. Weddings are booked months in advance.

Our Promise:
We will do whatever we possibly can to create a one-of-a-kind, unforgettable experience for you, your family, and your friends. Personal attention, attention to detail, the only thing we can't promise you is the weather of your dreams. The wedding of your dreams is a different matter.

The

Lilac Inn

53 Park Street, Brandon, VT 05733
800-221-0720 • 802-247-5463
Email innkeeper@lilacinn.com
www.lilacinn.com

"A romantic getaway." Best Places to Stay

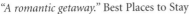

***One of Vermont's most romantic sites for your
wedding celebration in any season
— The Lilac Inn, Selected as one of the 100 best US wedding destinations***
100 Best U.S. Wedding Destinations by Kathryn Gabriel Loving

We invite you to have your wedding and reception at *The Lilac Inn,* the place for your romantic Vermont destination dream wedding ceremony, reception and unforgettable memories — in any season. Our completely renovated 1909 mansion has hosted over four hundred Vermont weddings —ranging in size from two to two hundred and fifty guests.

Since your Vermont wedding is a time of family sharing and reunions with friends from afar, we encourage you to plan for a multi-day event. This will provide time for laughter, conviviality, merriment, and reunion. Our Vermont weddings packages can include rehearsal dinner, reception and day after wedding brunch — each with a menu designed especially for you and your tastes. With only one reception scheduled per day, your Vermont wedding reception will be a special celebration.

Our tented courtyard can accommodate 250 seated guests and the historic, air conditioned grand ballroom, wrapped in oversized beveled glass French doors and windows which fill the room with soft sunlight from its southern exposure can accommodate 130 seated guests.

The Lilac Inn, Brandon, Vermont is a leading romantic luxury Vermont Country Inn Bed and Breakfast known for New England and Vermont weddings, Middlebury College events, Green Mountains recreation, corporate retreats and special occasions. Featured in Yankee, Country Living and Vermont magazines, the feel throughout is that of a "small luxury hotel with personal service to match". Each of the guest rooms has a unique personality — all have private bath, television and air conditioning, three have wood burning fireplaces.

***The elegant mansion, the courtyard and gardens, the fine food, the
attention to detail by all the staff and owners, plus the willingness to work
with the bride and groom to create their special dream wedding has made
The Lilac Inn, a favorite year round wedding site since 1991.***

65

MIDDLEBURY INN
❧ SINCE 1827 ❧

14 Court Sq. Middlebury, Vermont 05753
800-842-4666 ext. 582
weddings@middleburyinn.com
www.middleburyinn.com

A Romantic, Storybook Wedding.

Imagine gathering with family and friends in a picture-perfect Vermont Inn to celebrate your most special occasion. Whether you envision a celebration that's traditional, formal, intimate or grand, The Middlebury Inn has set the stage for memorable events since 1827. Boasting 70 beautiful newly renovated rooms, there is plenty of space for the whole family.

From elegant plated dinners served in The Founder's Room to a lovely outdoor courtyard, there is a special place just waiting for you to make your own history. The Founder's Room is a formal, luxurious ballroom ideal for weddings of up to 160 guests. The courtyard is the perfect venue for cocktail receptions and weddings up to 120.

Why rent a room when you can reserve a Mansion!

With 10 Rooms on two floors connected by a beautiful spiral staircase, the Porter House Mansion is the perfect place to lodge your wedding party and enjoy our gorgeous "Bridal Suite." Built in 1825 by Jonathan Wainwright, the Mansion is sure to impress and delight all your guests. Enjoy a special afternoon tea, or morning breakfast buffet, all in the intimate privacy of your very own historic retreat.

Let us pamper your guests with our "Historic Service", exceptional cuisine and relaxing on-site spa. The Waterfalls Day Spa at the Middlebury Inn offers exclusive services for your special weekend.

Call for more information on Mansion rentals, food service options and services available at the Waterfalls Day Spa.

Vermont ASSOCIATION OF
Wedding Professionals
MEMBER

VWA
VERMONT WEDDING ASSOCIATION
vermontweddingassociation.com

Mountain Meadows Lodge

285 Thundering Brook Road
Killington, VT 05751
Telephone: 802-775-1010
www.vermont-wedding.com
mountainmeadowsvt@hotmail.com
Contact: Anne or Bill Mercier

The best destination wedding site — lakefront property to share exclusively with your family and friends all weekend.

Lakefront lodge amid acres of private hills, bordered by National forest. Spectacular views of ski mountains and lake from many rooms. The Appalachian hiking Trail cuts through the property, leading to overlooks and waterfalls. On-site canoeing, kayaking, row boating to nearby islands, fishing in stocked lake, farm animal feedings, lake and pool swimming and yard games. Activities are included, offered in a relaxed atmosphere, conducive to bringing families and friends together.

Enjoy country lodging is a circa 1850's Vermont farmhouse and original dairy barn. The facility and activities become Bride and Groom's for entire weekend celebration, and they receive a complimentary suite and gift.

We can accommodate your event in any season and we offer flexible bar options, customized menus including vegetarian/vegan, "theme" menus, specialty wedding cakes, desserts and ice cream bars. Baby-sitting can be arranged during the weekend festivities, if desired.

Unique to Mountain Meadows:

Outdoor and small summer/fall indoor weddings include events such as lakeside campfire with marshmallow roast and guided morning hikes to waterfalls. Rehearsal dinners and full reception meals with strict attention to the couple's budget and tastes can be arranged. See our website for sample menus.

"Dear Bill and Anne, Thank you again for all of your hard work in making our wedding weekend turn out perfectly! It was everything we imagined and more. Our guests continue to tell us over and over what a great time they had and how beautiful the lodge and its surroundings are. Between the animals, the hikes, the lake, Mountain Meadows made everyone happy. The food, drinks, atmosphere and service were all terrific as well!
Thanks again,
Doug and Lisa Young"

SAINT PHALLE PHOTOGRAPHY

195 Mountain Top Road
Chittenden, VT 05737
802-483-2311
800-445-2100
www.mountaintopinn.com
stay@mountaintopinn.com
Contact: Khele Sparks

"Breathtaking Natural Beauty, Every Season, Every Wedding"

Imagine the perfect mountain top setting…you are surrounded by your family and friends amidst the majestic mountains of Vermont overlooking a serene lake, where everyone is dedicated to pleasing you and your guests. Arrive at your ceremony atop the meadow by romantic horse drawn carriage or handcrafted Austrian sleigh. Celebrate your reception with dancing under a bright starlit night or in the Dining Room with the moon reflecting through the window as the snowflakes drift quietly to the ground.

Throughout the weekend, your guests will appreciate the endless activities that we offer at the Resort, like horseback riding, kayaking, fly-fishing, clay bird shooting, hiking, cross country skiing, snowshoeing, and much more.

The Mountain Top Inn & Resort is the perfect place for your wedding. Our facilities accommodate weddings of all sizes, from an intimate gathering of the bride and groom to tented events with 250 guests. Every meal an affair, expertly prepared by an exceptional culinary team.

For your wedding the entire Lodge is reserved for you, your friends and family, enabling our staff to provide the most personal and attentive service. Wedding coordinators will assist with every detail, from the creation of an amazing and luscious menu with accompanying wines, to selection of your centerpieces, linens and gift bags…right through to the time you say farewell to your "new friends" at The Mountain Top Inn & Resort…with the splendid memories of the most special day of your life.

"You were an absolute pleasure to work with…our family and friends could not say enough. The consensus was that a weekend simply was not long enough to enjoy the Mountain Top Inn and all it had to offer. My five year old niece (the flower girl) has already made designs to marry there in twenty years."
–Lina & Dani, May 2009

OKEMO
MOUNTAIN RESORT

77 Okemo Ridge Road
Ludlow, Vermont 05149
functions@okemo.com
1-800-78-OKEMO
functions.okemo.com

Weddings at Okemo Mountain Resort

A stunning Southern Vermont mountain setting, legendary service, attention to detail, and creative menu selections are just the beginning of the *Okemo Difference.*

Okemo Mountain Resort provides several unique and beautiful locations for special celebrations. Nestled within the lovely Black River Valley, Okemo offers the perfect Vermont setting for your wedding.

A Special Setting for every Size and Taste

The newest offering at Okemo is at Jackson Gore. The Roundhouse is a unique room with vaulted ceilings, cherry columns, and a stone hearth fireplace. The one-of-kind octagonal shape provides an inviting, air-conditioned atmosphere with surrounding windows looking out to the carefully carved trails of Okemo Mountain. The Roundhouse is located in the new Jackson Gore Inn, an ideal, central location for overnight accommodations, dining, and wedding festivities.

For smaller celebrations Okemo offers the warmth and charm of the new Epic restaurant in the Solitude Lodge with cathedral ceilings and a circular stone fireplace, the new Wine Room at the Coleman Brook Tavern, or the elegant and tastefully appointed facilities of the Okemo Valley Golf Club. Okemo is also home to the Mid-Mountain Sugar House where the scenic views of the Black River Valley offer the perfect backdrop for your memorable event.

And there's more...but no matter which facility you select, you will enjoy personalized attention from your first meeting with the Okemo team, right through the tossing of the bouquet. That's the Okemo Difference.

Expert Catering with a Personal Touch

You will benefit from the extensive experience of our Sales and Culinary team. We will make sure that all the little details are addressed during the planning process so that your special day brings only enjoyment and warm memories.

SPECTACULAR VIEWS. RELAXING ATMOSPHERE. GENUINE HOSPITALITY.

The Okemo Difference.

The Old Lantern

www.oldlantern.com
802.425.2120
3260 Greenbush Road,
Charlotte, VT 05445

A CHARMING RUSTIC LOCATION
FOR WEDDINGS AND SPECIAL EVENTS.

We offer some of the finest food in Vermont made exclusively by our chef, Roland Gaujac. His background, training and specialties are the traditional and provencal cuisine of France. He is a graduate of the Grenoble Hotelry School in France and has spent many years expanding his knowledge of cuisine by working directly with the great chefs of San Francisco, Los Angeles, Detroit and New York.

The Old Lantern is an 8,000 square-foot Adirondack-style post and beam structure with the largest hardwood dance floor in Vermont. Excellently situated with plenty of parking, we are only 15 miles from Burlington and only 20 miles from Middlebury.

We can accommodate both small and large parties, up to 300 guests. We offer the finest cuisine, a charming setting for receptions and ceremonies, the perfect place to create the memory of a lifetime.

*"…just wanted to let you guys know that everything was wonderful!!
Thanks for making sure everything ran smoothly! The food was great and the
cake was beautiful!!! I'll make sure to recommend you guys to my friends!
Great job to all the staff!"* – Marijean (mother of the bride)

**All packages include tables, white chairs, linens, china, glassware,
utensils, candles and floral centerpieces.**

Samuel Read Hall House
The Old Stone House Museum
109 Old Stone House Road, Brownington Vermont 05860
802 754 2022 • Fax: 802 754 9336
www.oldstonehousemuseum.org

Samuel Read Hall House Weddings

Time has slowed down at this elegant 1831 mansion.
From every direction beautiful pastoral views enchant the eye.
There is an elegant center hall, two parlors, a library, and an old
fashioned kitchen. The house has a code-compliant kitchen for the
caterers, and a handicap accessible entrance and bathroom.
A bluestone terrace is perfect for viewing the pond. A sitting room,
bedroom and private bath are upstairs for the bride.

The grounds are designed with lawns adequate for a tent up to
100' long, a convenient place for a caterers' tent, and ample parking.
The house can seat 40 guests, the terrace 16 and the grounds
can accommodate a tent for groups up to 150 people.
For the ceremony, there are the lawns surrounding the house and
the site includes the historic Observatory, a unique belvedere
with magnificent views as far as Canada.
There also is a small white church built in 1841 across
the road that is available for ceremonies.

802 754 2022

Please visit our web site:
www.oldstonehousemuseum.org

72

One Park Street North Bennington, Vermont   802.442.5441   parkmccullough.org

BANQUET AND RECEPTION SITES

BANQUET FACILITY FOR **50–600** GUESTS
INDOOR OR OUTDOOR EVENTS
BEAUTIFUL UNIQUE VERMONT SETTING

360 Spear Street, South Burlington, VT 05403
Reservations: 802-862-5200 • www.Quarryhillclub.com
Email: Quarryhillclub@aol.com

Our Setting: The Quarry Hill Club is a beautiful Vermont reception setting located at the entrance to Burlington, just past the University of Vermont Campus. Our nicely landscaped grounds with flower gardens help create a truly unique reception atmosphere of casual elegance underneath the three-peak white tent, set up poolside or if you wish, you can have your reception in the Club House banquet room with a 90' covered deck overlooking the club grounds.

Outside Events: Exclusive use of our 3.5 acre site, five hour event to include; 40'x 80' white tent with lights, sides, hunter green carpeted floor, 20'x20' parquet dance floor, all of the set up, tables, chairs, table linens, dinner candles, cake service, welcome sign, banquet wait staff and manager on duty. Facility rental fee $1,800–$2,900.

Inside Events: Include Club House bar area, banquet room, 16'x18' dance floor and 16'x90' covered deck overlooking club lawn areas, all the set up, welcome sign, banquet servers. $900–$1,450.

Catering: Full service in-house catering offering a nice selection of beef, poultry or seafood dinner buffets, in addition to an extensive selection of hot and cold hors d'oeuvres. Our most popular reception buffet last season was Prime Rib and a Baked Stuffed Chicken breast dinner.

Bar Facilities: Indoor and outdoor bars available with full selection of liquor, select wines and ice cold beers.

Servers: Courteous and attentive, all servers wear black and white with black tie.

Lodging: There are over 1,200 rooms at 7 hotels within a 2 mile distance of the Club, with price ranges and room styles suitable for all your guests.

Call us for the perfect rehearsal dinner, ceremony and/or reception site offering a Vermont setting in the heart of Burlington. We will provide you and your guests a memorable occasion.

Riverside Farm

At the covered bridge
57 Tweed River Drive, Pittsfield, VT 05762
P: 802-746-8822   F: 802-746-8567
www.riversidefarmweddings.com
info@riversidefarmweddings.com

Along historic route 100, one of New England's most beautifully restored country estates warmly welcomes you. A perfect venue for a destination wedding, the property consists of 300 sprawling acres of exquisitely manicured grounds and mountain vistas. Ideally located in the heart of the Green Mountains, just 7 miles from Killington Ski Resort your guests will be able to take advantage of all that Vermont has to offer throughout all the seasons.

Destination Wedding — Specializing in the "destination wedding weekend" Riverside Farm offers every amenity a couple could ask for. Imagine your wedding as a three-day celebration, which includes a delicious rehearsal dinner, a beautiful outdoor ceremony, a magnificent reception and a farewell Sunday brunch, utilizing all the different locations on the property. You may select an elegant tented event in the fabulous landscaped grounds, for larger groups, or you may opt for the breathtaking post and beam Wedding Barn, which has been masterfully restored to seat 180 people or the Red Barn restored in 2003 to seat 120 people. Your guests may stay in the various accommodations throughout the property, including the Main House, the River House, the Guest House and the recently renovated Stables, as well as the stunning Bridal Suite and new Groom's House. More guest lodging is available at The Amee Farm, only ½ mile away (www.ameefarm.com). Riverside Farm and it's partner properties can accommodate your entire wedding party all within 1 mile of Riverside. We can provide you and your guests with a weekend they will never forget.

Wedding Concierge — More than an on-site coordinator, we are pleased to provide you and your guests with 100% personalized and attentive service during your stay. Our wedding concierge is here to assist you with every detail from beginning to end, so that nothing is overlooked, and that your day is stress free. From helping you design your wedding by offering unique suggestions and recommending vendors who will suit your needs, to facilitating and coordinating the flow of the event to ensure that your day runs smoothly and with precision. Our wedding concierge is available to schedule activities for your guests, negotiate hotel arrangements and assist with transportation.

Riverside Farm, the seclusion, elegance and natural perfection that every couple deserves on their wedding day.

Business Hours: 8:30 a.m. – 5:00 p.m.
Museum is open mid-May through October

Contact Person: Bruce Andrews

Route 7, P.O. Box 10, Shelburne, Vermont 05482
Phone: (802) 985-3346, ext. 3389 · Fax: (802) 985-2331
Email: bandrews@shelburnemuseum.org

Celebrate Your Future Surrounded by the Past

Nestled in the magnificent Champlain Valley of Vermont, the natural and historic beauty of Shelburne Museum's buildings, gardens, and grounds create a unique and pastoral setting for your wedding. The landscape includes sweeps of open lawn, panoramic views, and intimate gardens with a range of plantings that offer enjoyment throughout the seasons.

Sites available at Shelburne Museum include the elegant Brick House; the charming Charlotte Meeting House; the historic steamboat *Ticonderoga*; the romantic Bostwick Garden; and picturesque settings for tents in the heart of the Museum's grounds.

To receive an informational packet with color brochures and a complete description of Shelburne Museum's unique setting, please contact us.

Capacity: 50 to 400

Price Range: $1,000–$7,500

Catering: No in-house catering available. Approved caterer list will be provided by Museum.

Bar Facilities: To serve alcohol, caterer must be licensed.

Handicap Facilities: Please inquire for full accessibility information.

The Skinner Barn

Peter Boynton · 609 Common Road, Waitsfield, VT 05673
802-496-4422 · *pboynton@madriver.com* · *www.theskinnerbarn.com*

The Skinner Barn is a beautifully restored historic dairy barn originally built in 1891 by the Daniel Skinner family. Of classic post and beam construction, it offers a special environment for educational classes, cultural events, parties, and receptions. Flanked by the majestic Northfield Ridge to its east and the mountains that host the Sugarbush and Mad River Glen ski areas to its west, The Skinner Barn offers a quintessential Vermont setting and stunning views.

The upper floor of The Skinner Barn has been restored with loving attention keeping the historical character of the structure intact. This open space, originally designed for hay storage, is now used as an assembly space for a wide range of functions.

Our Season runs from mid-May to mid-October.

Facility fees for The Skinner Barn are as follows:
Weddings: $2,750.00
Rehearsals Dinners: $2,000.00
Brunch & party fees: $250.00/Hr.

The facility fee includes the use of the barn, parking supervision, and use of the meadows for ceremonies and receptions. The fee also includes (125) **indoor chairs** and (10) five foot round dinner tables. The fee does not include outdoor chairs, tableware, glassware, linens, or catering and beverage services.

The facility fee applies to the function date for which the barn has been rented. Any use of the barn or site *prior* to the event, (decorating, rehearsals, caterer set-up, etc.), will be billed separately and is based on the availability of the site.

Music for events at The Skinner Barn favors acoustic and lightly amplified instruments. Live music concludes at 9:30 pm with guest departure at 10 pm.

STOWE
MOUNTAIN
LODGE.

7412 Mountain Road, Stowe, VT 05672
888.4.STOWEVT (888.478.6938)
hmichel@destinationhotels.com
stowemountainlodge.com

BANQUET AND RECEPTION SITES

The perfect beginning to your happily ever after.

Whether you've always envisioned your dream wedding as a private mountaintop ceremony for two or a spirited gala of 300, Stowe Mountain Lodge offers the ideal location for your picture perfect wedding. Located slope-side at Vermont's most romantic and storied mountains, a wedding at Stowe Mountain Lodge means whimsical, inspired and personalized attention every step of the way.

With a selection of beautiful, private dining rooms, unique indoor and outdoor event spaces, outside terrace with fire pit and spectacular mountain views, Stowe Mountain Lodge has all that you have dreamed of for your wedding day celebration.

Your personal wedding specialist will coordinate all your wedding planning details. Our Vermont inspired, farm-to-table cuisine and our creative and customized wedding packages will make your decisions effortless.

For your out-of-town guests, all the comforts of home await. Private balconies with magnificent mountain views, custom furnishings with bamboo linens and goose down comforters, relaxation tubs and stone-framed fireplaces. Our par-72 championship golf course designed by the renowned Bob Cupp, world-class spa, state-of-the-art athletic facility and wellness center and ski-in/ski-out access to Stowe Mountain Resort will ensure that all your guests enjoy themselves.

To begin planning your fairytale wedding, please call our wedding specialist, Heidi at 802.760.4739

SPRUCE CAMP AT Stowe
MOUNTAIN RESORT

Shayne Lynn Photography

5781 Mountain Road, Stowe, Vermont 05672 • 802-253-3666 • 800-253-4754
www.stowe.com

Stowe Mountain Resort offers some of the most unique wedding venues in the northeast. The "Great Room," located in our stunning Spruce Camp base lodge and "The Cliff House," located at the summit of the Gondola, provide two of the most desirable locations in New England.

Wedding Planning:
• Our professionals will make planning your wedding as seamless as possible by assisting you with all of the details that make the perfect wedding.
• Choose from our distinctive wedding menu options or our Executive Chef and team will customize your own special meal.

Lodging:
• The Inn at the Mountain and Condominiums offer convenient slope-side lodging for all of your wedding guests.
• Fireside Tavern, a cozy gathering spot, located in the Inn, provides the perfect location for after hours private gatherings of friends and family.

Resort Amenities:
As a four season destination, the resort offers a variety of amenities and activities to enjoy all year long including:
• 8 Passenger, Gondola sky-ride winter or summer.
• Alpine Slide & Bungee Trampolines, summer/fall, at Spruce Peak
• 4.5 Mile Scenic Auto Toll Road to summit of Mount Mansfield
• Two 18-hole championship golf courses
• Cliff House Restaurant at summit of Gondola
• A "legendary" network of both Alpine and Nordic Trails
• Alpine Village located at Spruce Peak, featuring world-class luxury accommodations, restaurants and retail shops

AYER PHOTOGRAPHY

Stowehof Inn & Resort
434 Edson Hill Road, Stowe, VT 05672
(800) 932-7136 • (802) 253-9722
saunie@stowehofinn.com
www.stowehofinn.com

Experience the Stowehof Inn & Resort, an estate on twenty six acres of rolling hills that evokes the warmth and casual elegance of Vermont...winter, spring, summer or fall.

The Stowehof's Old-World charm and hospitality reflect our alpine heritage.

The Stowehof Inn & Resort provides casual elegance with spectacular scenery, sweeping mountain vistas and views of Mount Mansfield. Picturesque gardens, ponds and pools set the perfect scene for weddings, receptions and celebrations. Come experience delicious local cuisine and friendly service in a truly romantic setting.

Celebrate with up to 110 guests with a cocktail reception poolside and dinner in Emily's dining room both with amazing mountain views. Larger tented weddings for up to 200 or more are set in our wedding meadow overlooking breathtaking views of Mount Mansfield and the Stowe Valley. Hiking, biking, tennis, swimming and evening bonfires are just some of the many activities for your guests to enjoy while staying at the Stowehof Inn for the perfect Vermont destination wedding.

Each of our forty-six guest rooms is uniquely decorated, most featuring dressing rooms, sliding glass doors, and canopy beds. We also offer fireplace demi suites. You may reserve a block of rooms, or for a unique feeling of intimacy, relaxation and fun for you and your guests, reserve the entire inn for your wedding.

Immerse yourself in romance and beauty—
Come to the Stowehof Inn

1840 Sugarbush Access Road
Warren, VT 05674
800-53-SUGAR • 802-583-6300
www.sugarbush.com
e-mail:info@sugarbush.com

Sugarbush's NEW Lincoln Peak Village—
A mountain village that reflects the splendor of its surroundings.

LOCATION: Warren, Vermont. Located in the heart of the Mad River Valley, Sugarbush Resort is just minutes from Interstate 89 and less than one hour from the Burlington International Airport.

VENUES: In December of 2006, Sugarbush opened the luxurious Lincoln Peak Village. Relaxed yet refined, Vermont's newest mountain village features Clay Brook Hotel & Residences, Timbers restaurant – with 45-foot cathedral ceilings and upscale cuisine—and the Gate House Lodge, offering multiple room configurations for weddings of up to 350 people.

Smaller parties looking for classic country charm will find it all at the Sugarbush Inn. The Inn features multiple dining rooms, bars and dance floors for up to 130 people, as well as a poolside venue with a cabana bar, great for BBQs.

LODGING: Couples wishing to have a nuptial affair in total grandeur have Clay Brook at their disposal. The 61 refined slopeside residences feature studio to five-bedroom suites, a year-round outdoor heated pool and hot tubs, and walkout access to the 4,000-acre playground that is Sugarbush.

Other resort accommodations can be found at the cozy Sugarbush Inn, with 42 comfortable guest rooms, and at individually-owned Resort condominiums.

FEATURES: Winter opens over 53 miles of the best skiing and riding terrain in the East. With 111 trails, 16 lifts and 2,600 feet of vertical, Sugarbush's six mountain areas offer wedding guests endless avenues of exploration.

In the summer, you and your guests can challenge your skills on our 18-hole Robert Trent Jones, Sr. golf course, enjoy endless miles of lift-served and cross country mountain biking, ride the 800' zip line or recreate with an exciting round of disc golf. Those who prefer "off-the-links" pursuits can shop their way through historic villages, hike any number of 4,000-foot mountains or relax by Sugarbush's outdoor pools.

WEDDING SERVICES: Sugarbush has a wide selection of banquet services to accommodate any need. From an informal barbeque to a black tie affair, the Resort's attentive team of professionals and culinary experts will provide a personal, customized experience to guarantee no detail gets overlooked.

Trapp Family Lodge

A MOUNTAIN RESORT IN THE EUROPEAN TRADITION

BY THE FAMILY THAT INSPIRED "THE SOUND OF MUSIC"

700 Trapp Hill Road
Stowe, Vermont 05672
phone: 800-826-7000
www.trappfamily.com
Email: kd@trappfamily.com

Specializing in Outdoor, Tented Wedding Ceremonies and Receptions

Capacity

Indoors—a variety of locations provide the perfect setting for intimate occasions–up to 100 reception style.

Outdoors—the sky's the limit!

Price Range

Customized menus created for each wedding. Price determined by selection.

Catering

Executive Chef, Brian Tomlinson, and our Austrian Bakery offers exquisite options for your wedding reception.

Types of Events

Wedding Ceremonies, Receptions, Rehearsal Dinners, Sunday Brunches and Bridal Luncheons. The Lodge offers: in-house floral designers, elegant wedding cakes, wedding coordinator, horse-drawn sleigh and carriage and Honeymoon/Romance packages all customized to your request.

Resort Facilities

A 96-room Alpine Lodge featuring Austrian-style architecture and deluxe amenities, including duvet comforters and amazing views from every room. Roomy two bedroom Guest Houses and luxurious three bedroom Villas are available for larger families and groups. With three on-site pools, a modern fitness center, 100km of skiing, hiking and mountain biking trails, and three on-site restaurants directed by the resort's chef, there's no reason to leave once you've arrived.

A Mountain Resort in the European Tradition

Considered one of Vermont's top resorts, Trapp Family Lodge offers superior service in a pristine setting. On a 2,400 acre hillside overlooking the classic New England village of Stowe, Vermont, the Trapp Family Lodge is the perfect place for a wedding in any season. Whether you choose to marry in our Wedding Meadow surrounded by panoramic views of the Worcester mountains, on our concert stage nestled against the Nebraska Valley mountain range, or in the elegance of our Mozart Room, chances are excellent that your wedding will surpass your grandest expectations.

The Vergennes Opera House

PO Box 88 ～ Vergennes, Vermont 05491
Contact: Jackson Evans, Executive Director
Phone: 802-877-6737 ～ Fax: 802-877-1158
www.vergennesoperahouse.org
Email: rentals@vergennesoperahouse.org

An historic 1897 Landmark the beautifully restored Vergennes Opera House offers a uniquely elegant setting for your special event. Situated in lovely downtown Vergennes, Vermont's oldest city, the opera house provides a delightful venue for socializing, music and dancing. Just fifteen minutes north of Middlebury, and thirty minutes south of Burlington, Vergennes is situated at the heart of the picturesque Champlain Valley.

Capacity:

An Indoor Facility the opera house can accommodate up to 165 seated guests for weddings. Limited room for additional guests is available by special request. For private functions or concerts not requiring tables we are able to accommodate 300 guests. The Opera House is a fully air-conditioned and heated facility.

Catering & Beverage Services:

All catering & beverage services are provided by off-site caterers. We are happy to provide a list of recommended local caterers.

Types of Events:

Weddings (Ceremonies & Elegant Receptions), Rehearsal Dinners, Anniversary Parties, Luncheons, Private Functions and Corporate Events.

Reservations & Pricing:

Whatever you require, please call for more information. We will be happy to answer your questions and arrange an appointment for you to tour our lovely facility.

Special Services:

As a courtesy to our clients the opera house offers contact information for area accommodations, artists, craftspeople and businesses.

Laura Johnson Photography

The Vermont Inn

Route 4, Killington, VT 05751
relax@vermontinn.com
802-775-0708 ☎ 800-541-7795
www.vermontinn.com

The Vermont Inn is a 16 room country inn with original Vermont farmhouse charm. Set on 6 acres in the Green Mountains with breathtaking views, the Vermont Inn has the finest reputation for superior lodging. We feature an award winning, fine dining restaurant and a fabulous country breakfast.

Every celebration is customized to each couple's dreams. We are happy to be your Wedding Planner and can arrange for your flowers, balloons, wedding cake, music, photography, video, and even a Justice of the Peace.

We have special programs in place with many of our vendors and can either do the work for you or simply help you coordinate the communication with them.

Bring your friends and families to our Inn and enjoy the weekend while we take care of all the details for you.

Vermont State Parks

1-888-409-7579
www.vtstateparks.com

Host your wedding ceremony or reception in a Vermont State Park. Choose from over 40 unique locations across the state and make lush landscapes and romantic views the backdrop for your celebration, naturally enhancing the beauty of your day.

Vermont State Parks are perfect for weddings or any group event.

Shelters and picnic areas can accommodate groups from 50 to 700 people depending on location. All offer diverse recreational opportunities such as fishing, swimming, kayaking, canoeing and hiking, just to name a few.

Enjoy an indoor, tented, or open air gathering by the lake or mountain top. Festivities for you and your guests can include a stay in one our cozy cottages, cabins or campsites with varied amenities. For a truly special experience and memories your guests will treasure.

Shelters and pavilions prices range from $100 – $1,000.

Indoor facilities include Seyon Lodge, Kingsland Bay and Camp Plymouth State Parks.

Open-air pavilions can be found at Button Bay, Kill Kare, DAR, Mt. Philo, Allis, Ascutney, Coolidge, Camp Plymouth, Jamaica, Molly Stark, Silver Lake, Lake Bomoseen, Emerald Lake, Lake Shaftsbury, Knight Point, Underhill, Boulder Beach, Lake Elmore, Maidstone and Osmore Pond State Parks.

Spend a day, or a lifetime...

Woodstock
Inn & Resort

FOURTEEN THE GREEN
Woodstock, Vermont 05091-1298
800.448.7900 • 802.457.1100
MEM@woodstockinn.com
www.woodstockinn.com

CLASSICALLY VERMONT...UNIQUELY WOODSTOCK

Surrounded by the idyllic beauty of Vermont's Kedron Valley, The Woodstock Inn & Resort offers a storybook setting for weddings and receptions of all sizes. Let our professional Wedding Coordinator help you plan the perfect wedding. For added convenience and allure, The Inn can serve as your single venue for all your needs, such as the rehearsal dinner, ceremony, reception and farewell brunch. Our facilities include:

The Woodstock Ballroom – The Woodstock Ballroom offers an elegant setting for Weddings and can host groups of up to 225. This newly renovated space features glass French doors, which can open up to the Pre-Assembly Area or sheers that can be drawn for privacy.

The Garden Terrace – The airy Garden Terrace, with its adjacent outdoor patio and floor-to-ceiling windows overlooking the outdoor green, is ideal for rehearsal dinners, small gatherings, and receptions with hors d'oeuvres and desserts.

The Main Dining Room – The Main Dining Room, which has earned the AAA four-diamond distinction, lends sophistication to afternoon and evening receptions, with floor-to-ceiling windows overlooking the beautiful back lawn.

The Woodstock Golf Club – The Woodstock Golf Club, with its ballroom, dining room, lounge, and outdoor deck is a favorite for small to medium size groups. Experience your special day with a lovely view of Mount Peg and our Robert Trent Jones Sr. designed Golf Course.

The Front Lawn – The expansive Front Lawn is an ideal setting for an outdoor ceremony. Draw in the crisp Vermont air while overlooking the village green.

The pleasant setting and grounds are just the beginning. Allow our team of professionals to guide you in creating an event that is a true reflection of your distinctive style. The attentive staff will ensure that all of the details come together to create a seamless experience.

To learn more about our wedding services, contact our Wedding Coordinator at MEM@woodstockinn.com or call 802.457.6647.

NOTES

Photo courtesy of Portrait Gallery

How To Look Your Best

Beauty for a wedding can mean different things to different people. For the bride it may mean the perfect hair style, makeup and dress on her wedding day. For the groom it may mean losing a few pounds and gaining muscle. Many people use a wedding as they do the New Year, a time for new resolutions. Looking your best is an integral part of your wedding and you can achieve this outcome by taking the following steps.

Taking Care of Yourself

If a healthy diet and sufficient sleep are not part of your regular day, make this important to you at least two months before your wedding. Take care of yourself, when things start to get busy, you'll need the extra energy. There are numerous good books on healthy eating and exercise programs, or go to a gym and have a trainer start you on a program. Your engagement is a perfect time to start an exercise program and a healthy lifestyle.

Medical Tests and Travel Requirements

Vermont law does not require any blood tests, but if you are traveling abroad for your honeymoon, make sure you know if there are any requirements for shots.

Beauty Consultations

Your wedding is a perfect time to get treated like a star. You are going to have a gorgeous gown, a beautiful reception, and you want the perfect hair and makeup to accompany these. Make an appointment with specialists, one for hair and one for makeup, to discuss your upcoming wedding. First find out what their policies are on consultations. You may want to consult with a couple of salons before you make your selections, thereby you may incur an extra fee. But it's worth it to find the right place and person.

If you choose to do your hair and makeup yourself, make sure that you have the time to do it right the morning of your wedding. Perhaps you don't regularly wear makeup, but it makes a huge difference in photographs. Practice your makeup in advance. You certainly do not want any surprises the day of your wedding. It is worth applying it and have a professional or a friend who is good at it help you. Make sure your makeup is applied in natural light.

Two Weeks Before Your Wedding

Getting a massage and a facial are pure luxuries, and ones that you deserve. A facial will help prepare your face for the big day and a massage will relax and prepare your body. It is important that you do not schedule these too close to your wedding day just in case your face reacts to a facial. Massages help clean the toxins out of your body and it's best to give your body a few days to process these toxins out of your system.

The Day Before Your Wedding

This is the best day for the bride and bridal party to schedule a manicure and pedicure—there is less time between them and the wedding to mess them up. If you are treating your bridesmaids to a manicure, consider scheduling it with them so you can spend time together. This is a good time for the groom to consider a trim for his hair.

The Day of Your Wedding

You should know when all your appointments are and how long they will take. It is important that you have a good breakfast, snack on healthy food, and drink plenty of water. Give yourself enough time to get to all your appointments. Make sure that you are not rushed getting to the church on time; extreme anxiety and beauty will compete for a place on your face. It is not a good idea to delay weddings, this is the one time it is not fashionable to be late, especially if your reception must begin at a specific time.

Beauty Check List

Bring all the necessary equipment, such as makeup, hair sprays and brushes, nylons, safety pins, mirrors and blow dryer, to your final preparation site. If some of the items will be going on the honeymoon with you, make sure that you put them in a separate bag and get it back to your luggage. Have someone be in charge of all your things and get them to the proper place—your thoughts will be elsewhere.

Bathroom Check List

It is a nice touch to have baskets in the bathroom with special beauty needs. The men's basket can have mints, mouthwash, combs, hair gel and Kleenex. The women's basket can have mints, mouthwash, combs, gel, hair spray, Kleenex, feminine supplies and safety pins. These baskets will come in handy and show that you have planned for every detail.

Important Note

Do not try any new products on your wedding day if your skin is sensitive. A scented bath is a perfect way to start the day as long as you are familiar with the product.

Your Beauty Check List

- ❏ Massage
- ❏ Manicure
- ❏ Pedicure
- ❏ Haircut
- ❏ Hairstyling consultation
- ❏ Makeup consultation
- ❏ Wedding day hair appointment
- ❏ Wedding day makeup appointment
- ❏ Checkups
- ❏ Medications
- ❏ Facial
- ❏ New makeup
- ❏ Shampoo
- ❏ Conditioner
- ❏ Soap and bath oils
- ❏ Body lotion
- ❏ Facial lotion
- ❏ Facial cleanser
- ❏ Shaving materials
- ❏ Sunscreen
- ❏ Hairbrush
- ❏ Blow dryer
- ❏ Curling iron and rollers

- ❏ Hair spray
- ❏ Perfume
- ❏ Nail polish and remover
- ❏ Nail file
- ❏ Jewelry
- ❏ Toothbrush and paste
- ❏ Safety pins
- ❏ Travel sewing kit
- ❏ Travel bag
- ❏ Wedding bag
- ❏ Other
- ❏ Other
- ❏ Other

Michael DeMartino Photography

Post Office Box 525
Ludlow, Vermont 05149
Telephone: 802-226-7361
Fax: 802-226-7301
www.CastleHillResort.com
Email: sales@thecastle-vt.com
Contact: Lisa Cormier

Regal Elegance in Vermont

On a forested hill, overlooking Okemo Mountain sits a remarkable mansion. Built in the English Country House style, this exquisite building sets the standard for luxury...

Castle Hill Resort is perfectly suited for a wedding or special party with a formal entry hall, library and terrace. Castle Hill can accommodate up to 100 guests inside and 250 guests in our function tent; both locations have their own unique romantic and elegant atmospheres. You will receive impeccable service and gourmet food and the presentation that can only come with fine dining. The best of everything is available, no need to rent anything.

Castle Hill has ten luxurious private bedroom suites for overnight accommodations, with private baths, fireplaces or whirlpool tubs, plus all the modern conveniences. With our guest's comfort is always foremost in our minds, we have thought of every detail, including a new full service *Aveda* spa.

This incredible 100-year old castle is an architectural gem. With its' elaborate drawn plaster ceilings, paneled reception rooms and remarkable bedroom suites, your guests will more than enjoy their surroundings on your special day. Our professional social consultant on staff will make sure that every detail of your event is perfect.

To receive our beautiful information package call us at 802-226-7361.

MEMBER OF SMALL LUXURY HOTELS

93

The Hair Retreat

172 Spruce Street
Manchester Center, VT 05255

The Salon for the
Body, Hair, Hands & Feet

Hair ✳ Makeup ✳ Manicures ✳ Pedicures ✳ Tanning ✳ UpDo's

Our salon, with its peaceful atmosphere, friendly and talented staff of
professionals is the perfect place for you and your entire bridal party.
As the big day approaches you can look and feel your very best.
Our salon is the ideal setting to escape the stress from
wedding planning before your wedding day.
We will work with your hair's natural texture and your personal style to
make you look beautiful before and on your wedding day.

Your Wedding Day

In-salon or On-site

Our goal is to make you look your very best!

Located in Manchester Center, we encourage you to come in or call us
for a consultation for your wedding day makeup and hair styling.

(802) 362-5199

Cyndi Freeman Photography

Makeup Artists Etc

Sophisticated makeup artistry that enhances your natural beauty

166 Sycamore St, Suite 140
Williston, VT 05495
(802) 878-1236

www.makeupetc.com

Makeup artists etc is a division of
MD Cosmetic Laser & Botox.
www.mdlaserandbotox.com

The look that takes you anywhere...anytime.

The most beautiful cosmetic you can wear is healthy skin. That's why everything we have in our Jane Iredale mineral based makeup is a true extension of good skincare. Iredale products are not just a refinement of normal makeup. It is actually based on new technology. It is so effective that it is highly recommended by physicians and skincare professionals. At last, we are proud to introduce you to a makeup that's healthy for your skin and still makes you look beautiful.

- Makeup Instruction
- Makeup Previews
- Wedding Services
- Complete Skincare Services
- Convenient on-location services

Experience

Our licensed Estheticians and Professional Makeup Artists have over 10 years of experience and have provided services for the following:

- Local news channels
- TV Makeup for nationally known personalities
- Photo Shoots for Full Color Magazines: Fashion editorial and advertising
- Fashion Shows
- On-location Wedding Hair and Makeup at Vermont's exclusive resorts
- Bridal Shows

P.O. Box 369, Stowe, Vermont 05672 • Located on the Mountain Road
Telephone 802-760-1083 or 800-253-2232 • Fax 802-253-4419
Email: *spa@stoweflake.com* • Website: *www.stoweflake.com*
Contact: Amy Baraw, Wedding Sales

Weddings — Stoweflake style

The Spa at Stoweflake is here for you when you need us. Enjoy the utmost attention from our artists throughout the entire planning process, right up to your wedding day. Bridal hair and makeup consultations, veil fittings and wedding party French manicures are just a few of the services we offer for you and your wedding party.

Day Packages for the Wedding Party

Our spa day packages include access to our private sanctuary lounge area with fireplace, sauna, steam, whirlpool and juice/tea bar. You'll also enjoy use of our Aqua Solarium with signature Bingham Hydrotherapy Waterfalls and Hungarian Mineral Soaking Pool. Our spa day packages include:

Stoweflake Spa Bliss with five services to leave your entire body and mind in a state of bliss. Aroma Manicure, Aroma Pedicure, Aromatherapy Massage, Custom Facial and Roses all Over body treatment. Finish with a hair wash and style. A light spa lunch is included.

King for a Day is designed especially for men! Gentleman's Mountain Herbal Facial, Mount Mansfield Body Exfoliation, and Executive Stress Reliever. A light spa lunch is included.

Mountain Refresher lets you revitalize your face and soul. Aroma Manicure and Aroma Pedicure with Stoweflake Custom Facial.

Our Mother and Daughter Package will allow you to share this experience. Enjoy our treatment suite with side by side facials and massages, followed by Aroma Manicures.

The Stowe Escape for Bridal Parties gives unlimited use of the Spa's aqua features, fitness facilities and a fifty minute massage of your choice. A light spa lunch is included.

Also see the Stoweflake Mountain Resort & Spa listing in the
Banquet and Reception Sites.

The Essex Resort & Spa
70 Essex Way
Essex (Burlington), VT 05452

Toll free: 800-727-4295
Phone: 802-764-1452

Web: www.VtCulinaryResort.com
Email: info@VtCulinaryResort.com

A relaxing and rejuvenating Vermont spa escape.

A visit to Spa at The Essex is an escape to the ultimate retreat.

In the moments leading up to your special day, we offer services that ease your mind, renew your body, and soothe your soul. Our salon experts will work with you to design a treatment program that caters to your every need.

You are invited to enjoy pampering like you've never experienced before. Take advantage of our private relaxation lounge for a mini-getaway with the wedding party. A relaxing massage, a refreshing manicure, perhaps a full body relaxation ritual—there's no limit to the rejuvenation you can experience.

Our Recipe for Relaxation encourages you to arrive early to unwind and enjoy all of the Spa's numerous amenities, including our 25-yard indoor lap pool, oversize outdoor hot tub, steam rooms, saunas, and our state-of-the-art fitness center.

Bridal Services & Packages
From hairstyling to veil fitting to makeup, the professional staff at Spa at The Essex is read to make sure you look and feel perfect for your dream wedding. We also offer packages that include manicures, pedicures, and a wide range of other salon and body treatments.

NOTES

Photo courtesy of Portrait Gallery

Your Style of Wedding Attire

The Overall Style

Choosing attire plays a huge role in your overall wedding plans. The bride's gown, the attendants' dresses, the groom's and ushers' formal wear and the mothers' dresses all set the stage. The type of wedding you are having and your color scheme determine attire. It is hard to pick out a dress without knowing if it is a casual summer wedding or an evening black-tie reception. Once you determine that, everything will flow into place.

Remember, when choosing attire services, always make sure you feel comfortable with what they have to offer, their references and how they treat you. This is your wedding and you want to make sure everything feels right, including the businesses with whom you work.

The Bridal Gown

Once you have decided on the formality of your wedding, you need to select a gown. There are hundreds of gowns shown in the popular bridal magazines. Bridal shops also have books for you to look at and hundreds of dresses to try on. Get a feeling for styles that appeal to you before you start physically searching for the gown. You will need to try lots of dresses on, not only to determine a great style, but also to find one that fits your body. Bridal shops and dressmakers will help you find a style that compliments your body and your features.

When you go shopping for a wedding dress, it is a good idea to have one or two people with you who will give you honest opinions. Bringing too many people to "Poll the Audience" is a recipe for disaster that may cause you to miss out on your perfect gown. In the end, the only opinion that really counts is yours. You will be the center of attention at your wedding, and you want to look and feel amazing. Be true to yourself and don't be concerned about what others envision you wearing. (*Advice compliments www.MarryandTuxBridal.com*)

Start looking at dresses right away. If you order one, or have it made, it could take up to six to twelve months, not including the alterations. If time is an issue, bridal shops and dressmakers can help you find a dress that they have in stock or one that is easy to order or make.

There are many good reasons to have a dress custom made. You may want to design your own dress, or you have looked for the perfect dress but can't find it, or you have found the perfect dress but it is way out of your price range. Whatever your reason, there are talented dressmakers that can make your preferred dress from a picture. Make sure you have tried on a similar dress to see if it is truly the look you want and if it flatters you.

If possible, leave the gown at the seamstress or bridal shop after alterations. They have the facilities to take care of the dress and ensure it is pressed. Have someone in charge of picking up the dress and delivering it the day before the wedding.

Things to Consider When Choosing a Dress

Your budget, the dress ordering timeline, fittings and alterations, your style, the time of year for the wedding and the formality of your wedding, are all considerations when choosing a dress. Make sure when you determine the cost of the dress that you include the alterations, fittings, and any other incidentals, such as the petticoat underneath, a slip, a bra, nylons, etc. Are you comfortable with the dress arrival date, length of time for alterations and their cancellation policy? Ask for references before purchasing your dress, it is important to know what previous brides' experiences have been.

Creativity is encouraged at all times, especially if it will save you money. It is your wedding, your dream, and it should have your personality shining through at every moment. This holds true for your wedding dress as well, so just a word of warning as you are trying to find the wedding gown of your dreams without spending too much of your wedding budget. Be careful if you are considering ordering your wedding dress via the internet. One of the benefits of working with a local bridal shop is that they have already developed a relationship with many of the bridal gown manufacturers, and know which make quality dresses that will fit you well and look beautiful. It is not unheard of to spend more on alterations than you do on a wedding dress when you purchase from a manufacturer that does not make a quality garment. In some instances, dresses can be made in such a way as to make alterations nearly impossible. Save yourself some potential, unnecessary stress by finding a local bridal shop whose owner will ensure that your wedding dress is perfect for you, and that you will look as beautiful as you have always dreamed you would on your wedding day.

Important

Do not attempt to clean or iron your own dress or headpiece. The delicate fabrics will not handle regular washing and ironing. If you need to have your dress or head piece pressed, bring them back to the place you purchased them and ask them to do it. Once your wedding is over you can have your dress professionally cleaned.

The Bride's Attendants
Style
Choose the bride's attendants' dresses in the same manner as the gown itself. Consider the season, the colors of the wedding and the formality of the reception. If it is a brunch wedding on a sunny summer day, your attendants' dresses should reflect that. If you have them in black-tie attire for a day wedding, it may seem a little out of place.

If a number of people in your wedding will have the same dress, make sure the dress will flatter them all. Variations of the dress—same fabric, different style—might be the way to go. Even though it is the bride's choice, it is important that the attendants are happy with their dresses. Be conscious of the costs, it is important that you do not put your closest friends and family members in debt. Remember that on top of traveling costs they have to buy shoes, the dress, accessories, and a gift for you.

Businesses that sell formal attire will have books depicting a variety of dresses and will be helpful in selecting dresses that fit your occasion. Look carefully and choose what you want; do not be pressured into a certain dress or style and later regret it.

Size and Logistics
Once you choose the attendants' dresses, then you need to make sure your attendants get fitted with sufficient time to have any alterations completed. Get your attendants' exact measurements and regular dress size. You can either send them the dresses for alterations or have the attendants get them done at your dress shop. Be sure to give them lots of lead time.

The Groom and Attendants' Attire
The groom will pick out his attire and the attire of his attendants. It is important that the groom understand the style of the wedding and choose his outfit accordingly. For example, at an evening formal wedding, a black tuxedo may be the best choice. The bride may want to go along with the groom to help in the selection. Well dressed men add an element of class to any wedding—in addition to looking very handsome.

The groom may want to wear something slightly different to distinguish himself from his attendants. Just an added vest or a different cut jacket may be enough to be unique.

Size and Logistics

Once you have decided whether to purchase or rent, you will be able to work with your attendants on the fittings and sizings. If you are renting, you should make sure that the style you are renting is available for your wedding day and that the delivery service fits your needs. You will want to secure your rentals as soon as possible after the bride's attire has been chosen. The rental or formal wear shop will have a list of their sizing requirements. The groom's attendants should take their relevant measurements and give this information to the groom. The groom will then reserve the formal wear. If you have any special orders or fitting needs, confirm this in advance.

Choosing a Service for Bridal Wear

How long does it take to order the gown?

Are alterations an extra cost?

Do you carry accessories for the gown?

Will you deliver the gown?

What are your deposit and cancellation policies?

Can you special order a gown of my choosing?

Having a Gown Made

Can you design a gown from a picture?

Do you charge a set fee or by the hour?

What are your fabric costs?

How long does it take to make a gown?

Are alterations an extra cost?

What are your deposit and cancellation policies?

Bridal Attendants' Formal Wear

Are the dresses we want in stock?

How long does it take to order?

What are your measurement requirements?

Do you do alterations?

Will you deliver or ship dresses?

Can you do special orders for specific dresses?

What are your deposit and cancellation policies?

Groom and Attendants' Formal Wear

Are your styles in stock?

How far in advance do we order?

How do you do fittings for out-of-town groomsmen?

When should measurements be in?

Do you have a delivery service?

What are your pick-up and drop off policies?

How many days does the rental fee cover?

What are your deposit, cancellation and damage policies?

Can you do last minute alterations?

Wedding Attire Check List

- ❏ Type of wedding: formal, informal, semi-formal
- ❏ Day or evening wedding
- ❏ Style of attire
- ❏ Color scheme of attire

Bride

- ❏ Gown
- ❏ Headpiece/veil
- ❏ Gloves
- ❏ Jewelry
- ❏ Stockings
- ❏ Undergarments
- ❏ Petticoat/slip
- ❏ Handbag
- ❏ Garter
- ❏ Shoes
- ❏ Don't forget: "Something old, new, borrowed, and blue."

Bride's Attendants

- ❏ Formal wear
- ❏ Undergarments
- ❏ Stockings
- ❏ Shoes
- ❏ Jewelry and accessories
- ❏ Handbag

Groom and Attendants

- ❏ Formal wear
- ❏ Dress shirt
- ❏ Suspenders
- ❏ Cufflinks and studs
- ❏ Cummerbund or vest
- ❏ Tie, ascot or bow tie
- ❏ Shoes and Socks
- ❏ Belt

Hats by Mullé Designs

Custom Headpieces, Veils, Hats & More
for Your Bridal Party

Photo: www.silverimagesvermont.com

It's Your Special Day—and you should have it your way!

Jude Mullé will work with you, your colors and your budget to assure that yours will be a day to cherish forever.

She brings fifteen years of millinery experience, thirty years of floral design, a lifetime of custom sewing; and people skills that make her a joy to work with.

Whether you wish for beading, fresh or custom ribbonwork flowers in your headpiece(s), or wonderful hats for the mothers of the bride and groom, Jude can make it all come true.

Visit her website at www.mulledesigns.com to see the variety of her craftsmanship, then call for an appointment.

She is located in the Burlington Area, and her studio is in The Shelburne Art Center.

Hats by Mullé Designs
60 Harbor Road in Shelburne
802-985-5895 phone • 802-734-7337 cell
mulledesigns@yahoo.com • www.mulledesigns.com

107

Bridal and Formal Wear Directory

College Formals of West Lebanon
West Lebanon, NH
(603) 298-7868
www.collegeformals.com

Fiori Bridal
Essex, VT
(603) 872-9663
www.fioribridal.com

Lubiana's Bridal
Barre, VT
(802) 479-1966
www.lubianasbridal.com

McNeil & Reedy
Rutland, VT
(802) 773-7760
www.mcneilandreedy.com

The Tuxedo Gallery
Brattleboro, VT
(802) 257-7044
www.vttux.com

NOTES

NOTES

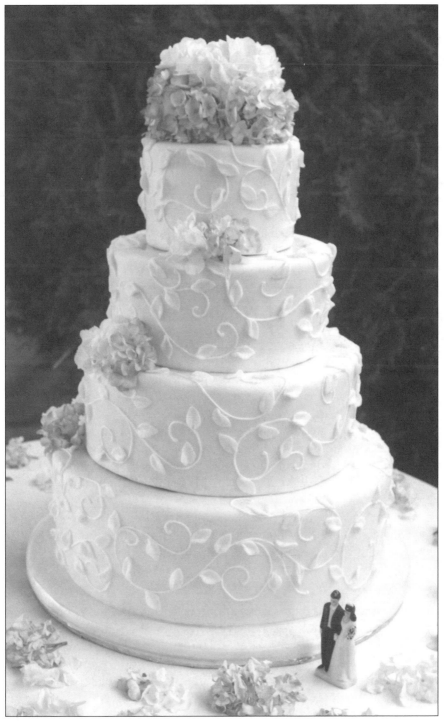

Photo courtesy of Cyndi Freeman Photography

Cake Choices

How to Choose a Cake

Here we are, at the tastiest part of the planning, the wedding cake. The wedding cake should reflect the bride and groom's style and their sweet future together. Choosing a wedding cake can be one of the most enjoyable parts of the planning. The style and look of your cake are just two of the many things to consider when choosing the perfect cake.

In choosing a wedding cake you must consider the flavor of the cake and topping, the size of the cake, how many guests will it feed, how large will the pieces be, the decorations and how will it be served.

Choosing a Baker

When talking to bakeries about creating your cake, have a basic idea of the size and formality of your wedding. The style and flavor of cake will vary depending on the structure of the cake and the number of people you want to serve. The most common flavor is a vanilla cake with a buttercream frosting. Other favorites are carrot cakes, spice cakes, marble cakes and chocolate cakes. Purchasing other types, such as cream or fruit filled, may depend on the size of your wedding. More delicate cakes may not hold up if you want a large tiered cake. Many bakeries will not only show you a portfolio of cakes they have created, they will ask you to sample some of their specialties.

You can have a beautiful cake and a tasty one too if you choose the right baker. Be sure to ask how they create the cake, how long in advance it is prepared and if they freeze it. Once again, ask for references.

Logistics

Once you choose a baker you will want to make sure that you coordinate all the logistics with them. If you are having fresh flowers on the cake, will they work with the florist? How and when will the cake arrive at the reception site? Does it need to be refrigerated? How long can it be in the sun or heat? Who will serve the cake? Do you have serving utensils? Do you plan to garnish the cake with anything? Can we bring the top of the cake home for our first year anniversary? All these questions need to be addressed well in advance of the wedding day.

Choosing a Baker

Do you have a portfolio of your cakes?

Do you have references?

Can we test a cake?

What are your specialties?

How big are the pieces to be served?

How will you charge for the cake, for the whole or by the piece?

Will there be delivery and set up charges?

Who will contact the florist if necessary?

What are your deposit and cancellation policies?

Cake Check List

- ❏ Flavor of cake
- ❏ Style of cake
- ❏ Size of cake
- ❏ Decorations on cake
- ❏ Cake table
- ❏ Decorations for cake table
- ❏ Cake table set up
- ❏ Cut and serve the cake
- ❏ Garnishes on cake plates
- ❏ Cake cutting knife
- ❏ Champagne with the cake
- ❏ Toasting glasses
- ❏ Top saved for first year anniversary

Cake Makers & Bakery Directory

The Cakery
Stowe, VT
(802) 253-0077
www.thecakeryvt.com

Fischer's Fancies
Colchester, VT
(802) 598-9699
www.fischersfancies.com

Irene's Cakes by Design
Ludlow, VT
(802) 228-4846
www.irenemaston.com

Hindinger Cakes
Perkinsville, VT
(802) 263-5924

Sharon Myers Fine Catering
Brattleboro, VT
(802) 254-2480
www.sharonmyers.com

"DELECTABLE...ELEGANT...INSPIRED."

SUSAN HINDINGER CAKES

855 Quarry Road, Perkinsville, Vermont 05151
802-263-5924 • shindinger@tds.net
www.susanhindingercakes.com

Wedding cakes, made from scratch with the finest Ingredients, and custom-tailored to order. From traditional to whimsical, our creations are as delicious as they are beautiful.

Some comments from satisfied customers:

"That was the best cake I've ever had. I'd recommend you to anyone!"
— Wedding guest, 1 year later

"The cake was delicious. My father ate three pieces!"
— Bride, September 2008

"The cake was fantastic! I received so many compliments on how great it looked, and it tasted amazing too!"
— Bride, August 2009

"The cake was the best I've ever tasted."
— Mother of the Groom, September 2008

115

NOTES

Photo courtesy of Cyndi Freeman Photography

Having Your Reception Catered

If the location hosting your wedding does not provide the food, and/or allows your own, deciding to use a caterer is a wise choice. Caterers not only provide a wide menu selection, but their service and presentation also plays a major role in your reception. With this in mind, you can find a caterer that fits your budget and culinary needs.

Facility Considerations

When choosing a caterer there are many things to consider. The caterer must not only fit your culinary needs but your facility needs. If you are having an outdoor wedding, the caterer will have to provide the equipment to refrigerate and heat the foods. They will also need to provide the plates, linen and serving utensils for the meal. Many caterers also provide the tables, chairs and numerous other decoration items.

Your Menu and Service Selection

Once you decide on the type of meal (a sit-down or buffet reception) and what your facility provides, you can choose a caterer. Together you can determine the menu and the appropriate type of food setting for the degree of formality of your wedding. Make sure you feel comfortable with the price quotes and the number of cooks, servers and bartending facilities they are suggesting for your wedding.

Choosing a Caterer

When meeting with caterers have them provide you with a portfolio of weddings they have done in the past. The pictures will show you the presentation of their food and the professional attire of their servers. You may even want to request visiting an event they are serving to see them in action.

When finalizing a contract with a caterer make sure you are perfectly clear on the amount of food that will be served, when they will arrive, how they will set up and service, and how you will be charged for the food and beverages (know the costs of all additional items). Be sure to include the taxes and tips in your total costs. If your caterer is providing your liquor and beverages be sure that they have a liquor license and liability insurance.

Beverages and Bartending

Some caterers do not have a liquor license and will recommend a bartender who can serve your beverages. In this case, you can purchase your own liquor and provide your own bartender. You might save money this way, but you want to consider the liability. If you hire a bartender, she or he should be the one to carry the liability insurance. Be sure you know who assumes the liability for alcohol service. If you choose to serve it you may want to consider a rider on your insurance policy. If someone else is serving your liquor make sure they have a proper liquor license and insurance coverage.

Questions to Ask When Choosing a Caterer

Do you do a lot of wedding receptions?

What is your specialty food service?

Do you have a specific menu?

Can you prepare food that I select?

How do you charge for your meals?

What is included in your costs?

What are the additional costs?

Do you provide liquor and beverage service?

What are your policies and provisions for serving alcohol?

Do you have a liquor license and insurance?

How many servers and bartenders do you provide?

How will you prepare and serve the food?

Will you need a kitchen facility?

Will you need electricity?

Is cleanup included in your fee?

Are tips and taxes included in your costs?

Do you have references I can call?

Catering and Bartending Check List

- ❏ Hors d'oeuvres
- ❏ Main Meal
- ❏ Servers
- ❏ Cooks
- ❏ Tables
- ❏ Chairs
- ❏ Table settings
- ❏ Buffet and food tables
- ❏ Table linens
- ❏ Table silver
- ❏ Glasses
- ❏ Coffee and tea
- ❏ Cake and dessert
- ❏ Cake cutting
- ❏ Cake plates and cake table
- ❏ Bar
- ❏ Bartender
- ❏ Liquor and beverages
- ❏ Champagne toast
- ❏ Champagne glasses

"Dear Henry & Dina,
Everything was wonderful, delicious, beautifully presented, fresh, perfect, amazing.
Every guest I've spoken with commented on the food! Your staff was courteous and caring. It was a pleasure to work with you.
See you at the restaurant!
Fondly,"
Mary & Walt   October 2003

THE BEST WEDDING YOU'VE EVER BEEN TO SHOULD BE YOURS... AND WE GUARANTEE IT.

YOUR WEDDING will START with

EXPERT PLANNING & ATTENTION TO DETAIL, MOVE ON TO A CUSTOM DESIGNED MENU FEATURING VERMONT PRODUCTS PREPARED with OUR SOUTHERN FRENCH/NORTHERN ITALIAN FLAIR, be SERVED by PROFESSIONALS WHO GENUINELY CARE about YOU and YOUR GUESTS and be ACCOMPANIED by FIRST CLASS BEVERAGE SERVICE.

IN OTHER WORDS,

Everything You Want At Your Party

CALL HENRY (CHEF-OWNER) OR

DINA (OWNER-CAKE BAKER-PLANNER EXTRORDINAIRE)

802-362-4982

OR EMAIL, weddings@bistrohenry.com   facebook.com/bistrohenry

Also....REHEARSAL DINNERS   WEDDING BRUNCHES   BRIDAL SHOWERS

GENUINE BBQ   CUSTOM WEDDING CAKES

ROUTES 11/30, MANCHESTER CENTER, VERMONT www.bistrohenry.com

WE INVITE YOU TO SAMPLE BISTRO HENRY TO TASTE WHAT WE DO EVERYDAY.

OUR WEBSITE, www.bistrohenry.com HAS MENUS and PHOTOS.

specialty linens • custom available

local food • licensed bar service

cozy central Vermont dining
off premise bar catering

13 School St. Rochester | 802-767-3272 | occasionsvt.com | thevillageporchvt.com

"I would like to thank you both immensely, for all of your wonderful work to make our wedding weekend so special. We know how hard you and your staff worked at all three events, and we couldn't be happier with the service, presentation, and quality of food that we received. It felt so good to know that everything was being taken care of, and at the highest quality. It truly helped us stay relaxed and happy the entire time." ~ Aimee Paulson

We specialize in country tent weddings offering fresh salads and entrees grilled on-site. We also offer "custom" catering allowing us to create a menu specifically for you. Depending on your reception site, we can provide a meal that is plated and served, a buffet or several stations. A FULL SERVICE LICENSED BAR IS AVAILABLE FOR YOUR RECEPTION through our restaurant, The Village Porch.

Experience: We have been in the food industry for over 25 years with experience that includes private chef dinners for an exclusive resort community, restaurant baker, corporate catering and consulting of many weddings. Occasions has done in-home dinner parties, weddings of all sizes and cocktail parties in New York City for three hundred guests! Our reference list is always available.

Customer Service: We can handle the details of your special occasion by providing names and vendors for you to contact or a complete consulting service where we take care of everything from tents to flowers. Our catering service provides for wait staff, rentals, decorating, food presentation and wedding coordination. Connie Mendell and the staff at Occasions are excited to make your catering experience one of joy and confidence, knowing that your day will be filled with special memories.

The Linen Shop at Occasions
A seamstress as well as a cook, owner Connie Mendell has created a unique line of rental linens in response to requests from many of her wedding customers. The inventory at the Linen Shop has grown rapidly over the past few years and now boasts one of the largest selections of rental linens in Northern New England! In addition to stocking a rainbow of colors and prints, offering custom work to individual customers allows us to continually increase our selection with interesting combinations that include silks, taffeta, sheers, and cotton organza. Please call to request swatches or schedule a visit.

We make it happen with style.

744 Meadowbrook Road
Brattleboro, VT 05301
(802) 254-2480
www.sharonmyers.com

FINE CATERING

A full service caterer, renowned for her mouthwatering food exquisitely presented,
Sharon Myers Fine Catering has been voted
Greater Brattleboro's #1 Caterer 6 years running.

We will work with you to create a special theme.
Your ideas and preferences for taste and color form the basis for the food and décor.
We create an entire experience...with panache.

Full Service can include:

- Flowers – We arrange with florists for flowers for tables, cake, garnish, and tent decoration.
- Cakes and Pastries – Sharon loves to bake. It is her specialty. She makes all her own cakes and pastries in many flavors.
- Rentals – We coordinate with rental firms to take care of details. Tents, whether elaborate peaks or simple poles are decorated with garlands, hanging pots, and potted trees.
- Other – We suggest photographers, florists, bed and breakfasts, country inns.

We provide the service level you need at a cost that fits your budget.

- For 10-400 people
- Passed, plated or stations
- Wait staff or delivery
- New ideas for delicious dishes and elegant presentation.

Sharon Myers Fine Catering....

Caring attention to create lasting memories of special events.

NOTES

NOTES

Photo courtesy of Cyndi Freeman Photography

Ceremony Sites and Officiants

The Importance of Your Ceremony

When you are in the thick of your wedding planning, especially the details of the reception, it is easy to forget that the purpose of a wedding is all about the vows you exchange. The ceremony is where you make your commitment to each other for the rest of your lives; this is where your family and friends witness your exchange of love. With careful planning, you can make the ceremony fit your needs, and simultaneously provide a lasting remembrance for your family and friends.

Vermont Ceremony Sites

Vermont's wedding sites are among the most spectacular ceremony sites in the world. Options include historic churches, scenic rural settings, mountains full of wildflowers and state parks with babbling brooks. The choices make Vermont an ideal setting for a very romantic wedding.

The three primary considerations in choosing a ceremony site are: your religious preferences, your wedding style and the comfort of your guests. Several religions require that you get married in the church of your worship. Vermont has beautiful churches and synagogues, a site for virtually every denomination.

A Church Ceremony

The clergy of the church you are considering will know the type of service that is allowed and the requirements you must meet to get married in their church. When you decide on your location, ask the clergy to give you a copy of the traditional service and find out where you can make changes and additions. The church may have specific requirements regarding your music, readings, flowers, candles, video and photography. Make sure you know the requirements.

A Non-Traditional Ceremony Site

Whether you get married in a church or not, you still can have a religious ceremony. Many clergy will perform the ceremony at your chosen ceremony site. The clergy may have a specific ceremony outline that they follow and will let you know what parts must be included in the service. You will need to coordinate with the clergy on what you can add, delete or change. Make sure you get your music, readings and any other special items approved by the clergy.

Your Marriage License

Wherever you get married, bring your marriage license to present to the officiant! You will not have a legal marriage without it. Your officiant and witnesses, usually the best man and maid of honor, must sign it. Have your marriage license put in a safe place; it's a very important document. You will use this document when changing your name.

Officiant and Ceremony Site Fees

Before you secure a ceremony site be sure to find out their fees. Some fees at churches may include an organist, changing rooms, a cleaning service and church decorations such as an aisle runner and candelabras.

The fee for the officiant may be separate, especially if they are going off site. It's polite to ask what the standard fee and tip policy is. Some clergy may request that your fee be a donation to the church. Ask the clergy member for suggested donation amounts.

You should ask the same questions for non-traditional facilities as you did for churches. If it is an outdoor site, ask if they have restroom facilities and if they provide coverage in case of weather. If they do not, you will need to provide these items.

Etiquette requires that the officiant be paid on the day of your wedding. Typically the groom asks the best man to handle that responsibility. The groom should have prepared in advance the fee, tip and thank you card and given it to the best man. Many times this can be done at the rehearsal; the officiant will inform you which is best.

Your Outline

You have selected a site and an officiant. Once you have decided how you want your ceremony to flow, it is important that you prepare an outline for the officiant, the musicians, and everyone playing a role in your wedding. The outline will allow them to work together and you will feel comfortable knowing that your service will follow a plan.

Justice of the Peace

We would like to list the Justices of the Peace that are available for your ceremony but it is difficult since they change constantly and number in the hundreds throughout the state. An easy way to find a Justice of the Peace for your specific ceremony location is to contact the *Secretary of State's Office* at 802-828-2363 and ask for your specific Town Clerk's office number (make sure you know the name of the town your ceremony will be in). Or you can contact *Vital Records* for your local Town Clerk's office number at 800-439-5008 or 802-863-7275. The Town Clerk's office will have a list of Justice of the Peace for their own town. Or get online at www.sec.state.vt.us and search for your Town Clerk's office and you can find the information there.

Choosing a Ceremony Site

What dates and times do you have available?

How many guests can your facility handle?

What are the requirements to get married at your location?

Is the officiant available?

What are the costs for the facility?

What is included in the costs?

What are the costs for the officiant?

Are there any restrictions?

Do you have changing rooms?

Will the officiant work with us on our vows?

Are there any vow or service restrictions?

How long will the service be?

How long do we have the facility for?

Do we need to attend any meetings or consultations prior to the ceremony?

Ceremony and Officiant Check List

- ❏ Ceremony location
- ❏ Officiant
- ❏ Ceremony program
- ❏ Vows written
- ❏ Marriage license
- ❏ Music
- ❏ Readings
- ❏ Attendants
- ❏ Ring bearer
- ❏ Flower girl
- ❏ Processional formation
- ❏ Recessional formation
- ❏ Decorations
- ❏ Seating for guest
- ❏ Ceremony outline to key people
- ❏ Parking
- ❏ Changing area
- ❏ Rehearsal time and location
- ❏ Receiving Line

Historic Vermont Church Buildings

Vermont has a wealth of well-preserved historic church buildings owned by local historical societies and similar organizations that are suitable for wedding ceremonies. They are found in small historic villages and in scenic rural settings, and date from the 1787 Rockingham Meeting House, the oldest standing public building in Vermont, to the early 20th century Beaver Meadow Union Chapel. All retain their architectural character and appear untouched by time. Some are only available for seasonal use and may not have electricity or plumbing.

Call or write contact people for particulars on fees, interior accommodations, availability of musical instruments, such as organs or pianos, and other information.

PLEASE NOTE: This list was compiled by the Vermont Division for Historic Preservation. It is not inclusive. Listing does not constitute endorsement.

✪ = Listed in the National Register of Historic Places
✤ = Listed in the State Register of Historic Places

Northern Vermont

Burlington
✪ First Unitarian Universalist Society
✤ At the top of Church Street in downtown Burlington at 152 Pearl St., Burlington, VT 05401. Contact: Christina Fulton, 802-862-5630, ext 22.

Fairfield
✤ North Fairfield Brick Church (President Chester A. Arthur Historic Site) Off Chester Arthur Road, Fairfield. Built c.1840, brick. Contact: John Dumville, VT Div. for Historic Preservation, National Likfe Building, Drawer 20, Montpelier, VT 05620. 802-828-3051

Fletcher
✪ Fletcher Union Meeting House Fletcher Village. Built 1872, Vernacular style. Contact: Lisa Rock, 92 Cambridge Road, Cambridge, VT 05444. 802-849-6417

Holland
✪ Former Holland Congregational Church, West Holland Road. Built 1844-54, Greek Revival style. Contact: Penny Tice, 591 Page Hill Road, Holland, VT 05830. 802-895-2917

Lunenburg
✤ Lunenburg Congregational Church, US Route 2, Lunenburg Village. Built 1850, Greek Revival style.

Newark
Newark Union Church, Newark St. Built 1862. Contact: John Findlay, 2234 East Hill Road, Newark, VT 05871. 802-467-3036

Richmond
✪ Round Church, Round Church Rd., Richmond Village. Built 1812-1813, sixteen sided church. Contact: Sally Singer, 1233 Kenyon Road, Richmond, VT 05477, or Richmond Historical Society, P.O. Box 253, Richmond VT 05477. 802-434-4119

Shelburne
Old Charlotte Meeting House Shelburne Museum, off US Route 7. Built 1840, Greek Revival style. Contact: Public Relations & Devel. Dept., Shelburne Museum, Shelburne, VT 05482. 802-985-3346

Weathersfield
✦ Weathersfield Meeting House and First Congregational Church, Weathersfield Center Historic District, Weathersfield Center Road. Available for events April through December. 802-263-5146

Stannard
✪ Former Stannard Church, Stannard Mountain Road. Built 1888, Victorian Gothic style. Contact: Rachel A. Hexter, 41 Old Pasture Road, Greensboro Bend, VT 05842. 802-533-7082

Williston
✪ Old Brick Church, US Route 2, Williston Village. Built 1832, Gothic Revival style. Contact: Carol West, 7900 Williston Road, Williston, VT 05495. 802-879-1176

Central Vermont

Bradford
✪ Old Goshen Church, Goshen Rd. Built 1834, Gothic Revival style. Contact: Diane Smarro, PO Box 778, Bradford,VT 05033. 802-222-9391

Calais
✪ Old West Church, Old West Church Road. Built 1823, Vernacular style. Contact: Dr. Wayne D. Whitelock, P.O. Box 200, Calais, VT 05648-0200. 802-456-8129

Cavendish
✪ Old Stone Universalist Church, VT Route 131. Built 1844, Greek Revival style. Contact: Carmine Suica, Tarbel Hill, Cavendish, VT 05142. 802-484-7498

Manchester
✪ First Congregational Church, 3624 Main Street (Historic Route 7A) Contact: Linda Hueckel, Wedding Director, P.O. Box 588 Manchester Village, VT 05254. 802-362-4904 or 802-362-4329 (home)

Newbury
✪ Former Newbury Methodist Church, On the Common, Newbury Village. Built 1829, Federal/Gothic Revival style. Contact: Martha Knox, Newbury, VT 05051. 802-866-5380

New Haven
✦ The Union Church of New Haven Mills, River Road and East Street. Built 1851-52, Greek Revival style. Contact: Susan Bennett, 1080 Munger St., New Haven, VT 05472. 802-453-5300

Norwich
✪ Beaver Meadow Union Chapel, Beaver Meadow Road. Built 1915, Vernacular style. Contact: Raymond Royce, Sr., RR #1, Box 458, Sharon, VT 05065. 802-649-3814

Plymouth
✪ Union Christian Church (Calvin Coolidge Memorial Foundation), Cheese Factory Road, Plymouth Notch. Built 1840, Greek Revival style. Contact: Karen Mansfield, Box 97, Plymouth Notch, VT 05056. 802-672-3389

Royalton
✦ St. Paul's Church, VT Route 14, Royalton Village. Built 1836, Gothic Revival style. Contact: John P. Dumville, 4184 Rt. 14, Royalton, VT 05068. 802-763-8567

Rutland
✦ Chaffee Center for Visual Arts, built in 1896, Queen Anne Victorian mansion. Contact: Nick Raeburn, 16 So. Main St., Rutland, VT 05701. 802-776-0356

Starksboro

✪ Starksboro Village Meeting House, VT Route 116, Starksboro Village. Built 1838-1840, Gothic Revival style. Contact: Cynthia Kling, 141 Brown Hill West, Starksboro, VT 05487. 802-453-5227

Strafford

✤ Universalist Church, VT Route 132, South Strafford Built 1833/1860, Greek Revival style. Contact: Lori Wolfe, P.O. Box 134, Strafford, VT 05072. 802-765-4295

Southern Vermont

Arlington

✤ Chapel on the Green, West Arlington Village. Built 1804/ 1850, Greek & Gothic Revival. Contact: Rev. Richard Gratz, 41 E. Main St., Cambridge, NY 12816. 518-692-2560

Bennington

✤ White Chapel, Chapel Road. Built c.1858, Vernacular-Greek Revival. Contact: Alice Sausville, Chapel Road, Bennington, VT 05201. 802-442-4508

Guilford

✪ Guilford Center Meeting House Guilford Center Road. Built 1837, Gothic Revival style. Contact: Fred Humphrey, Tater Lane, Guilford, VT 05301. 802-257-7306

Halifax

✤ Halifax Community House West Halifax. Built c. 1854, Greek Revival style. Contact: Joan Courser, P.O. Box 27, West Halifax, VT 05358. 802-368-7733

Putney

✪ Putney Community Center Christian Square, Putney Village. Built 1884, Victorian Gothic/ Queen Anne. Contact: Heather Maples, Community Family Center, Putney, VT 05346. 802-387-8551

Rockingham

✪ Rockingham Meeting House Off Route 103, Rockingham. Built 1787-1801, Federal period Contact: Town Manager's Secretary, PO Box 370, Bellows Falls, VT 05101. 802-463-3964

Shaftsbury

✪ North Shaftsbury Community Club Hall, Depot Road. Contact: Mrs. Robert Cornwell, RR Box 221, Shaftsbury, VT 05262. 802-375-6636

Sunderland

✤ Sunderland Union Church, Hill Farm Road. Built c.1880, Queen Anne style. Contact: Pauline Hill, 634 Ondawa Road, Arlington, VT 05250. 802-375-6955

Vernon

✪ Pond Road Chapel, Pond Road and Huckle Hill Road. Built 1860, Vernacular-Greek Revival style. Contact: Barbara Moseley, c/o Vernon Historians, Inc., P.O. Box 282, Vernon, VT 05354. 802-254-8010

Woodford

✤ Former Woodford Hollow Church (Woodford Town Hall), Woodford Hollow. Built 1871, Vernacular style. Contact: Aileen O'Neil, Town Clerk, 1391 VT Rte. 9, Woodford, VT 05201-9410. 802-442-4895 a.m. only

List Prepared by Vermont Division for Historic Preservation, 135 State St., Drawer 33 Montpelier, VT 05663-1201. 802-828-3226

FIRST CONGREGATIONAL CHURCH
of
Manchester, Vermont

◆

3624 Main Street
(Historic Route 7A)
P.O. Box 588
Manchester Village, Vermont 05254

CONTACT:
Linda Hueckel, Wedding Director
Tel: (802) 362-2709 or
(802) 362-4329

First Congregational Church of Manchester (FCC), listed on the National Register of Historic Places, is one of the loveliest and most sought-after wedding venues in New England. Established in 1784, the church is the heart of Manchester Village, located directly across the street from the historic Equinox Hotel and down the road from other memorable reception sites such as the Wilburton Inn, the Southern Vermont Arts Center and Hildene, Robert Todd Lincoln's summer estate.

If a couple desires a picture-perfect church wedding, FCC is an ideal location. This reality is made apparent when you step inside the nave of the church and experience the wonderful wood of the sanctuary and see how beautifully the light plays off the magnificent stained glass windows. At once you are warmed to the experience. You and your loved ones sense that you are in the presence of God. This is precisely the feeling you should have on your wedding day.

Seating Capacity: 350 in church nave, 25 in Chapel

Type of Ceremony: Our FCC ministers offer their services for traditional wedding ceremonies and civil unions. We welcome couples of all faiths and will gladly work with outside ministers if the family so desires.

Special Features: Our wedding director is on site and is available to help you with all aspects of the wedding ceremony. She is able to guide you in obtaining a wedding license and can also help select a printer, photographer, florist and musicians.

Fee: $1500 includes church rental, facility prep and clean-up, ministerial, music and wedding director fees. Fee is reduced to $1,200 if you supply your own minister. Chapel weddings are available for a $800 fee.

First Congregational Church of Weathersfield, Vermont (UCC)

Weathersfield Center Road
Weathersfield, Vermont 05156

Contact:
Cynthia Porter
Tel: (802) 263-5397

The First Congregational Church of Weathersfield, also known as the Weathersfield Meeting House, is located in the Weathersfield Center Historic District and is listed on the National Register of Historic Places.

Located in a secluded area in the geographical center of the town, the red brick Meeting House was constructed in 1821 and is one of the finest in Vermont. It stands in an ancient maple grove facing the Civil War monument and to the north the peak of Mt. Ascutney is visible from the grove.

The facade of the building has three entrances. The center entrance leads to a large meeting hall with two bathrooms (access requires three steps), a stage and fully-equipped kitchen. It is used for public and private functions and gatherings. The doors on either side open to stairways that lead to the upper sanctuary. On the east side there is a wide granite ramp and an incli-nator for handicapped access which climbs alongside the stairway to the first floor. The organ is at the south end of the sanctuary facing a center pulpit with two side aisles.

Seating capacity: 150 in the pews (additional chairs may be added to hold approximately 175).

Ceremony: The church does not have a resident minister. For traditional ceremonies and civil unions couples of all faiths make arrangements to provide their own minister or a Justice of the Peace to conduct services.

Additional Information: The Center Church is seasonal. Services are held from June to September but it is a popular venue for weddings from April through November.

There is additional parking across the Center Road.

Contact information for the resident organist is available upon request.

Fee: $200 includes the church rental. $100 covers the use of the downstairs meeting house for gatherings and wedding receptions

Jeudevine Falls

2259 Craftsbury Road
Hardwick, Vermont 05843
(802) 472-5486
www.weddingfalls.com
www.waterfallswedding.com

Just 2-1/4 miles from the jct. of VT
Route 14 North & VT Route 15

Why Have Your Special Day at an Ordinary Place?

GET MARRIED IN HEAVEN AND HAVE THE RECEPTION OF A LIFETIME AT JEUDEVINE FALLS

Your special day. You found the perfect dress, the perfect rings, and the perfect flowers. Most importantly, you found each other. May we suggest the perfect place? Tree branches spread over you and the music of the rushing waterfall, a soft breeze and native songbirds fills the air. You stand together in a gazebo that looks like it may have grown there as your guests wait for the two of you to be united as one.

Jeudevine Falls in Hardwick, Vermont offers all of this and more. The pride and love we feel for this place shows through in every little detail. We invite you to share your ceremony with those who matter most to you at the falls. We are happy to advise you on lodging for out of town guests, caterers or anything else to help make your special day, your perfect day.

> *Our search for a beautiful, romantic and fun outdoor location for our recent Wedding ended when we discovered Jeudevine Falls. With its beautifully constructed Gazebo, breathtaking waterfalls and meticulously maintained grounds and gardens we found just what we had been looking for. Bob Edebohls, the owner had just installed a large wedding tent along with a great dance floor. He was also great at helping us with our final details and preparations. We would highly recommend this site for any couple looking for a unique Wedding location...*
>
> *Thanks again Bob!*
> *Sincerely,*
> *Jim and Ann Severance*

Greg Trulson
607 Crossett Hill Rd
Waterbury, VT 05676
802-244-5378
Contact: Greg Trulson
Greg@moosemeadowlodge.com

Stephanie Koonz
2096 Ward Hill, Box 575
South Duxbury, VT 05660-0575
802-496-2276 or 802-249-2838
Contact: Stephanie Koonz
stephaniekoonz@hughes.net

Greg Trulson

I work closely with couples to create a truly personal and memorable ceremony. I will help you develop all the elements, from the opening introductions to the exchange of rings and vows, and from poetry readings to expressions of blessings. You will receive samples of beautiful ceremonies from which you can start to form your own. Since 2001, I have had the privilege of officiating at over 500 ceremonies throughout Vermont. I would be honored to serve as your officiant.

Stephanie Koonz

Since 1994, I have been officiating weddings and starting in 2000, civil union ceremonies throughout Vermont. After getting to know the couple a bit, I help develop a unique ceremony that reflects their personalities. I enjoy incorporating words by Robert Frost and other Vermont poets. Whether at a private home, local inn or on the shores on the Waterbury Reservoir, I would be honored to serve as your Justice of the Peace.

Vermont ASSOCIATION OF
Wedding Professionals

United Church of Dorset and East Rupert,
United Church of Christ, Congregational
143 Church Street, Dorset, VT 05251
802-867-2260
E-mail: dorsetchurch@gmail.com

Office Hours: Tuesday -Friday 8:30 am – 4:30 pm

Selecting the location for your Wedding Ceremony is one of the first items on your to-do list. If your looking for a classic New England setting, our beautiful Vermont Marble Church located just off the Dorset Green may be the location you are looking for. Our building has beautiful Tiffany stained-glass windows that bring a rainbow of color to our sanctuary.

Our minister, Rev. Dr. James H. Gray enjoys assisting couples with their wedding plans. Every May a Wedding Workshop is held. Every couple that has scheduled a wedding during the year is encouraged to attend. The workshop offers insight into Marriage Communications.

Our Minister of Music, Jane Wood is a talented pianist/organist that can enhance your ceremony with your musical selections.

Our Administrator, Jane LoBrutto will be happy to discuss your plans and see you through the complete planning of your ceremony, from meeting with the Minister to sending the bride down the aisle.

We invite you to stop by for visit during our office hours or join us at Sunday worship at 10:00 AM.

Rev. William Wintersteen

INTERFAITH
NON-DENOMINATIONAL
ECUMENICAL

(802) 434-2876

I have over twenty-five years of experience working with couples to create enjoyable wedding ceremonies.

Each service is individually crafted with the Bride and Groom. I enjoy helping each couple create a meaningful and contemporary wedding. I value each couple's input into the creation of their service.

I am willing to perform services in any setting indoors or outdoors, especially in non-denominational historic buildings like the Round Church (Richmond, VT) and the Brick Church (Williston, VT) or in natural settings at a destination resort or a state park.

There is a spiritual aspect in all my wedding services. I am willing to travel anywhere within approximately one-hour of my home in the greater Burlington area.

You may contact me at 802-434-2876.

Sincerely, Rev. Bill Wintersteen

Vermont State Parks

1-888-409-7579
www.vtstateparks.com

Host your wedding ceremony or reception in a Vermont State Park. Choose from over 40 unique locations across the state and make lush landscapes and romantic views the backdrop for your celebration, naturally enhancing the beauty of your day.

Vermont State Parks are perfect for weddings or any group event.

Shelters and picnic areas can accommodate groups from 50 to 700 people depending on location. All offer diverse recreational opportunities such as fishing, swimming, kayaking, canoeing and hiking, just to name a few.

Enjoy an indoor, tented, or open air gathering by the lake or mountain top. Festivities for you and your guests can include a stay in one our cozy cottages, cabins or campsites with varied amenities. For a truly special experience and memories your guests will treasure.

Shelters and pavilions prices range from $100 – $1,000.

Indoor facilities include Seyon Lodge, Kingsland Bay and Camp Plymouth State Parks.

Open-air pavilions can be found at Button Bay, Kill Kare, DAR, Mt. Philo, Allis, Ascutney, Coolidge, Camp Plymouth, Jamaica, Molly Stark, Silver Lake, Lake Bomoseen, Emerald Lake, Lake Shaftsbury, Knight Point, Underhill, Boulder Beach, Lake Elmore, Maidstone and Osmore Pond State Parks.

Spend a day, or a lifetime...

NOTES

NOTES

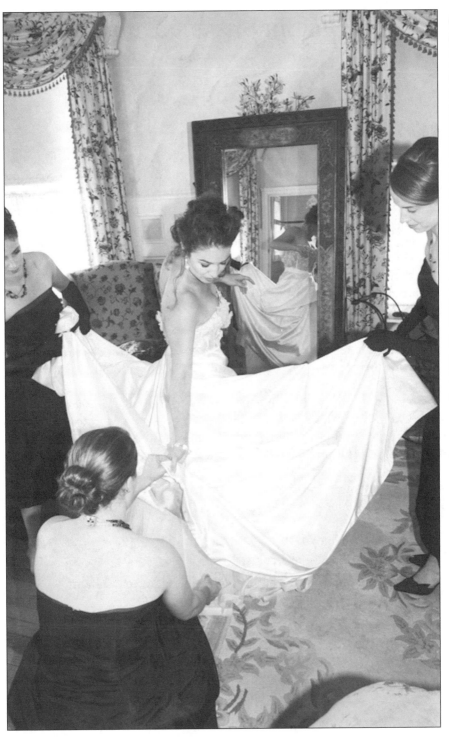

Photo courtesy of Emma Dodge Hanson Photography

Choosing a Consultant

What a Consultant Can Do For You

There are many good reasons for hiring a wedding consultant, the foremost being that they will make your wedding planning much easier. The details are endless, a consultant is trained to handle them and follow your wedding plans. Consultants know the services that are just right for your style and your budget. Because of this, they can save you money. When presented with your budget, they can help you stick to it. They can share valuable ideas on ways to save time and money. They will save you endless hours of planning, calls, attending to details and worry. This way you can enjoy overseeing your wedding without all the stress—that alone is worth their fee.

Choosing a Consultant

Checking references is the best way to see if this person is right for you. Asking for their last two or three wedding references should give you a feel for his or her services.

You want to work with someone you are comfortable with and who will allow you to have your style. Consultants can give you great ideas and hints to make your wedding even more spectacular. However, it is important that you don't feel pressured into adopting a different style or type of wedding.

With your consultant, work out who will be responsible for what details. You don't want any surprises, especially if you are responsible for a big piece and you forget about it, such as your cake!

Consultants Check List

- ❏ Do you have references?
- ❏ How many years have you been a wedding consultant?
- ❏ Do you have a portfolio?
- ❏ Do you have consulting options?
- ❏ What are your fees?
- ❏ Can you provide a detailed responsibilities list?
- ❏ Can you work within my budget?
- ❏ What do you need from me to do your job?
- ❏ Will you oversee the day of my wedding?

Julie Ireland Photograph

Woodstock Productions
WP Event Planning

~ Consultations
~ Three Day Support
~ Full Service Planning

"Your services were by far our best investment... *because we were really able to turn the reins over to you and relax during the wedding weekend. I thought I would not be able to do that, being a planner myself and this being my big day, but it was easy to do because you gave us the confidence that you could handle every little detail and that you understood our vision."*

Sincerely,
Eleanor Pessin, August 2009 Bride

(802)356-5060
www.woodstockproductions.com
sabrina@woodstockproductions.com
P.O. Box 291, Woodstock, VT 05091

Consultants & Wedding Planners Directory

Annellie Vallone Events, llc
South Burlington, VT
(802) 859-0110
www.annellieevents.com

Central Reservations of Vermont
Waitsfield, VT
(800) 451-4574
www.vtvacation.com

Megan Schultz Events & Designs
Moretown, VT
(802) 496-6466
www.meganschultz.com

VT Weddings by Kim
North Troy, VT
(802) 988-4730
www.vtweddingsbykim.com

The Wedding Wizard
South Burlington, VT
(802) 865-8989
www.weddingwizardusa.com

Woodstock Productions
Woodstock, VT
(802) 356-5060
www.WoodstockProductions.com

NOTES

NOTES

Photo courtesy of Lauren Stagnitti Wedding Photography

Decorating & Rental Information

Decorating and rental shops provide a wide array of wedding items to please everyone: this includes balloons, streamers, champagne fountains, and even arches under which the couple may wed. When you are looking for a particular item, most decorating and rental shops will probably have it. The major pieces, such as tents, tables and chairs, can always be found at major rental shops. It is always best to plan as far in advance for these items as possible.

Put Together a Plan

When planning your rental and decoration needs for the ceremony and the reception, it is important to get a visual picture of how you want everything to look. Be sure to ask permission from the sites to confirm what you can and cannot do. Once you have the concept, write down all the items you will need. If you are using balloons, are you going to rent a helium tank or have them delivered blown up? A rental shop or decorating store can give you an idea of how many balloons it will take to decorate a certain area. Know the size of the spaces you will decorate, and don't be afraid to use your imagination!

Outdoor Settings

If you choose to use an outdoor setting and caterer, you can rent all your table needs from rental shops if it is not already provided. They carry all the accessories needed for a beautiful table setting. This includes the linens, china, glassware, silver and centerpieces. Be sure to rent candles or lights for an outdoor wedding. Some of your guests may have trouble seeing in the dark, you don't want them to trip or miss part of the beauty.

Bridal Accessories

Bridal accessories such as toasting goblets, cake-cutting knife, the ring pillow, candles and any other special items you may need can be rented if you choose not to buy them.

Tent Rentals

We have mentioned before the importance of renting a tent for an outdoor reception. Be sure to include sides on your tent too. In high winds the rain

150

doesn't just come down from the sky. Even on a sunny clear day it's nice to provide shade protection for your guests. It is always good to be prepared. You don't want to be up all night wondering if it is going to rain. Today's tents are so elegant they can make a wedding look like the mythical King Arthur's court.

Finding the Right Tent

Your options are endless—but only if you book early! Do you want it extra big for a large dance floor and a big band? Do you want it small and intimate for a candlelight rehearsal dinner? Tents are used for a variety of functions and have become so popular that they are booked years in advance. The moment you know you want to use a tent, talk to the tent-experts; they will help you decide on what is best for your wedding style and size.

The Right Location

Tent location is very important. Many sites that you are considering have been used by the tent companies before, and they can give you great advice as to the exact layout of the tent. You want to make sure that you have the perfect view, and also the best spot in case of bad weather. Request that the tent set-up person make a special visit to your location to get measurements and your layout requirements. You don't want any surprises—tents are not easy to move.

Tent Sizes

Before deciding on the tent size, you will need to know approximately how many guests you will be having, what type of tables, if the meal is buffet or sit down, and how large your dance floor will be (if you have one). All of these things will help your rental company choose the best tent for your needs. Use the following chart as a good rule of thumb for determining the size of the area you will need to cover. Be sure to consider any special needs you may have.

Cocktail Party/standing/seating; five to six square feet per person

Cocktail Party/seated; ten square feet per person

Reception/partial seating; eight square feet per person

Dining/oblong tables; ten square feet per person

Dining/round tables; twelve square feet per person

Cathedral seating (in rows); six square feet per person

Dance area; two to four square feet per person

(Information provided by Vermont Tent Company)

Choosing a Decorating and Rental Service

Do you have the items we need in stock?

Do you have a list of wedding items available?

Can you order the items?

How long does it take to get the items in?

Can you deliver?

Do you have bridal accessories available?

When do I need to return rental items? Do you pickup?

What is the deposit amount?

Choosing a Tent Rental Service

Do you have a tent available for my date?

What size do I need?

Do you have a portfolio of tent choices?

Have you been to the location before?

Will you do a site visit?

When do you set-up the tent?

When do you take the tent down?

How long is my rental for?

Can I lengthen the rental time if necessary?

Can you supply my table and chair needs?

Can you supply any other rental needs?

What are your deposit/cancellation policies?

Decorations, Rental Items and Tent Check List

❏ Reserve a tent early

❏ Choose the size of your tent

❏ Choose all necessary items

❏ Tables

❏ Chairs

❏ Dance floor

❏ Linens

- ❑ Table settings
- ❑ Centerpieces
- ❑ Lanterns
- ❑ Heaters
- ❑ Candles
- ❑ Lighting
- ❑ Restrooms
- ❑ Decorating for ceremony site
- ❑ Decorating for reception
- ❑ Decorating for other locations
- ❑ Other _____
- ❑ Other _____
- ❑ Other _____
- ❑ Other _____
- ❑ Other _____
- ❑ Other _____
- ❑ Other _____

154

BLOOD'S
CATERING & PARTY RENTALS INC

"When you want your event done to Perfection"

1147 Hartford Avenue • White River Jct., VT 05001
www.bloodscatering.com • 802.295.5393

Family owned and operated for over 60 years.

***When you want your catering and event rentals done to perfection –
you will find everything you need at Blood's.***

Blood's is the only company that can provide you with both catering and party rental services for your wedding which will save you time and money during the planning process. We own all of our own equipment so we can assure our clients of the best possible quality products and service available. Here is just a sample of the items that we rent:

◆ Beautiful White Wedding Tents with cathedral "French Window" Side-walls
◆ Complete Event Generator Power Services
◆ Chairs – Garden and Elegant White Wooden Padded Chairs;
   Plastic Folding – White and Brown
◆ Tables – Round and Banquet, Cocktail and Dining Heights
◆ Parquet Dance Floors, Staging, Tent Flooring, Carpeting
◆ Elegant Linens, Complete China and Flatware Service – 4 china styles to choose from
◆ Fancy Glassware – Champagne, Wine, Punch Cups, Cocktail, Water Goblet, Pilsner, etc.
◆ Specialty Lighting for Evening Receptions
◆ Portable Tent Heaters, Grills and Ovens
◆ Chocolate Fountains

*Blood's offers computer assisted drawings for you
to see your wedding layout before the day of the event.*
Call the event planning experts at Blood's today
Michael Blood – 802.295.5393 ext.103
to schedule your consultation and watch your dreams become a reality.

Don't trust your special day to just any company…
Trust the experts at Blood's Catering & Party Rentals.

***Visit our website at www.bloodscatering.com to view our selections
or visit our showroom – the largest of its kind in the Upper Valley.***

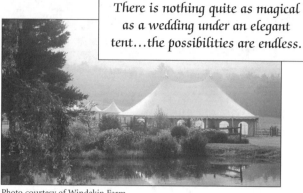

There is nothing quite as magical as a wedding under an elegant tent...the possibilities are endless.

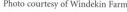

Photo courtesy of Windekin Farm

Celebration Rentals, Inc.

A Full Service Wedding and Special Event Rental Company

86 Park Street, PO Box 387, Brandon, Vermont 05733-0387
802-247-0002/Fax: 802-247-2893 • www.celebrateinvermont.com

With over 20 years of experience, our staff at Celebration Rentals has the knowledge and experience to make a wedding from 10 to 300 people a truly memorable experience.

We have provided services throughout Vermont, as well as New England. We are familiar with weddings at Resort Hotels, Country Inns, historic setting as well as individual settings.

We consider every event a unique affair and pride ourselves with the flexibility in satisfying customer needs.

With extensive inventory, we can assist you with all aspects of your wedding.

Contact: Melissa or Robert
11 Hedding Drive, Randolph VT 05060
802-728-3805 · Toll free:1-888-224-3426 · Dewater91@msn.com

Specializing in quality restroom rentals for
Weddings and Special Events

Featuring:

Elite Series Portables

White and Green Deluxe Units
Self contained
Complete privacy
Flushing toilets
Fresh water sinks
Interior lighting and mirrors
Soap dispenser
Paper towels

Portable Restroom Trailers

Separate men's and women's
   accommodations
China flushing stools and urinals
Steel partition locking doors
Trash receptacles
Florescent lighting
Exterior lighting
Mirrors
Air Conditioning/heat
Stereo System

We provide exceptional sanitary flushable outdoor convenience.
We work closely with our customers to insure the continued
cleanliness of our restrooms during the entire rental period.
Please contact us to discuss how we can facilitate the
complete satisfaction of your special event.

157

Green Mountain Tent Rentals, LLP

Townshend Park, Route 30, Townshend, Vermont 05353
800.691.8368 • 802.365.7839
www.GreenMtnTents.com • gmtents@svcable.net
Evans Family
John • Luke • Ross

Green Mountain Tent Rentals is a family owned and operated rental company that specializes in Weddings and Outdoor Events. From the smallest rehearsal dinner to the largest reception, Green Mountain Tent Rentals has you covered. For questions or a quote give John, Luke or Ross Evans a call or visit us online.

• Tents	• Portable Toilets
• Tables	• Flush Toilet (regular)
• Chairs	• Flush Toilet (deluxe)
• Lighting	• Portable Sinks
• Sides for tent	• Portable Tent Heaters
• Dance floors	• Barbeque Grills
• Staging Platforms	• Tableware

What size tent you need depends on several factors. We will be glad to discuss your event with you and help you in any way we can. Referrals for food catering are also available. For a quote, call (800) 691-8368 or locally, (802) 365-7839, between 7:00 am and 9:00 pm.

Serving Southern Vermont and Surrounding Areas

Rain or Shine

TENT AND EVENTS

14 Hull St., Randolph, VT 05060
ph 800.640.8368 • ph 802.728.3630
info@rainorshinevt.com
www.rainorshinevt.com

We are a full service event rental company specializing in
customer service and high quality rental products

Tents	Custom rental furniture
Tables	Unique lighting fixtures
Chairs	Clearspan structures
China	Power generation and distribution
Glassware	Different flooring options
Dance floors	Advanced decorating capabilities

155 Carroll Road, Waitsfield, VT 05673 • 802-496-3545 or 888-898-3839
Amyw@weddingstentsevents.com
www.weddingstentsevents.com

Weddings, Tents and Events can provide the perfect balance of beauty with value. From Mikasa china to specialty linens and beautiful peaked tents, we take care of it all.

We have over twenty years in the business, bridal consultants on our staff and an extensive inventory.

We rent only the very best!

Tents, Huppas, Dance floors, Linens, China
Crystal, Silver, and more!

Call to set up a meeting with a planner in our event showroom.

*Meet with our Event Rental staff for a free on-site visit
and computer layout of your event.*

• • • • • • • • • • • • • • • • • • •

*"We are delighted with the new equipment which is much more fitting
with our contemporary brides. From the event to the tent crews, the
Weddings Tents and Events staff is courteous and willing to deal with the
last minute changes. Our clients report having their guests exclaim how
beautiful their events and tents are!"*
— Anne Marie Defreest
*Cooking from the Heart Catering at the Inn at the Round Barn
A&A Hospitality, Inc, Waitsfield*

*"Thank you for your seemingly endless hours of work on our wedding.
We couldn't have done it without you."*
— A.C. Vermont

NOTES

NOTES

Photo courtesy of Raiche Photography

Favors and Special Touches

Adding A Favor

There are so many unique ways to add a favor or special touch to your wedding. Vermont has something special for each season and an abundance of unparalleled quality products and services that will help you create personalized gifts for your guests. Add a touch of Vermont to your wedding by choosing a few of the ideas below to add to your special day.

Wedding Favors

Favors are used to symbolize your appreciation for the many guests who have honored you with their presence on your wedding day. There are hundreds of ways to show your appreciation and we have gathered a few ideas that will remind your guests of Vermont. Whatever you do as a gift, choose an appropriate way of giving the gift to your guests. You can place your gifts in a basket by the door, or place them at each table setting. Couples have even passed out favors themselves, to ensure that they talk to each of their guests individually. Whatever works best for you, make sure that you save a couple for yourself as keepsakes.

Special Touches

Whether you have a family tradition or add a special Vermont touch to your wedding, your guests will enjoy the uniqueness. On the next page we have listed some interesting ideas that other couples have done at their Vermont wedding. Please be sure to let us know of other unique ideas when you fill out the survey in the front of the book.

Favors and Special Touches Check List

- ❏ Favors Selected, Delivered and Set Up
- ❏ Arranged and Delivered Special Gifts for out-of-town Guests
- ❏ Special Touch Confirmed
- ❏ Special Touch Made
- ❏ Special Touch Delivered
- ❏ Other _____
- ❏ Other _____

Unique Favors and Special Touches

Many states are noted for special products that are unique to their region. This is especially true of Vermont. Listed below are just a few ideas. We would love to hear about the special Vermont touches you used to distinguish your wedding. When you fill out the survey in the front be sure to include your special touches!

- Give guests small bottles of maple syrup with special labels commemorating your wedding. Place them in big baskets by the door and have servers hand them to exiting guests, or put one at each place setting at the tables. Choose any tasteful way to give this touching Vermont gift.

- Maple candy served with your wedding cake adds a distinctive Vermont garnish.

- Candles make beautiful decorations. In Vermont, citronella candles are the most popular, since they help keep bugs away. If you are having an outdoor evening wedding, these candles can be put on tall iron rods throughout your lawn. (Be careful if there are kids around). Light up the night while keeping your guests comfortable and bug free.

- Wildflower seeds are a nice touch, especially for outdoor weddings. You can buy a Vermont mixture in bulk and put the seeds in pretty baskets, decorated boxes or wrapped bundles for your guests to take home as a gift. Your guests can plant their seeds back home and be reminded of your wedding with a collage of colors.

- During the fall foliage season, Vermont is one of the most splendid places in the world to hold a wedding. In addition to the spectacular colors, Vermont is well known for its delicious fall apples. Send a basket of apples, with a note, to all your guests that are staying overnight. Get a list of places where everyone is staying and have one person spend a couple hours delivering the baskets.

- Champagne poured in a picturesque Vermont field is a very romantic way to start the receiving line. Consider serving champagne in beautiful flute glasses to the guests while they wait in the receiving line.

- How about brewing your own Vermont beer! This is a fun and distinctive idea for couples who want to serve their own beer, adorned with their own label, at their reception or rehearsal dinner. Your own micro-brewed beer also makes a great gift for your guests or wedding party.

- Place a Polaroid camera next to your guest book, have guests take each other's picture, and tape it to the book with their best wishes and signature. It is a lot of fun to look at afterwards.

- ☺ Make a picture collage of the wedding couple's life history and include photos of family, friends and guests. Your guests will love to look at these pictures—especially if they are in them.

- ☺ Have your photographer take an outdoor panoramic photo of the entire wedding. Use this picture for thank-you or holiday cards.

- ☺ Use a variety of fall leaves on your individual place cards and on the tables. One table can be maple leaves, another beech leaves, etc. This is a beautiful way to help your guests find their seats.

- ☺ Another interesting way to assign table seating is to use the Vermont Mountains. Place a card at each table with a name of a mountain. At the entrance table place a large decorative placard with the table's mountain name and the guests that are sitting there.

- ☺ Baskets full of birdseed at the end of the ceremony is a perfect touch. When the guests come from the church or to the ceremony site have them take a handful of seeds and throw them as the couple drives away. It is much better than rice—which can actually hurt birds.

- ☺ A friend of mine, and her fiancé, purchased framed Vermont artwork and had it laid out on a table at their reception. All the guests signed the matte that surrounded the lovely artwork. They now have this piece hanging in their home and every time they look at it, it reminds them of their special day.

- ☺ Baby pictures of the couple placed at the gift table or the head table is always a big hit. Try and get a 5x6 or 8x10 of each person and have them in similar frames.

- ☺ Another couple used rocks as place cards—this was especially helpful at their outdoor setting. This idea can be time consuming so play around with a few markers and some clean rocks.

- ☺ Individual miniature terracotta pots with names painted on them. Each place setting has a terracotta pot filled with flowers personalized for each individual guest. This favor for each guest also becomes the instant table decoration. This idea is perfect for an intimate garden wedding.

- ☺ Consider an old fashion, classic-style photobooth rental. This provides both great entertainment for your guests and great memories for everyone.

Comfort Cookies

Food made naturally to soothe the soul!

Vermont based bakers
Laura Walker and Scott Sewell
Toll free: 877-700-8822
802-425-4283
www.ComfortCookiesInc.com

Getting married in Vermont is a celebrated and beautiful decision. Your wedding favors should be as memorable as your "special day"!

Comfort Cookies, with more than 20 flavors, are as unforgettable as they are delicious. Each cookie is lovingly molded by hand using Vermont butter, eggs, and gourmet chocolate while adding no preservatives or anything artificial.

Our Comfort Cookies are always individually wrapped, allowing us to easily customize the label to honor your day. Whether you want to simply add Comfort Cookies to your own gift bag, feature them on your dessert table, or desire us to provide colorful organza and silk favor bags, we are happy to work with you to make your wedding remarkable.

We promise that your guests will know how truly appreciated they are once they taste Comfort Cookies.

 Truffles

Erle R. LaBounty
Waterbury, VT • 802.793.9033
www.farmhousetruffles.com
info@farmhousetruffles.com

A Mood Mending Indulgence

"Farmhouse's truffles are rolled rather than poured and they whispered their flavor..."

–Seven Days

Farmhouse Truffles, artisanal, hand-made truffles, are all produced with high quality Belgian couverture in small batches with great attention to texture, taste, and temptation. A silky smooth ganache combined with fresh fruits, nuts, and liqueurs, all hand-dipped in dark chocolate: this is the trademark of Farmhouse Truffles. E.R. LaBounty Confections also produces delectable pralines made with a rich, buttery caramel studded with toasted almonds and enrobed in a dark chocolate.

We specialize in confections perfect for wedding favors. We work with you to create a bespoke package that coordinates with your wedding design. Contact us for more information.

www.farmhousetruffles.com
info@farmhousetruffles.com
802.793.9033

From start to finish we're here to help you celebrate your special day. Start with our huge selection of invitations, then select from elegant cake tops, guest books, unity candles, toasting glasses and so much more. Add beautiful balloon decor and you're ready for the most important day of your life.

Largest In-Store Bridal Selection

Custom Invitations	Guest Books
Balloon Decorations	Unity Candles
Cake Tops	Toasting Glasses

...and so much more

Visit the location nearest you:

129 Strongs Avenue	Towne Marketplace	178 Washington Street
Rutland, VT	Susie Wilson Road	Claremont, NH
802.773.3155	Essex Jct., VT	603.543.1795

www.thepartystores.com

169

Favors With Flavor

VT Made Richard's Sauces
richardsauces.com/promo.html
sauce@vtmadebbqu.com
802-524-3196

Favors with flavor…that is how we describe our unique
and delicious party/wedding favors.
Personalized with your photo, symbol of love or message of gratitude.
Richard's Gourmet Sauces in 3 flavors, packaged in 5oz bottles is
Vermont quality given with pride. Create a Gift Basket
for your special guests or wedding party.

Steve and Martha have been married for 38 years and are the proud owners of VT Made Richard's Sauces. What began as a family recipe developed by brother Richard some 17 years ago is now a wonderful New England favorite.

Steve and Martha have owned and operated VT Made Richard's Sauces for the past 7 years and have enjoyed developing additional flavors along the way. Their **5 ounce Party Favor** filled with their delicious, all natural Barbecue Sauce is the perfect way for you to give your guests a special memory from your special day. With all the planning for perfection that will go into your wedding day, this **FUN, UNIQUE and PERSONAL** gift will be the memory talked about for years to come.

Because we understand the importance of presentation and personal response, we have committed, local professionals always ready to assist in a timely manner, to make sure we can meet your personal needs. If you order on-line, we can have any number of favors at your door within 3 weeks.

Favors for weddings, showers, engagement parties, specially personalized with your photo, symbol or message of thank you to guests, are a token of appreciation that will be memorable and fun and as unique as your special day.

Vermont Elegance

Special wedding keepsakes for your guests.

Telephone: (802) 822-5500
Email: info@VermontArtStore.com

VermontArtStore.com

Artisan Bob Burke has created a new line of beautiful, stainless steel ornaments designed to celebrate a couple's special day. This personalized touch will be appreciated by guests and will be enjoyed and remembered for a lifetime.

The ornaments are individually hand crafted with no two exactly the same. Bob's designs are made of high quality stainless steel, brush finished and professionally electro etched to aircraft quality standards. They are then accented by hand polishing to bring out the three dimensional shape of each ornament.

Please check our website to review the designs available for your special day. We would be happy to send a sample of our "Wedding Favor" ornament to you. Please contact us at info@VermontArtStore.com.

Banquet and Reception Sites are invited to join our sponsorship program of this new "Wedding Favor." Participants in the program can choose to have their Company name, location or logo permanently etched on the reverse side as a reminder of where the special event was held. Our special event ornament can also be used as part of Wedding Packages to prospective brides.

If you have a special need, contact us at info@VermontArtStore.com. We have also created beautiful handmade Vermont Stainless Steel and Candle Centerpieces for your special event. They are available for purchase or for rent.

Special wedding keepsakes for your guests.
Visit us on the web: www.vermontartstore.com

Vermont by the Bushel

*Theme, Thank You, Wedding, Welcome &
Vermont Specialty Food Baskets*

P. O. Box 644
Proctor, Vermont 05765
T 802.459.2897 • F 802.459.2804
www.vermontbythebushel.com
info@vermontbythebushel.com

Custom Crafted Signature Baskets

Brides Wedding Basket *Maple Lovers Basket*
Grooms Wedding Basket *Snack Lovers Basket*
Wedding Welcome Basket *Coffee Lovers Basket*
Classic I Love Vermont Basket *Tea Lovers Basket*
Classic Fall Apple Basket *Canine Lovers Basket*
Italian Feast Basket *Feline Lovers Basket*
Chocolate Lovers Basket *Anniversary Basket*

Custom Crafted "Personalized" Gifting

We will customize your ¼ peck, ½ peck, peck or full size bushel to meet your needs with Maple Products, Cheese, Jam & Preserves, Mustard, Relish, Coffee, Tea, Fun Candy & Chocolate, Chocolate and Caramel Sauces (sugar free sauces too) Dip Mixes, Pancake, Muffin and Scone Mixes, Chips and Salsa, Pepperoni, Venison Sausage, Crackers, Hot Sauces, Trail Mix, Nuts and more. And yes…these are all Vermont products!

Couples are sending Wedding Attendants heartfelt thank you baskets with a personal touch and Wedding Welcome Baskets for their out of town guests. Send us a sticker, pen, mug or memorabilia from your hometown, almamater or your favorite team and we'll incorporate it into your basket.

Call or email Judy about customizing baskets for your wedding, birthday, anniversay or special occasion.

NOTES

NOTES

Photo courtesy of Portrait Gallery

Selecting the Right Florist for You

Flowers play a vital role in creating the romantic mood of a wedding. Adorned with the right flowers, your wedding site can become a Garden of Eden. The price of flowers varies greatly, so before you get your heart sold on specific arrangements, consult with a florist—and, of course, your budget. There are many beautiful flower options that can make your wedding gorgeous and fragrant. Finding the ones that will match your wedding needs may take a little shopping around.

Your Style

When deciding upon your floral design, you will need to know your wedding style and the locations of your ceremony and reception sites. Knowing that, you can visit a florist who will help you design beautiful arrangements. They know which flowers will be in season, and how to match your wedding style and type. Summer wildflowers are gorgeous at an outdoor summer wedding but might be impractical at an evening winter wedding.

Choosing Your Flowers

Before approaching a florist, have a few specific ideas of flower arrangements that you like. This will make it easier for the florist to work with you and know your style. If your budget is an issue, you can select primarily low-cost flowers, they are still beautiful, and limit the expensive ones to where they really show such as the bride's bouquet.

The Bride's Bouquet

At almost every wedding, the entire flower arrangement scheme is woven around the bride's bouquet. The bride's bouquet is the centerpiece of the wedding decorations. All your attendants and the groom's flowers should get their style and design from the bouquet. The bouquet will be seen, touched and smelled, more than any other flowers. Choosing the bouquet first will help your florist immensely. Take the time to make it meet your dreams.

Choosing a Florist

There are many florists who specialize in weddings. They will have portfolios of their work, and provide you with references. Put together a list of all the items you need and ask for a cost estimate from the florists with whom you would like to work with. If you want to work with a particular florist, jointly design beautiful arrangements that fit your budget.

Choosing a Florist

Do you do a lot of weddings?

Do you have a portfolio I may review?

Do you have references?

May we come in for a consultation?

What are your deposit/cancellation policies?

Will you deliver and arrange the flowers?

Have you seen the reception/ceremony sites?

Would you be willing to look at them?

Flower Check List

❏ Ceremony site flowers

❏ Main alter flowers

❏ Aisle pews

❏ Bride's bouquet

❏ Tossing bouquet

❏ Attendants' bouquets

❏ Flower girl

❏ Mothers' corsages

❏ Grandmothers' corsages

❏ Hairpieces

❏ Other _____

❏ Other _____

❏ Other _____

Boutonnieres for:

❏ Groom

❏ Ushers

❏ Ring bearer

❏ Fathers

❏ Other _____

❏ Other _____

Reception site:

❏ Tabletops

❏ Head table

❏ Buffet table

❏ Cake table

❏ Cake

❏ Other _____

❏ Other _____

178

Hawley's FLORIST

We will create beautiful floral designs for your very special day.

We create designs for the ceremony, reception, rehearsal dinners, barbeques, and anything else you need.

Lovely natural bouquets using native flowers and foliages, along with calla lilies, roses, mokara and dendrobium orchids, gerbera daisies, or lilies. We work and guide you in designing the perfect flowers for you.

We service the resort areas of Central Vermont in the Killington-Okemo areas, Mountain Top Inn, Mountain Meadows, Killington Grand, Jackson Gore, Bates Mansion, Echo Lake Inn, Riverside Inn, and more.

Call, stop in or e-mail us for personal service for this very special occasion in your life. We are here to help in every way.

Bonnie Hawley and Staff
29 Center Street
Historic Downtown Rutland, VT
hawleyb@sover.net
florist.com
800-841-4601

179

Maplehurst Florist

since 1943

10 Lincoln Street
Essex Junction, VT 05452
62 Church Street
Burlington, VT 05401
802-878-8113 or 800-777-8115
www.maplehurstflorist.com
maplehurstflorist@verizon.net

Congratulations!

Let us help you celebrate one of the most important days of your life.

Our wedding flowers have graced beautiful ceremony and reception venues in the greater Burlington area for over 50 years. From casual to formal, indoors or outdoors, Maplehurst Florist will create floral designs to accent the beauty of your wedding. Our creative and talented staff will make sure your day is as special as you have always dreamed.

What Makes Maplehurst Unique

Vermont is brimming with perfect venues for any size wedding and we've worked with many of them over 50 years. This expertise allows us to offer guidance as to what will enhance your selected site. We have the most extensive selection of flowers available, from roses to tulips to exotic tropicals. No matter the style or size of your wedding, we offer exceptional service to assist you in selecting the perfect flowers for your special day. We will work within your budget and strive to assist you in all your wedding needs. Knowing planning can be very hectic, our wedding consultants work within your schedule.

What we offer

Let our designers create breathtaking bridal and bridesmaid bouquets, gorgeous centerpieces and stunning ceremonial displays. Their creativity will be directed by your flower, style and color desire whether unique or reproduced from a photograph. We put as much perfection into the corsages and boutonnières as we do the bridal bouquets.

We understand that weddings are very personal, that each one is unique and consider it a privilege to be included in your special day.

We look forward to meeting with you and your fiancé!
Schedule your consultation today.

Florist Directory

Abbott's Florist
White River Jct, VT
(800) 613-3294
www.abbottsflorist.com

Creative Muse Floral Design
Enosburg Falls, VT
(802) 933-4403
www.creativemusevt.com

From Maria's Garden
Stowe, VT
(802) 345-3698
www.frommariasgarden.com

Hawley's Florist
Rutland, VT
(802) 775-2573
www.hawleysflorist.com

Maplehurst Florist
Essex Junction, VT
(802) 878-8113
www.maplehurstflorist.com

NOTES

NOTES

Photo courtesy of Portrait Gallery

Gifts for the Wedding Party

Special Thank You Gifts

As you read through this book, you begin to understand that planning a wedding or special event takes time, money and a lot of help. Whatever your situation, it is important that you thank those who made your special day such a success. Parents help out a tremendous amount, whether it is financially, emotionally or physically. Special friends and family that are part of your wedding party, and even those who are not, need to be thanked for their contribution. Did a friend or family member make your favors? Did they deliver gift baskets all day? Did they oversee all the final touches on the last day? Did they pay for your entire wedding? Think about those who really went the extra mile and thank them. No matter what you decide, whether it is a unique Vermont made product, artwork, a bouquet of flowers or even a card, they will certainly appreciate the effort.

As you think about the many special friends and family that you want to thank, you should try to make your gift both a wedding remembrance and a token of your appreciation for their time and efforts.

You should always try and remember that what works for one person might not work for another. Don't feel as though you have to get everyone the same present.

Try to make sure your gift is timeless and something useful after your wedding day. While accessories to be worn for the wedding make lovely gifts, try not to make them too wedding-specific. If it is important to you that your wedding party all wear the same jewelry and that it matches their wedding attire, think about packaging it with something useful, such as a beautiful jewelry box.

Take the "would I want this?" test. Before picking up something that seems totally adorable or creative, stop to think if it's something that you would like to receive and/or display in your home. Cute monogrammed silver or gold trinkets may catch your eye, but depending on their usefulness they could surely end up in the back of a drawer for the next 25 years.

When to Get Them

Well for once there are no rules or specific timelines. The shopping for these gifts can fit into your schedule as you plan the other appointments necessary to planning your wedding. Of course, it is always better to buy them sooner rather than later—in general, aim for no later than one to two months prior to the wedding. This way you are no trying to fit the shopping for these gifts into the week before your wedding.

In the months leading up to your wedding, keep an eye out for something that you know will touch the person for whom you will be buying a gift. By planning ahead, you will be able to take advantage of sales or you may even come across a hot item while compiling your own registry.

What to Spend

Well, this is certainly a question only you can answer. There is no right or wrong answer. Your thoughtfulness will be what is important to each of the recipients.

It is typical for the maid of honor to receive a gift that is a little more significant than the other bridesmaids, since it's normally her job to coordinate the shower and the bachelorette party. Don't forget about the flower girls, what a wonderful chance to give them something they will remember for many, many years.

Sometimes the best gifts are those you can't put in a box. If expenses for your bridal party are running a bit high, consider offering to pay for their wedding-day hair and makeup, for a suite upgrade at the hotel, or for their bridesmaids dress.

When to Give

It is traditional for the wedding party gifts to be handed out at the rehearsal dinner, when everyone is together in one place. Of course, if you prefer a more intimate moment, you can set aside some time in the one or two weeks leading up to your wedding and hand them their gifts in private.

Vermont ᵇʸₜₕₑ Bushel

*Theme, Thank You, Wedding, Welcome &
Vermont Specialty Food Baskets*

P. O. Box 644
Proctor, Vermont 05765
T 802.459.2897 • F 802.459.2804
www.vermontbythebushel.com
info@vermontbythebushel.com

Custom Crafted Signature Baskets

Brides Wedding Basket	*Maple Lovers Basket*
Grooms Wedding Basket	*Snack Lovers Basket*
Wedding Welcome Basket	*Coffee Lovers Basket*
Classic I Love Vermont Basket	*Tea Lovers Basket*
Classic Fall Apple Basket	*Canine Lovers Basket*
Italian Feast Basket	*Feline Lovers Basket*
Chocolate Lovers Basket	*Anniversary Basket*

Custom Crafted "Personalized" Gifting

We will customize your ¼ peck, ½ peck, peck or full size bushel to meet your needs with Maple Products, Cheese, Jam & Preserves, Mustard, Relish, Coffee, Tea, Fun Candy & Chocolate, Chocolate and Caramel Sauces (sugar free sauces too) Dip Mixes, Pancake, Muffin and Scone Mixes, Chips and Salsa, Pepperoni, Venison Sausage, Crackers, Hot Sauces, Trail Mix, Nuts and more. And yes…these are all Vermont products!

Couples are sending Wedding Attendants heartfelt thank you baskets with a personal touch and Wedding Welcome Baskets for their out of town guests. Send us a sticker, pen, mug or memorabilia from your hometown, almamater or your favorite team and we'll incorporate it into your basket.

Call or email Judy or Marie about customizing baskets for your wedding, birthday, anniversary and special occasion.

NOTES

NOTES

Photo courtesy of Portrait Gallery

Choosing Registry Locations

Where to Register

You will be pleasantly surprised at the number and type of stores in which you may register for gifts. Today, registering does not have to be just for china and silver, even though those are still the most popular items. As a couple, you can choose what your needs and wants are and plan your gift registry accordingly. Remember all your guests and choose items for every price range. You will want to register as soon as possible since many people will want to get your engagement and shower gifts through your registry. Register at several locations to give people a selection. Kitchen shops, linen stores and even outdoor stores are fun places for registries.

Thank-you Notes

Have thank-you notes on hand so that as soon as you receive a gift you will be able to send a personalized note. Always send handwritten thank-you cards; never type them. It is proper to thank people promptly for their gift. Sending a thank-you right away will also save time later on when you get lots of gifts all at once. Keep a list of who sent you what gift in the Wedding Worksheet section. This will allow you to keep track of gifts and enable you to mention the gift in your thank-you note.

As a special touch, if you will be sending out greeting or holiday cards in the future, you can again mention their gift and how much you enjoy it. If they attended your wedding, thank them again for coming.

Registry Card

Inform your families where you registered, so that they can let their friends and other family members know. The best way to do this is to have a neatly printed 3x5 registry card with the locations, addresses and numbers of the places where you have registered. Many locations will provide their own individual registered cards for you. This will make it easy for families and attendants to send them out in shower invitations. Your guests will ask where you registered; don't be shy about this. It is just as much fun for your guests to pick out your gift as it is for you to receive it.

Damaged Items and Return Policy

Make sure you know the stores policy regarding damaged items and returning duplicates. You don't want to be stuck with five teapots.

Gift Table

If you decide to have a gift table, it is important that you have someone oversee this table. Your guests will enjoy having someone greet them at the table and help them display their gift. Make sure their card is properly taped to their gift. Many guests will just bring envelopes, you should have a basket for these. The envelopes should be removed and given to a parent or a close relative for safe keeping once all the guests have placed their gifts. Many couples like to open and display their gifts; decide if this is appropriate for you. Make sure someone gets the gifts back to the location you have designated. If you are bringing the gifts back to your home before heading off on your honeymoon, make sure you do not leave them by the door. Put them under a bed, in a closet or the basement—not in public view.

Choosing Registry Stores

Do you have a bridal registry?

How can I register?

Do you have the items in stock?

What is your duplicate policy?

What is your damage policy?

Will you ship gifts?

Can you provide us with a list of our register items?

Do you have a phone number for our guests to call?

Do you have register cards?

Gift Registry Check List

❏ Choose locations to register

❏ Choose items to register for

❏ Create register cards

❏ Damage and return policies

❏ Thank-you notes

❏ List of gifts and who gave them

❏ Decorate gift table

❏ Basket for envelopes

❏ Assign person to gift table

❏ Person to hold envelopes

❏ Get gifts back from reception

NOTES

Photo courtesy of Echo Lake Inn

Guests Accommodations

Planning Ahead

This category becomes particularly important in Vermont. Whether you live in Vermont or are just choosing it as the perfect wedding destination you need to realize that planning ahead is important. In the fall, locals frequently open up their own homes to tourists who had no place to stay because all other accommodations were booked. Advise your guests to reserve their accommodations far in advance.

As we discussed in the "Out-of-Town Guests" section, the variety of Vermont's accommodations is outstanding. By planning ahead, you will be able to find just the right accommodations for all of your guests. Check first with the location you chose as your reception site, do they have accommodations? Many places will temporarily reserve rooms for your wedding. If you reserve rooms, make sure that there is a date at which time they are offered back to the public. You do not want to pay for rooms that went vacant. If you choose not to block out rooms, ask your guests to call and state they are with the wedding party, they may get a discount that you prearranged.

When researching the variety of accommodations available for your guests, consider every price range. Guests traveling from afar may want to stay a few days and prefer moderately priced accommodations.

Put a list together of lodging near your wedding site well in advance of your wedding. If your wedding is at a busy tourist time, you will want to send this list out early. Let your guests be responsible for booking their own accommodations, but be sure to let them know they should do so as quickly as possible. Review the Banquet and Reception section for locations that have rooms.

The Bride and Groom's Lodging

You should consider where the wedding night suite will be. Frequently, couples who have an evening wedding do not travel straight to their honeymoon destination. It is wise to find a beautiful place close by to stay. This way you will get more rest and be able to see family and friends again the next day before you travel. If you are holding your reception at a site that also has rooms, the site may provide a free newlyweds room as part of the package. This room also comes in handy when the bride and her attendants prepare for the wedding.

A Little Advice

If you truly want privacy the evening of your wedding, do not let anyone know where you are staying. This is a perfect opportunity for all your practical-joking friends to get back at you for anything you previously did to them in kindergarten! If you are the partying type, and do want a few friends around, choose a place that accommodates a little noise.

Choosing Accommodations

Do you have rooms available on these dates?

What are your price ranges?

Do you give a discount for a number of rooms?

Can we temporarily block off rooms?

Will we be charged for blocked rooms you do not rent?

How far in advance should someone book a room with you?

How long will you let us block off rooms?

Do you have an airport shuttle service?

Do you have a honeymoon suite?

Accommodations Check List

❏ Put together list of places and prices

❏ Confirm that there are rooms still available

❏ Block off rooms if necessary

❏ Accommodation for your immediate family

❏ Accommodation for your wedding party

❏ Honeymoon suite for bride and groom

❏ Gift baskets for out-of-town guests

❏ Transportation issues regarding guests

❏ Check that you are not being charged for any rooms you may have temporarily blocked off

❏ Your travel bags are delivered to honeymoon suite

Accommodations & Information

Directions, Maps and Accommodations

Okay, you spend a great deal of time planning your wedding, designing your invitations and then you include a hand-drawn map to your ceremony and reception sites with lists of accommodations—all we can say is Yuck! If you are not going to make this piece match your invitations, then send it separately.

The service that provides your invitations can help you design an extra enclosure for directions and other information. If you choose to mail this piece early, perhaps you can create it on your computer. Exact directions can be found and printed directly from the internet... aah, technology.

For your convenience we have listed some wonderful spots to house your guests. You may also call the Chambers of Commerce listed in the Vermont Section and ask for accommodations lists, upcoming events and nearby interests and attractions.

Guest Accommodations Site Map

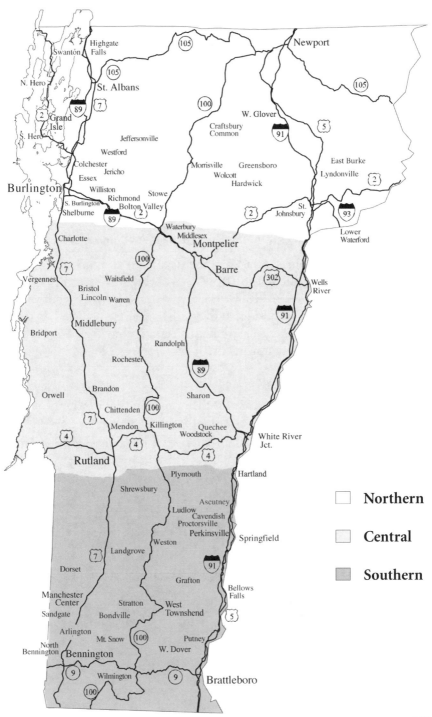

Highgate Falls
Swanton
N. Hero
Grand Isle
S. Hero
Burlington
Colchester
Essex
Williston
Jericho
S. Burlington
Shelburne
Charlotte
Vergennes
Bristol
Lincoln
Waitsfield
Warren
Middlebury
Bridport
Orwell
Brandon
Chittenden
Mendon
Rutland
St. Albans
Jeffersonville
Westford
Richmond
Bolton Valley
Stowe
Waterbury
Middlesex
Montpelier
Barre
Randolph
Rochester
Sharon
Killington
Woodstock
Quechee
White River Jct.
Newport
W. Glover
Craftsbury Common
Morrisville
Wolcott
Greensboro
Hardwick
East Burke
Lyndonville
St. Johnsbury
Lower Waterford
Wells River

Plymouth
Shrewsbury
Hartland
Ludlow
Ascutney
Cavendish
Proctorsville
Perkinsville
Springfield
Weston
Landgrove
Dorset
Grafton
Manchester Center
Sandgate
Arlington
North Bennington
Bennington
Stratton
Bondville
Mt. Snow
West Townshend
Bellows Falls
Putney
W. Dover
Wilmington
Brattleboro

Northern

Central

Southern

199

818 Charlestown Road
Springfield, VT. 05156
Toll Free: (800) 465-4329
Phone: (802) 885-4516

www.vermonthi.com
hixpress@aol.com

We Do...take care of your out-of-town wedding guests!

Congratulations on your special wedding day! With so much to coordinate and arrange, let the Holiday Inn Express — Springfield team help with the accommodations and extra details. Have your out-of-town wedding guests stay with us, with peace of mind that they will be comfortable and experience a true Vermont atmosphere. Our intimate meeting room is ideal for rehearsal dinners or private wedding luncheons.

Our Wedding Package includes:

- A complimentary guestroom for the bride and groom when your wedding party reserves 10 or more rooms
- Complimentary bottle of chilled Champagne for the bride and groom
- Late check-out
- Free parking

FOR THE FINEST IN ACCOMMODATIONS

Holiday Inn Express – Springfield
www.vermonthi.com • hixpress@aol.com

Guest Accommodations Directory

Best Western Windjammer Inn
South Burlington, VT
(802) 651-0635
www.bestwestern.com/windjammerinn

Echo Lake Inn
Ludlow, VT
(802) 228-8602
www.echolakeinn.com

Holiday Inn Express Springfield
Springfield, VT
(802) 885-4516
www.vermonthi.com

Tabor House Inn
West Swanton, VT
(802) 868-7575
www.taborhouseinn.com

Vermont Inn
Killington, VT
(802) 775-0708
www.vermontinn.com

NOTES

Photo courtesy of Lauren Stagnitti Wedding Photography

Planning the Perfect Honeymoon

Honeymooning in Vermont

Spending your wedding night or your entire honeymoon in Vermont can be one of the most relaxing and romantic vacations. Some of the top romantic inns in the country are nestled in the green mountains of Vermont. Many inns and resorts have wonderful honeymoon packages that will fit all your activity and relaxation requirements.

The Vacation of a Lifetime

Your honeymoon is a perfect opportunity to take a once-in-a-lifetime vacation. The challenge is to find a trip which meets the ideals of both the bride and groom. Going to the Caribbean for a beach vacation may be ideal for one partner but not so great for the other who has problems with the sun. Because you both like to do fun, but sometimes different things, it is a good idea not to surprise your fiancé with the honeymoon destination. Half the fun is discussing all the possibilities and things you can do on your honeymoon. For both of you, a honeymoon may just be a relaxing week in a beautiful state like Vermont.

There are so many ways to research great honeymoon destinations. There are books and magazines that have articles on particular spots and all the activities you can do in that area. Once you have decided on a destination, or two, research pricing and reservation information for the trip.

The honeymoon is one vacation that will help you relax and start to set the mood for your future together, therefore it is a good idea to spend some extra time to ensure the trip goes off effortlessly. An early start guarantees the best rates, the availability of locations and transportation, and the ability to explore alternate plans if necessary.

Things to Consider When Planning a Location

What is your ideal romantic setting? City or country; sunny and warm or snowy and cold; relaxing or full of adventure; small tent in the woods or the Ritz Carlton; these are just a few of the choices. Make sure what you choose matches both your needs.

You will need to consider the length of time it takes to get to your destination. If one of you do not like long plane rides you may want to consider something closer. And of course, you cannot forget your budget. You will need to compare prices, decide what your priorities are and what you can do without. No one wants to think of a budget on a honeymoon but if you plan ahead you won't have to think of it during the honeymoon because you have budgeted for all your costs.

Honeymoon Packages

It is sometimes hard to tell if honeymoon packages are a good deal or not. It truly depends on whether or not you want to deal with any of the planning. Packages can be great because they require very little work by you. Often resorts or locations offer one-price all-inclusive packages which often take the pressure off monitoring and planning considerations. Remember to confirm what is included in the package such as airfare, airport shuttles, meals, sporting activities, etc. It is important that you feel comfortable with the reputation of the company with which you are working. It may be best to work with a travel agent when looking at package deals.

Consider Purchasing A Vacation/Timeshare Ownership for Your Honeymoon

So you have done the preliminary planning and made some decisions regarding the type of honeymoon you would like to have and you have a general idea of where you would like to go. At this point, depending on the budget you have set aside for your honeymoon, before you make the final arrangements, you might want to consider if a vacation/timeshare ownership makes sense for you.

If you are the type of person who will want to return to the location of your honeymoon for many years to come, a vacation time share offers a great way to do this.

There are many different companies that offer vacation/timeshare ownership. It is important to deal with well known, established companies and research your preferred location carefully. It is important to check references and to visit the properties before you make your purchase. Usually you can visit the properties for a discounted price by contacting their sales departments.

Special Requirements

Make sure to check the local legal requirements for your destination. Many countries require passports, special visas and drivers' licenses for age requirements for driving. It is also important to inquire about any medical considerations, such as shots. If you have a special medical consideration you may want to inquire about local hospitals.

Carrying Cash

The only thing we can say about carrying cash is don't do it—or at least very little. You should only travel with credit cards and travelers checks/cards. Credit cards are the best, especially in a country that uses foreign currency because you will get the best exchange rate and not the local exchange rate. Make sure you leave copies of all your credit cards, contact telephone numbers and any other information with your families just in case your wallet gets lost or stolen. It is also best to clean out your wallets before you go and only bring the necessary items.

Have A Great Time

Just relax and enjoy yourself. You are on vacation. The word "honeymoon" adds a certain expectation to your trip but if you are relaxed and don't set unrealistic goals about your trip—it will surely be filled with lifetime memories.

Your Wedding Night

Before you travel for your honeymoon it is important that you feel well rested, especially after an energy-filled reception. Stay near the location of your wedding reception but take the time to choose a romantic and relaxing location to stay on your wedding night.

Honeymoon Check List

- ❏ Location
- ❏ Destination
- ❏ Availability
- ❏ Reservations
- ❏ To and from transportation
- ❏ Car rental
- ❏ Official requirements
- ❏ Medical requirements
- ❏ Proper attire for destination
- ❏ Travelers checks
- ❏ Credit cards

- ❏ Camera and film
- ❏ Person watching home and pets
- ❏ Stop mail and newspaper
- ❏ Double check all reservations
- ❏ _____
- ❏ _____
- ❏ _____

Photo by Natalie Stultz www.nataliestultz.com

Dream Escapes Travel

117 Allen Drive, Milton, VT 05468 • (888) 802-7364
www.honeymoon-travel-ideas.com

"Making your dream honeymoon a reality"

Your engagement is a wonderful period in your life and you want to spend time enjoying it. But there is so much planning to do! When it comes to planning your honeymoon, Dream Escapes Travel will make the process stress-free and enjoyable. We are honeymoon planners and we make sure your honeymoon is as special as your wedding. Whether you want to go on a small, Vermont honeymoon or a grand European tour, we can help you plan every detail. We have over 10 years of travel experience and will make sure that your honeymoon is exactly what you dreamed it would be.

Your honeymoon is the first and most important trip you'll take together as a married couple. It's easy nowadays to book a trip on the Internet, but these trips can lead to disappointments. We personally make sure that you will be treated to all the extras because you are on your honeymoon. Here are some of the advantages of booking a honeymoon with Dream Escapes Travel:

- Personalized service, including a free honeymoon planning session.
- $50 credit towards a future travel booking with Dream Escapes Travel.
- Concierge services such as restaurant bookings available for a small fee.
- Help resolving problems such as lost luggage and passports.

Our travel planning and booking services are free. We try to save you money since we know getting married can be very expensive. Our goal is to help you plan a honeymoon that will meet all of your needs.

Please consider Dream Escapes Travel when planning your honeymoon. We will make sure your dream honeymoon turns into a reality!

www.honeymoon-travel-ideas.com

Guest Accommodations Directory

Crown Reef Resort at South Beach
Myrtle Beach, SC
(877) 704-5219
www.crownreef.com

Dreaming Mountain
Johnson, VT
(802) 279-8946
www.dreamingmountain.com

Milne Travel
Barre, VT
(802) 479-0541
www.milnetravel.com

Mountain Edge Resort & Spa
Mt. Sunapee, NH
(877) 468-3343
www.mountainedgeresort.com

Northeast Kingdom Travel & Tourism Association
East Burke, VT
(802) 626-8511
www.travelthekingdom.com

NOTES

NOTES

INVITATIONS AND ADDRESSING

Photo courtesy of Raiche Photography

The Importance of Invitations

Whom to Invite

Determining your wedding list will be one of the most difficult jobs involved with your wedding. The number of people at your wedding will be governed by your budget and your families' lists of guests. Traditionally, the bride (and her family) and groom (and his family) each get to choose half of the guests. You will need to consider co-workers, friends, neighbors, and distant relatives. Decide what you can do, how large you want your wedding to be and make your selections accordingly.

The Invitations

Your invitations should reflect your wedding style. Whether you have a casual or formal wedding, the invitations should reflect that just by their style. Specialty invitation shops will have many books to look through and you will see a variety of choices. With the assistance of an invitation expert, you will be able to choose the invitations and the necessary accessories.

Invitations require a degree of formality and a specialist can help you choose the right wording for all the pieces that go in the invitation. The basic elements that are included are an outside envelope, an invitation (reception card), a response card, a return envelope. Additional pieces are directions to the ceremony and reception site and accommodations listing.

Thank-you cards and any other accessories should match your invitation style. Other accessories that you may consider are napkins, matches, place setting cards and ceremony programs. Many couples are moving away from traditional accessories to more unique gifts that reflect their individual tastes.

You should order your invitations three to four months before the wedding. Make sure that you order a few extras for keepsakes and mistakes.

Addressing

You will have put a lot of time in to selecting the best invitation—make sure your addressing is just as classy. Get the proper titles, spelling and addresses for all your guests. You can learn the proper ways to address envelopes from your invitation specialist or an etiquette book. Calligraphy is always an elegant way to distinguish your invitations.

Accommodations List

When planning a wedding you have to consider not only where and when, but if there will be overnight rooms available for your guests. Many couples who plan Vermont weddings send their accommodation list well in advance of their invitations. This is something you should consider, especially if you are getting married in a popular resort town. This consideration is discussed in detail in the Guest Accommodation Section.

Save the Date Cards

While Save the Date Cards are not necessary, they are a wonderful way to share the excitement and, more importantly, allow your family and friends plenty of time to make arrangements to share in your special day. Especially important for friends and family who will be traveling to your wedding location, Save the Date cards allow travelers to schedule time off from work, take advantage of travel deals and make any other necessary plans sooner rather than later.

If your wedding date falls on or around any holidays, or if it is taking place at a popular vacation or destination location, you should consider sending out your Save the Date notices at least five to six months (even possibly twelve months) in advance depending on your wedding location. This is a nice way to allow your guests to combine attendance at your event with a vacation and they will appreciate having the time and information to plan accordingly.

Save the Date cards can be viewed as a preliminary invitation to your wedding. There are a variety of options available to suit your taste, style and budget. A very popular form of Save the Date notice is a decorative magnet, but a simple postcard is also a very nice alternative.

A Save the Date card should not serve as an engagement announcement and should not be sent to anyone who will not be receiving an invitation to your wedding.

When to Send Out Invitations

Invitations are sent eight to ten weeks (sometimes even up to twelve weeks) before the wedding. This gives guests plenty of time to set the date aside for the wedding. It allows you to receive the RSVP's and work with your reception site on the number of guests you need to prepare for. Remember, even the stamps on your invitation should reflect your wedding. Ask the postal service to weigh your invitation and show you the choices for that postage amount. Invitations are usually at least 60¢ mailings so be prepared for the extra postage.

Invitations Check List

- ❏ Choose an invitation specialist
- ❏ Hire a calligrapher
- ❏ Guest list and addresses
- ❏ Save the Date cards
- ❏ Invitations
- ❏ Wording for invitations
- ❏ Ceremony program
- ❏ Announcements
- ❏ Addressing
- ❏ Directions
- ❏ Accommodations list
- ❏ Thank-you cards
- ❏ Place seating cards
- ❏ Proper postage
- ❏ Napkins
- ❏ Matches
- ❏ Other_____
- ❏ Other_____

215

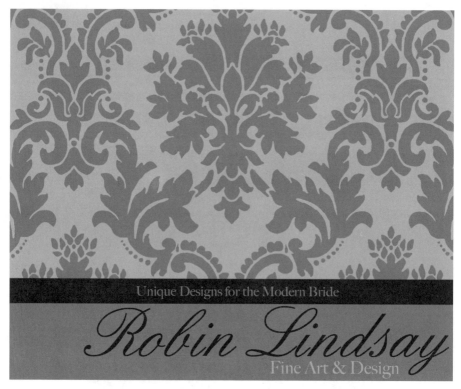

Invitations and Addressing Directory

Capitol Stationers Inc.
Montpelier, VT
(802) 223-2393
www.capitolstationers.com

Heather Hill
13 Pine Court
Essex Jct, VT
(802) 872-1678

The Party Store
Rutland, VT
(802) 773-3155
www.thepartystores.com

Robin Lindsay Fine Art & Design
Concord, NH
(603) 727-8581
www.robinlindsay.net

Vermont Calligraphy
Manchester, VT
(802) 362-3818

NOTES

Photo courtesy of Jeff Schneiderman Photography

Choosing Quality Jewelry

Jewelry for a wedding ranges from the engagement ring to gifts for the bride's attendants. The engagement has become less traditional and more of a shared discussion and that sometimes includes selecting the engagement ring. Yes, sometimes the bride is included in picking out the engagement ring. Still today, most men spend many hours on their own looking for the perfect ring.

Engagement Rings

If you choose to purchase a diamond engagement ring, it is important that you understand a little bit about how diamonds are priced to be sure you are getting what you want. One of the best ways to do that is to talk to a diamond expert. There are many quality jewelers who will take the time to explain diamond details to you. The four main items that determine the cost and quality of a diamond are Cut, Clarity, Color and Carat.

The Definitions of Cut, Clarity, Color and Carat

Cut: *Refers to the arrangement of a diamond's facets. A diamond which is "ideal cut" captures and releases the maximum play of light.*

Clarity: *The degree to which tiny marks of nature called inclusions are present in the diamond.*

Color: *Diamonds range from colorless—the rarest and most valuable— to yellowish, with a range of shadings in between.*

Carat-Weight: *Standard measurement for diamond size.*

Choosing the Right Ring

This may seem like a lot to learn, but a reputable jeweler will be able to explain the value and quality of a diamond. It is important that you know what you are buying. Not only is this for your marriage but it could very well be an heirloom for your children and their children.

Let the jeweler know your budget so that you are not shown rings that are way out of your price range. Choose the ring which is valued the highest and which looks the best to you for your price range. Certification will provide you with proof of the diamond's grade and identity. Be sure to get the certification for your records and make sure your insurance agency gets a copy of it immediately to add to your policy.

A Little Advice

Ask detailed questions regarding the diamond and the setting. It is important that you know the quality of the gem you are getting.

Family Rings

One of the most sentimental engagements rings is a family heirloom. They are beautiful but sometimes the prongs that hold the diamond are not as strong as they used to be. You may want to replace or repair them to a more modern or just a more sturdy setting. It is important that you, at the least, get the ring cleaned and appraised for insurance.

Wedding Bands

Whether or not you choose to purchase an engagement ring, picking out the wedding bands together is a romantic and exciting adventure. There are many jewelry experts who can guide you in this important endeavor. Your rings will be forever, a daily reminder of your commitment to each other; choose your jeweler and your rings wisely.

Bridal Party Gifts

Many brides purchase earrings, necklaces or even bracelets for their wedding party as their appreciation gift. If they are to wear your gift during your wedding, pick something complementary to the bride attendants' dresses and, as always, your budget. For other types of gifts, refer to the specialty companies in the Favors and Special Touches and Gift Registry sections.

Choosing a Jeweler

Do you do consultations regarding rings?

May we see examples of your engagement rings?

Can you design rings?

What are your deposit/cancellation policies?

Do you have any warranties, guarantees?

What do I do if I need a repair?

Do you provide a certificate of authenticity?

Will the sales receipt and certification be specific regarding the ring's qualities?

Can you design matching wedding bands?

How long does it take to order a ring?

How long does it take for a custom ring?

Do you inscribe bands with a message or wedding date?

NOTES

Photo courtesy of Lauren Stagnitti Wedding Photography

Setting the Tone with Music

Choosing the Right Music For Your Wedding

Music is one of the most important choices in creating the ambiance for your wedding. Whether you choose traditional wedding music, more modern favorites, a soloist or a small group of musicians, make sure that each song contributes to the overall tone you want. The sound of pleasant music helps create a great first impression for arriving guests.

Musicians also play a large role in the flow of the ceremony and reception. Many couples will choose a soloist or a single musical instrument to be played at the ceremony. Be sure that what they play matches your needs and the requirements for the ceremony site.

For your reception you will want to consider a more lively type of music. You need to consider all your guests at your wedding. Hard rock may be your favorite kind of music but it may not be your grandparents. Hire musicians that will appeal to all your guests.

Music Considerations

Coordinate with your officiant and the musician on which pieces are appropriate for your ceremony. It is important that the music fit with the ceremony. Having a twenty minute soloist piece in the middle of the ceremony might not be appropriate. Once you have determined the songs and their length of time, you can determine the flow of your ceremony.

When planning your reception music you have two requirements. One is background music for when guests arrive and during the dinner service. You don't want loud or rock'n roll music during dinner. Soft, easy, romantic music is best during this time. When it's time to dance, remember, if the majority of your guests are older they may enjoy big band, orchestra or waltz music. If you have a mixed crowd you will want a band or D.J. with a broad repertoire, this will allow for some popular dancing songs and the waltz songs everyone enjoys.

You will also need to confirm with your reception site what they allow. You may want the musicians to play until midnight but 10 p.m. may be the facility's stopping time.

Master of Ceremonies Duties

Think carefully about who you have as the Master of Ceremonies. You may want the musicians to announce the wedding party, the first dance, the parents' dance and the cake cutting, but you need to make sure they have done it before and do it with class. You can easily disrupt the style of your wedding with a risqué or loud Master of Ceremonies. You may want to learn more about the musician's skill in that category. If you do have a musician play this role, make sure he or she understands exactly the wording and tone you expect.

Choosing Musicians

Always ask if you are able to hear the musicians you are considering. A live performance is the best, but if that is not possible, then ask them for a tape. Most musicians will have a tape and a list of the songs that they play. Also ask for references—it is good to hear other opinions about their music, setup, appearance and style. If you are considering a group of musicians, ask how long they have been performing together and if they can guarantee that they will be the same ones playing. It can be quite a shock to go listen to a band and have different members show up at your wedding. If that does happen, they are usually just as good as the members picked before.

When you sign a contract with a band, make sure it includes all the items you have discussed, including the names of the musicians who will play at your wedding. You will need to consider meals, tips and taxes along with deposit requirements. When you are certain, make a deposit and sign a contract with the musicians you chose so they are booked for your date and cannot accept another offer.

Set-up Requirements

Different ceremony and reception sites will have specific set-up requirements and areas. Put the site manager and musicians in contact with each other to coordinate necessary arrangements. Double check this, especially for outdoor ceremonies and large groups of musicians.

Playing Time

Before you decide on musicians make sure their playing and break times work with your ceremony and reception outlines. Some musicians will double book a wedding day—just make sure they will arrive in plenty of time to set-up and be ready. Musicians usually have a specific amount of time they play, if you would like to have them longer, ask them what they can do and what the additional fee would be.

Consider Dance Lessons

Even only a couple of hours of lessons will help you feel more confident and look good dancing together to your special song. Whether you join a group class or take a private lesson, dancing lessons are just plain fun and the benefits are noticeable. In just a couple of hours you can learn a few simple steps, how to keep proper form, stick to the beat of the music and how to work together to glide across the dance floor. Always remember…smile while you're dancing!

Choosing Musicians

Do you perform at weddings?

How many years have you been a musician?

Will you be the one performing at my wedding?

Can I hear you play?

Do you have a tape available?

Do you have a list of songs that you play?

Can you suggest some songs?

What are your fees?

What is the length of time you will play?

Can you work with the ceremony site for set up?

What are your requirements for set up?

Do you dress according to the wedding style?

What are your deposit, cancellation policies?

What are your contract requirements?

Music and Entertainment Check List

❏ Ceremony Music
❏ Beginning of ceremony
❏ Processional
❏ During the ceremony
❏ Additional songs
❏ Recessional
❏ Reception music
❏ Background at reception
❏ During dinner

- ❏ Main musicians for dancing
- ❏ Master of ceremonies
- ❏ List of songs to play
- ❏ List of songs not to play
- ❏ Outline for the master of ceremonies
- ❏ Wedding party announcement song
- ❏ Bride and groom first dance
- ❏ Bride and father's dance
- ❏ Groom and mother's dance
- ❏ Announcement for all guests to dance
- ❏ Cake cutting announcement
- ❏ Toast announcement
- ❏ Set-up and breakdown
- ❏ Meal for musicians
- ❏ Electricity
- ❏ Music list
- ❏ Order of events
- ❏ List of names and roles to give to musicians
- ❏ Place for musicians to change
- ❏ Meal for musicians
- ❏ Beverages for musicians

BestBands

Vermont's Finest Wedding and Function Bands 1-800-639-6380

New England's premiere entertainment agency, specializing in wedding receptions, corporate functions and private parties.

Our Commitment to You

Through fastidious attention to detail, vast musical knowledge, and a personal touch, Best Bands will help you find the most inspiring and appropriate band for your event. Best Bands also offers solo performers and an unparalleled DJ service.

The Finest in Wedding and Function Bands

Phil Abair Band	Glow
Alessi Band	As You Like It
A House On Fire	Sandra Wright
Pulse	Search Band
G Funk Band	Good Soul
DT Fever	DC Project
High Rollers	Shake It

and many more…

User Friendly Information Package

We will send you a free information package which will include a custom burned CD of the bands that are available on your date, that fit your musical preferences and are within your budget. Just fill out an ASAP Inquiry Form on our website:

www.bestbands.com
or call
1-800-639-6380

EVERGREEN ERB

35 Old Pump Road
Jericho, Vermont 05465
Phone: 802-899-3231
Cell: 802-488-0183
evergreen@heartslonging.com

WEDDING MUSIC

Celtic Harp ∾ Classical Music ∾ Personal Compositions

Evergreen's harp music has been heard at over one hundred weddings in the last fifteen years. These weddings include traditional settings such as churches, and nontraditional settings, such as lakeside, on boats, in the forest, seaside, and even on top of Mt. Mansfield.

> *"I feel honored to play at all types of commitment ceremonies, representing many different religions and life philosophies. It is a pleasure to be part of one of life's most joyous transitions."*

Evergreen understands when she is hired to play at someone's wedding, that she in going to be a small part of a very significant event for the couple she will play for. She encourages people to hear her play in person to see if she is the right person for them, and if she is, she will work hard to play just the music the couple wants for their ceremony.

> *"I encourage people to come to my home to hear me play, but I will also travel reasonable distances with my harp. I have a CD of my music (mostly my compositions) that I am glad to lend to couples to listen if for some reason we can't get together".*

Evergreen has references if you need them, and also the endorsement of some local businesses. She will be happy to share some of these with you.

LET ME MAKE YOUR EVENT MAGICAL

> *"Thank you for playing your beautiful harp music during our wedding ceremony. My family enjoyed your playing as they assembled up top the mountain."* — Erica S.

> *"Your music was beautiful, bringing great pleasure to all those who attended."* — Frank I.

www.HeartsLonging.com

₣ull Circle

Celtic, medieval and Renaissance music
for your wedding ceremony and reception

We are available as a duo of harp and hammered dulcimer, or a quintet that also includes recorders, pennywhistle, guitar and percussion.

The Duo

Susan and Mary Ann have played for weddings, libraries, farmer's markets and festivals for more than 10 years. Their unique blend of harp and hammered dulcimer is featured on their recent CD, *"All Alive"*.

"The love for the music and each other comes shining through!" – Mark S.

The Quintet

Full Circle is a group of five women who have been making music together for more than 10 years, friends whose paths have separated and who have come together again, full circle.

"Your concert made us want to plan a trip to Ireland" – Saul J. & Laura C.

"..the instrumental playing…is gorgeous and gives me...delicious shivers."
– Tony S. (after listening to a CD)

Fees range from $300 – $750

contact: Mary Ann at
msamuels@burlingtontelecom.net
or 802-658-0832

Find us on Facebook at Vermont Folk Weddings

Lisa Carlson

Flute: Solo or with
Harp, Piano, Strings, or Winds

802-229-9901   lisa@lisaflute.com

"I just wanted to say thank you SO much for playing so beautifully at our wedding. We loved the music and it just made the ceremony that much more special." —Tanya and Dean

"Thank you both for the beautiful music you provided for our ceremony. Many people commented on how terrific it was – especially the special pieces you learned and played for my family. These extra touches and all of your help made our ceremony so special!" —Rebecca and John

"Thank you so much for a beautiful job at our wedding. It was the most magical wedding ever and you had a big part in that!" —Marina and Todd

Biographical information, more testimonials, and further detail about all of my solo, duo, trio and quartet options is available at:

www.lisaflute.com

Marina Carter

SOLO • DUO • TRIO • BANDS

Versatile and entertaining, Marina Carter is well known in Vermont and New York's Capital District region. Marina's career has spanned over 25 years which has afforded her the experience of playing as a soloist, a duo, a trio and also with her larger band presentations. Marina's musical flexibility has her entertaining at weddings, corporate events and private parties throughout New England. She can accommodate any indoor or outdoor event.

Marina is dedicated to working closely with her wedding clients to get to know their personal style and musical preferences. Her versatility allows couples to design their music from ceremony to cocktail hour, and through the reception to reflect their unique personalities and love.

Come to Marina's studio to relax and enjoy the creative process as you design your days music together. Marina offers an eclectic mix of current pop music, classic rock, R&B, jazz, show tunes, classical and new age music. Log onto her website **http://vermontpianomusic.com** and listen to the many possibilities that she can offer you for your special day.

Contact Marina today to discuss how you can create your ultimate wedding event. And if you're thinking of having a DJ for your reception, Marina can also provide you with the ultimate romantic singer to add that personal touch for your special first dances to make the beginning of your reception that much more memorable.

802.362.8124 • mcarter@vermontpianomusic.com

Barrie Fisher Photography

Vermont's #1

PEAK DJ.COM

PEAK ENTERTAINMENT INC.

802-888-6978 • email@peakdj.com • www.peakdj.com

Serving Vermont, New Hampshire and the Adirondacks

Professional Disc Jockeys specializing in elegant weddings since 1995

Peak Entertainment is Vermont's full-time DJ company—*referred* and *preferred* by every major inn, hotel and wedding facility in Vermont, New Hampshire and the Adirondacks. Our office staff and eleven professionally trained and properly equipped DJs are dedicated to producing personalized, superbly orchestrated weddings…**without the "cheese" factor.**

The *only* Vermont DJ company listed in
Modern Bride Magazine's
"150 Hottest Bands and DJs in the U.S."

- The finest professional grade gear
- Complete backup systems on-site at every event
- Flexibility: from announcing to formalities and music selection, we will do everything as you wish

"Mark did a great job. We were impressed with his professionalism and his ability to keep everyone dancing. He didn't try to steal the show like other DJs sometimes do and let the music do the work. We'd recommend Peak Entertainment to our friends. Well done!"

–Rich and Heather Inserro, Wedding
at the Wilburton Inn, Manchester, VT

"The wedding went great! Nick did a nice job of following our wishes during dinner and dancing. His care in making sure to pronounce names correctly was much appreciated. Thanks for helping us create a memorable occasion."

–Laurie and Dave Tilgner, Wedding
at Trapp Family Lodge, Stowe, VT

233

Samuel Guarnaccia
Classical Master Guitarist

MonteVerde Guitar
1699 Irish Hill Road
Shelburne, Vermont 05482
(802) 985-2917
Voicemail: (802) 453-5460
Email: sguarnaccia@msn.com

Type of Music

Sam's repertoire includes Renaissance, Baroque, Classical, Romantic, 20th Century, Chamber and Concerto. Samuel is a professional guitar soloist who often accompanies Voice, Flute, Violin, Harpsichord, Strings or other chamber combinations.

Professional Experience

Mr. Guarnaccia has studied and played classical guitar throughout the U.S. and Europe for over twenty years. Along with being an expert performer, he also teaches guitar and conducts workshops. As a professional, Samuel will make your special day memorable.

Special Services

Samuel is available as a soloist or in a wide spectrum of chamber or multimedia settings for your ceremony or reception. Call for a consultation and for a list of music and styles Samuel can play to make your wedding day perfect. He will also arrange and perform any special songs or music at your request.

Just a Few Words About Samuel's Performance

"We are always amazed at the extraordinarily high level of excellence in his music and at the passion and warmth with which he plays. He possesses a wonderful ability to read his audience and respond to them. He has, without fail, met and exceeded all our expectations." Catherine Studley

"Guarnaccia's skill and profound artistry…from the depths of the soul." Springfield Reporter

"He is talented, personable and very reliable…I would recommend him highly." Rita McDowell, Basin Harbor Club

"It was the most romantic wedding you've ever seen. Sam was great!" Teresa Swan, Mother of the Bride

St. J. Jazz

P.O. Box 53, St. Johnsbury, Vermont 05819
802.748.8150 • stjjazz@sover.net • www.stjjazz.org

St. J. Jazz offers 30 years of experience providing live classic swing, dance standards, traditional jazz and blues for lovers of the dance and dancers in love. If dancing and romance are in your wedding plans our experienced, professional musicians can give your reception that special touch that only comes with live music and personal attention. From solo jazz piano to a swinging big band, St. J. Jazz has an ensemble to fit your hall and budget. Our premier bands include:

Swing North – Our 19-piece Big Band with female and male vocalists, 14 horns, full rhythm section and a professional M/C. From Count Basie to Blood, Sweat & Tears we offer music that swings and rocks along with Latin, waltzes and beautiful ballads for your special "first dance".

Maple Leaf Seven – Our busiest band playing traditional jazz, blues and classic swing. Good time music provided by four horns, piano, bass and drums with male vocalist / MC. Request a copy of our newest CD "Tappin' Time."

Twilight Jazz Group – The quintessential wedding band playing dance standards, classic swing and contemporary jazz. Based on a sax, trumpet and rhythm quintet, the band can go smaller or larger depending on your needs.

Visit us online at www.stjjazz.org or call Phil Brown at 802-748-8150, stjjazz@sover.net to request a demo CD or discuss options.

St. J. Jazz also has several options for music for your wedding ceremony including handbells, vocalists, pianists and flute & guitar duo.

TONY'S MOBILE SOUND SHOW

Tony Lamoureux
TOLL FREE 888-821-3511
www.tonysmobilesoundshow.com

Tony has entertained over 200 hundred wedding receptions since 1989. If you are looking for the best music entertainment for your wedding, you have found it with Tony. His energy, state of the art equipment, and full selection of music will inspire your guests to tap their feet and get up to dance!

Consultation
Tony offers free consultations to plan your big day. He has seen what works well and can give very helpful advice. Excellent references are available.

> *"Just wanted to say thanks again for the awesome job you did DJing our wedding! We knew you'd do a great job with the music, and we were so impressed with how you keep things flowing. We had zero worries all night! And you received tons of compliments from our guests, it was great. Thanks again!"*
> *Erin & Chris*

> *"Thank you so much for everything. You really pulled our wedding together and made everything happen so wonderfully. We really appreciate everything. Everyone commented on how great our DJ was, and we were so glad!"*
> *Ryan and Krystal*

Service
As Master of Ceremonies, Tony will coordinate with all of your wedding professionals (photographer, caterers, etc.) to ensure the timely progression of your special moments. He has the experience to observe your guests to play the music they love. Tony is not just a DJ, he is your entertainment!

Cost & Terms
Tony will give you the finest entertainment around at a price you can afford. Call now for reservations.

TOP HAT
ENTERTAINMENT
DJs for Perfect Weddings

www.tophatdj.com
802.862.2011

When you hire Top Hat…you get
Professionalism, Experience and Versatility.

We encourage you to meet with us in our
conveniently located South Burlington office.
Sit down with one of our DJ's in person to ensure that you will get the
wedding you deserve.

Winner of the 2006
Small Business of the Year Award
(Lake Champlain Regional Chamber of Commerce)

Top Hat Entertainment is pleased to offer the best DJ service in Vermont.
We take pride in providing superior service.

"Thank you for everything!
From day one, you made planning our wedding a breeze. It was truly a
pleasure having you at our wedding. Music is such an important part of
a wedding, and you got everything just right. If you'd like to use me as a
reference, please do because it will be easy to rave about your work.
Your passion for your work shows, and we truly
appreciate everything."
–Wiita/Spear Wedding Reception, 3/17/07

Let us set the mood…

NOTES

Photo courtesy of Lauren Stagnitti Wedding Photography

The Importance of Photography and Video

When all the guests have gone home, and the honeymoon is unfortunately over, the wedding photographs and video will always serve as a joyful reminder of your celebration. Selecting the right photographer and video professional are two of the most important decisions of your wedding. These professionals capture the moments forever on film and record a lifetime of memories.

Choosing a Photographer

The format, personality, style, formality and price of the pictures are issues to consider when choosing a photographer. The best way to evaluate photographers is to look at their portfolio. Remember, the portfolios represent the photographers best work. If you like what you see, then explain what you want and ask if the photographer can fulfill your requests.

Fees for photographers' services can vary greatly. Ask for a breakdown of all the costs to understand what they will provide. Always choose a photographer with whom you feel comfortable! It's a must that you meet with the photographer in person. One photographer may be less expensive than another, but don't let price be the only consideration; go with the quality and the package with which you feel confident. These pictures are forever.

Must Have Photos

Once a photographer has been selected, specify a list of photographs which "must" be taken. Make sure you and the photographer know the layout of your wedding and the type of photographs that you envision. Wedding photographers are professionals and have a great deal of knowledge when it comes to the perfect shot and poses.

When the day finally arrives it is usually a good idea to assign a friend or a relative to assist the photographer. Once you have introduced the friend to the photographer, the friend can point out who everyone is. If the photographer has a question, they will feel comfortable that they have someone they can approach without bothering the bride and groom.

A Little Advice

Hey, you look great! You're both as handsome as ever—get lots of photographs! How often are you going to hire a professional to take your picture? Catch the two of you in all kinds of poses: loving, silly, in action, and be sure to include interaction with family and friends. Get some great shots of you both in close up, informal, loving poses. Get a great picture of the bride and her closest friends all in one big hug. This is a perfect holiday gift for your friends. Think of special pictures besides the normal list and make them happen!

Video Production

Many couples also choose to have a video made of their wedding. A video can capture your celebration in a totally different way than photos do—if you choose the right service. Unfortunately, it is often a waste of time and energy to have a friend videotape your wedding for you. There are so many integral details associated with videotaping, an amateur video is seldom the quality you want.

When choosing a video professional, make sure they understand the details that it takes to video a wedding. The best way they can demonstrate this is to show you a wedding they have previously filmed. It is important to look at the quality of the video and not just the people in it. Be sure that the lighting and sound is good and that the flow of the video is smooth. There are many inclusions that can be added to the video, but usually at an additional fee. Be sure to know exactly what is included in the cost of the video.

Preparing For the Video

Inform the video professional where you will be having the ceremony and reception, so he (or she) can determine in advance their lighting and set-up requirements. It is best if they have a good quality cordless microphone so that your guests will not be bothered with a cord. You will also need to give the video professional an outline of ceremony and the reception so he may set up at the best locations before the action starts. Be sure to let him know everything you want to be filmed in addition to the ceremony and reception. Many couples like to have their guests talk into the camera and give toasts. Your video professional can give you suggestions for the layout of your video. You may want to assign the same person who is assisting the photographer or consider a second person if they need a lot of assistance.

Choosing a Photographer

Is our wedding date available to you?

How many years experience do you have?

May I see your wedding portfolio?

Can we set up a consultation?

Will you visit the ceremony and reception locations?

What type of packages do you offer?

Do you own the negatives or can I purchase them?

What are your deposit and cancellation policies?

What are your reprint costs?

What are some of the additional services you offer?

Choosing a Video Professional

Same questions as above

Do you have wedding videos we may review?

What are your video copy charges?

What are some additional elements you can add to the video?

Must-Take Photograph and Video Check List

❑ Bride in dress

❑ Bride with mother

❑ Bride with father

❑ Bride with siblings

❑ Bride with whole family

❑ Bride with bridal party

❑ Groom in formal wear

❑ Groom with mother

❑ Groom with father

❑ Groom with siblings

❑ Groom with family

❑ Groom with attendants

❑ Bride and father arriving at ceremony

❑ Groom with attendants at ceremony

- ❏ Bridal party coming down the aisle
- ❏ Bride and father coming down the aisle
- ❏ Groom meeting bride
- ❏ Bride and groom during ceremony
- ❏ Bride and groom exchanging rings
- ❏ Bride and groom kiss
- ❏ Bride and groom walking down aisle
- ❏ Bride and groom with guests after ceremony
- ❏ Bride and groom
- ❏ Bride and groom and bride's family
- ❏ Bride and groom and groom's family
- ❏ Bride and groom with grandparents
- ❏ Bride and groom with all attendants
- ❏ Bride and groom with entire wedding party
- ❏ The receiving line
- ❏ Bride and groom in receiving line
- ❏ Bride and father dance
- ❏ Groom and mother dance
- ❏ Best man toast
- ❏ The cake table
- ❏ Cake cutting ceremony
- ❏ Bride and groom toast
- ❏ The bouquet toss
- ❏ Couple leaving reception
- ❏ Couple saying good-bye to parents

BARRIE FISHER
PHOTOGRAPHERS

www.bfisherphoto.com

802.496.5215

A Visual Journey

Productions

PO Box 234, Waitsfield, Vermont 05673
Phone: 802-583-2410 • Fax: 802-496-7800
EMAIL: cbrown@madriver.com
www.charliebrownspage.com

Wedding Packages and Prices We offer a variety of Photography and Video options that cover everything from the rehearsal dinner to the reception. A 10% overall savings can be realized by booking us for **both Photography and Video**. Packages range in price from $595 to $6,995. Please inquire about package options, or let us customize a package for your specific budget.

Experience and Equipment Charlie Brown has over 25 years of experience in making your wedding day memorable. We use Canon D-10 digital still cameras for photography and Sony HD 1000 – 1080 HIGH DEFINITION output to DVD or HD DVD – NO BRIGHT LIGHTS

Videography for Your Rehearsal Dinner: Customized Video production containing material culled from the celebrants early years, romance, family, friends…whatever. These vintage photos, film, & video are then edited & choreographed to music of your choice and presented on a large screen at the Rehearsal Dinner or Wedding Reception…(not a dry eye in the house). Not only that, but the DVD remains in the family archives to be viewed & enjoyed by future generations to come.

Convert digital Wedding images to DVD video presentations,
complete with music of your choice.

Every package includes a DVD with the photos from your Wedding.

Charlie Brown Productions has captured hundreds of Weddings & Celebrations in churches, private homes & lakeside in Vermont & throughout New England. From the historic ROUND BARN FARM in Waitsfield, to SHELBURNE FARMS overlooking Lake Champlain, we capture the magic of your celebration. Charlie Brown offers you the best in HD digital video capture & post production services. His uncanny ability to recognize what is going to happen before it actually happens is not just luck, but a result of over 25 years of covering events around the World.

Wedding, Special Event, Portrait and Nature Photographer

Moments captured for a lifetime of memories.

Life changes with the blink of an eye. Special moments last a lifetime with beautiful images capturing the emotions of the day. My specialty is to capture those emotions with enthusiasm, excitement and passion.

With 25 years experience and the joy of being mother-of-the-groom, I know foremost how vital it is to relive this precious event. When the dancing is done and the day is over you will have an album created with cherished images that truly allow you to bring to life your memories.

Serving VT and NH

(802) 333-9812
dlcook@live.com
www.donnaleecookphotography.com
PO Box 321
East Thetford VT 05043

EMMA DODGE HANSON
PHOTOGRAPHY
518-587-4282

EMMADODGEHANSON.COM

JEFF SCHNEIDERMAN PHOTOGRAPHY

www.jeffschneiderman.com

802.878.0769

"We want to take a moment and thank you for the exceptional work and pictures you took of us on our wedding day. We cannot begin to tell you about the comments we have received regarding our pictures. Our day was perfect and you managed to capture the beauty of it all." Kristina Clay

2393 Oak Hill Road, Williston, VT 05495   jsphotos@aol.com

Landwehrle Photography

504 north hill

Stowe Vermont 05672

802.253.8831

weddings@llphoto.com

www.llphoto.com

Capturing the Magic of each Moment

For over 25 years, Don and Kathleen Landwehrle have spent their lives capturing breathtaking moments — with sophistication and style. Through true artists' eyes, they seize the moments — your moments. The passion they share for photojournalism is transposed, enhancing the images of a most important day in your romantic journey.

Educated in the fine arts, Kathleen and Don remain on the crest in their use of the most advanced equipment and digital techniques to assure the highest quality images.

Sought-after wedding photographers-- the Landwehrles are astute at capturing setting and emotion. With warmth, insight and expertise. Whether pensive or playful, enchanting or celebratory...every Landwehrle picture tells a story. Yours.

PORTRAIT *PG* **GALLERY**
GEOFFREY McLOUGHLIN · WENDY McLOUGHLIN
Wedding Photography Specialists

1500 Hinesburg Road
South Burlington, VT 05403
802-864-4411
800-286-4418
www.portraitgallery-vt.com
pgallery@comcast.net

Browse our website for recent weddings. Select "Wedding Portfolio" to view recent weddings. We typically have 50 or more entire weddings online for your viewing.

This is what our customers say:

"We couldn't be happier! Please use us as a reference for future couples; there isn't anyone else who compares!"
- Mandy and Joe

"We were so glad you were able to take photos for us. When we look back at them 50 years from now, we will remember you."
- Kristina and Matthew

"Please add us to your list of references; we would confidently suggest you to photograph any wedding."
- Leah and Keith

All packages come with high resolution digital files delivered on DVD. You own full reproduction rights. We also put your best images online. Family, friends and guests can view images and order reprints.

Our famous 2-photographer package gives you twice as many photos to select from! Solo photographer packages are also available. 7-hour packages from $1,400 to $5,000. Shorter or longer coverages are available.

FREE DOWNLOADING: Online viewers can download any or all images directly to their computer, free of charge, as part of all packages! The bride and groom's finished album and a dramatic slideshow dubbed to elegant music, can also be downloaded free of charge!

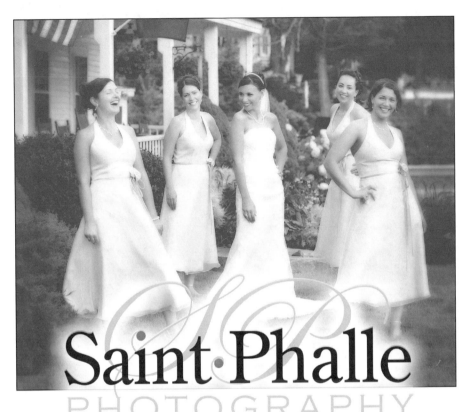

- complimentary studio engagement portrait session
- double wedding day photography by two award-winning photographers
- online gallery + slideshow with easy print ordering
- 700+ unmarked 4x6 proofs in a leather presentation box
- 700+ full-resolution JPEGs on DVD with license for personal use

please visit ·
http://spwed.com/playground
to experience our real-time interactive
price quote and booking form
or call us toll-free at 1-800-781-0255 or locally at 1-802-635-2262

VERONICA + ANDRÉ de SAINT PHALLE

International WPJA Award Winning Wedding Photojournalist

NOTES

Photo courtesy of Barrie Fisher Photographers

The Importance of Your Rehearsal

Purpose

The purpose of the rehearsal is to ensure that your wedding is as perfect, stress free and enjoyable as possible. A practice run-through will put everyone at ease—and yes—you will probably discover a few little glitches you might not otherwise have anticipated.

Scheduling Your Rehearsal

It is usually held the night before your wedding for the convenience of the officiant and wedding attendants, plus the availability of your wedding ceremony site. Be sure to ask the officiant how long the rehearsal will take so you can plan the rest of your evening.

Who Coordinates the Rehearsal?

The wedding couple, or the person they delegated, makes all the arrangements for the rehearsal (reserving the site, getting everyone there, sending out directions, etc...) but once the actual practice begins, the officiant takes over and guides the process. If you have musicians or other wedding service providers present at the rehearsal, make sure you know if their presence requires an additional fee or if it is included with the wedding fees. Bring any necessary payments and your marriage license (your officiant may ask to see it or hold it for you).

The Mood

Make the rehearsal attendants feel relaxed and comfortable, but let them know this is a serious moment and they should pay close attention, dress appropriately and act accordingly. If possible, get everyone together before the rehearsal for refreshments to put everyone at ease. This also enables everyone to travel to the rehearsal site together and to arrive on time.

Rehearsal Dinner

Vermont offers the entire array of rehearsal dinner possibilities: elegant formal settings, friendly charming inns, country buffet in an old barn, catered outdoor Bar-B-Que or catered affairs in a private home. Traditionally, the rehearsal dinner is hosted by the groom's parents. The dinner is a special occasion for all the guests to get to know each other. Be sure everyone is introduced. This is also a perfect time for the wedding couple to give gifts to everyone who helped coordinate the wedding and to the wedding attendants.

Formal Rehearsal Dinners

If you are planning a formal rehearsal dinner, it is customary to send out invitations, announce appropriate attire and plan the menu and the seating arrangements.

Toasts

Whether the rehearsal dinner is formal or informal, it is appropriate to propose toasts. Traditional toasts are: the best man to the couple; the groom to his bride and her parents; the bride to her groom and his parents. Another nice touch is to have the host of the rehearsal dinner toast the bride and groom and their guests.

Whom to Invite

Attendants and their spouses or partners; parents of any children participating; the officiant and their spouse; special out-of-town guests; the parents of the couple; and the bride and groom, are all traditionally invited to the rehearsal dinner. However, you don't have to be restricted by tradition. You and the rehearsal dinner host can expand or reduce the invitee list as suits your personal desire and budget.

Locations

We have kept all reception and rehearsal dinner sites in the Banquet and Reception Site Category. This allows you to conveniently find both rehearsal and reception sites at the same time.

Rehearsal Check List

- ❏ Officiant available
- ❏ Ceremony site available
- ❏ All necessary fees paid
- ❏ Musicians available (if necessary)
- ❏ Marriage license
- ❏ Invitations to all necessary individuals to rehearsal
- ❏ Rehearsal dinner location reserved
- ❏ Menu and time chosen
- ❏ Invitations to rehearsal dinner
- ❏ Transportation coordinated
- ❏ Gifts for wedding party
- ❏ Asked specific individuals to make toasts
- ❏ Thank rehearsal hosts

Portrait Gallery

öeCHO®
LAKE AQUARIUM
AND SCIENCE CENTER
LEAHY CENTER
FOR LAKE CHAMPLAIN

BURLINGTON WATERFRONT
TOLL FREE 1-877-324-6386
EVENTS@ECHOVERMONT.ORG
ECHOVERMONT.ORG

Only ECHO provides this unique and memorable experience for your wedding day.

Capacity

With our lakefront location, breathtaking views of the Adirondacks, 3 floors filled with sparkling aquariums, and elegant indoor and outdoor spaces for ceremonies, dining, and dancing, you'll find ECHO to be the most unique and memorable location around. ECHO's innovative and elegant architecture can seat up to 242 for a plated dinner or up to 228 for a buffet. If you'd like a dance floor these accommodations drop to 170 for a plated dinner or 156 for a buffet. Up to 750 can be accommodated for a standing cocktail reception.

Location

Located on the Burlington Waterfront just 3.71 miles from the Burlington International Airport, one block from several premiere hotels, and walking distance from the Church Street Marketplace, ECHO is a premier lake aquarium and science center where the traditional reception is mixed in with the benefits of your own private tourist attraction.

Special Features

You and your guests will also feel good knowing your event's actually helping the environment and community. ECHO is LEED certified, which means it's designed to minimize water and energy consumption. Additionally, we encourage all our event partners to follow environmentally friendly practices. So, by hosting your event at ECHO you are actually reducing the impact your event has on the environment as well as helping provide our nonprofit with critically needed financial support to continue our mission, to educate and delight guests about the Ecology, Culture, History, and Opportunities for stewardship of the Lake Champlain Basin.

Please contact Private Event Sales for more information and come explore ECHO as a location for your wedding and reception!

Vermont ASSOCIATION OF
Wedding Professionals
MEMBER

259

Echo Lake Inn

P.O. Box 154 • Ludlow, VT 05149
802-228-8602 • 800-356-6844 • FAX: 802-228-3075
EMAIL: echolkinn@aol.com
WEB: www.echolakeinn.com

Capacity
- Exterior (lawn with tent)—225 sit-down
- Interior — 120 standing or 75 sit-down
  — 75 standing or 55 sit-down

Price Range Customized wedding packages and menus available.

Catering Full service in-house catering.

Types of Events
- Wedding
- Elegant Buffets
- Full Service Dinners
- Cocktails and hors d'oeuvres
- Rehearsal Dinners

Availability and Terms
Our banquet facilities are available year round.
Please contact us for specific deposit information.

Description of Services
Seating: Outdoor/Indoor/Veranda
Bar Facilities: Two Bars/Lounges
Parking: 50 Car Capacity

Special Services
We are located across the street from a historic church (1860's) that is perfect for wedding services. Nestled at the edge of our woods is an old wishing well, a perfect spot for a romantic ceremony.

A Sophisticated Country Inn
Located in Vermont's beautiful central lakes region, the Echo Lake Inn with 24 rooms and 6 condos was built in 1840 as a Victorian summer hotel. Today it remains one of the few authentic country inns operating in Vermont. Every year the Echo Lake Inn hosts many weddings and other important events. Chef Kevin and his staff were recently featured in *Gourmet* and *Bon Appetit* magazines for their excellent food and the quality of service that they provided. The warm, sophisticated hospitality of the Echo Lake Inn awaits you on your special day!

NOTES

NOTES

Photo courtesy of Emma Dodge Hanson Photography

The Best Transportation Ideas

There is such a variety of transportation needs during a wedding that it's best to assign this overall responsibility to a reliable friend or family member. In addition to getting the bride and groom to the ceremony on time, there's pick-ups, appointments, out-of-town wedding attendants without cars and grandparents who don't drive. Most of your guests and wedding party will plan their own transportation. Give them suggestions, but let them do as much as possible—you'll be busy enough. In the "Worksheets" section there is a sheet for transportation and airport pick-ups; be sure to follow this outline and you should have no problems.

The Wedding Day

You have planned the perfect wedding, now you need to make sure you arrive in style. Most couples choose to hire a limousine service because it adds a touch of luxury to the wedding and they are large enough to hold your entire wedding party. One way to coordinate transportation is to have the bride with her parents in one limousine and the bridal party in another. The limousine will then depart with the bride and groom when the reception is over.

Τhe bride should travel to the wedding with her parents, especially if her father is walking her down the aisle. It also gives them precious last moments together. Try not to get too emotional during this time—you don't want to walk down the aisle with tears on your face!

Other favorite types of transportation are unique cars such as classics or a Mercedes convertible. A horse and buggy is one of the most romantic ways to arrive and depart your wedding.

Choosing a Transportation Service

You may choose more than one source of transportation. You may choose a horse and buggy for the bride and her parents' arrival and for the bride and groom's departure. You may want your bridal party to arrive in a limousine, however you are not required to arrange transportation for your bridal party. Be creative—there are no rules.

It is important when choosing a service that you inspect closely what they have to offer. Set up a time to look at your chosen mode of transportation and be sure it meets your quality standards. State your exact choice of transportation along with the exact pick-up and drop-off times and locations in the contract. Ask what the service includes and what is extra, such as tip and champagne. Be sure someone is prepared to tip or add it directly to the bill so you do not need to worry about it that day.

Choosing Transportation

What is your selection of transportation?

Does the cost include the driver?

How will the driver be dressed?

How do you price your service?

Can you fill my transportation needs?

Is the date available?

Will I get the exact car I choose?

What is included in the service?

What is extra?

Do you know where the ceremony and reception sites are?

Do you need directions to our location?

When will you arrive to pick us up?

What are your deposit and cancellation policies?

Transportation Check List

❏   Bride and parents to ceremony

❏   Wedding party to ceremony

❏   Bride and groom to reception

❏   Parents and wedding party to reception

❏   Bride and groom leaving reception

❏   Parents and wedding party leaving the reception

❏   Directions

❏   Confirm times and date

❏   Type of transportation

❏   Champagne and other special items

❏   Tip for driver

NOTES

BURLINGTON LIMOUSINE
AND CAR SERVICE
(Formerly Limos For Less)

South Burlington, VT 05403
(802) 861-2600 1-888-666-3471
Email: limo@sover.net
www.burlingtonvtlimo.com

Contact Us Today
for More Information

Make it Even More Memorable...

Our Service

When it comes to quality service, you don't want to take any chances with your wedding. Our customers demand superior service and Burlington Limousine & Car Service delivers! With our extensive fleet of well appointed, late model vehicles and our courteous and professional staff, you can be assured of first class transportation to and from your wedding event- regardless of whether it is a rehearsal dinner, bachelor or bachelorette party or the wedding itself! Our company's steady growth over the years is a direct result of our superior service and friendly approach, our repeat customer loyalty and our consistent attention to detail.

Our Vehicles & Our People

From nine passenger stretch Lincolns and Cadillac sedans, to our custom vans and 14 passenger "longer-than-a-city-block" stretch Excursion SUV- our extensive fleet of well appointed vehicles feature comfortable, luxurious interiors with great sound systems, DVDs or VCRs, and so much more. And when it arrives, our luxury vehicle's gleaming finish will surely be the perfect complement to your wedding party. Then out steps the formally attired and groomed chauffeur to quietly and efficiently attend to your every need. *Perfect!*

Our Service Area

Our customers hail from all over the world and our database is filled with clients from all walks of life and every corner of the globe. Our wedding event capabilities extend throughout all of Vermont, upstate New York and northern New Hampshire as well as southern Quebec. Wherever your wedding will be, we will be there on time and ready to make it the most wonderful occasion!

Reservations

We encourage you to contact us early as the wedding season is a very busy one. We will be happy to consult with you to help you with your wedding transportation needs and to assure you of a quality experience for your special event. We will do everything we can to make the most wonderful day of your life the one that will truly live long in your memory.

Classic Limo Service

Vermont's Original Classic Car & Limo Service

www.classiclimos.org

Featuring
the 1950 Chrysler
Windsor Limousine
used by the
Rockefellers

Brad Kirby
802-985-5460

Now Offering
Vermont's Only
White Cadillac
Superstretch

Our Company

Established in 1994, we are a Vermont family owned and operated business. Classic Limo Service is the only Limo company to offer a variety of transportation needs. Our vehicles are ideal for any occasion. We maintain high quality standards—a reputation that we have become known for.

Our Cars

Of our three vintage cars, we have a 1951 Chevy Styline Deluxe sedan that has been restored to its original elegance. We also offer a stylish black 1950 Chrysler Windsor limousine that was used by the Rockefellers! Our latest vintage edition is a red 1969 Oldsmobile convertible with white leather interior.

Our white Cadillac Deville superstretch is one of a kind equipped with a flat screen TV, DVD player, walnut bars and accommodates up to ten passengers.

Coming soon a new black Cadillac or Chrysler 300 stretch offers an alluring interior fully loaded and also seats up to ten passengers.

Our silver five passenger Yukon Denali custom SUV has heated seats, back controls and a Bose six disc CD player.

Our Service

Our drivers are in full tuxedo dress complete with white driving gloves and chauffeur's cap. Our Classic Limo Service wedding package includes three hours or more of service.

An upfront 50% deposit and contract allows us to personalize your service with optional champagne bar, ice, glasses, your favorite music and a white rose with weddings and anniversaries.

The Yukon Denali, the Cadillac and Lincoln limos are available year round while the vintage automobiles are stored during the winter season.

Please contact Brad or Dinah at 802-985-5460
www.classiclimos.org

BBB
ACCREDITED
BUSINESS
bbb.org

We accept Visa, MC, Amex, cash or checks.

ETHAN ALLEN COACHWORKS
Luxury Transportation at Affordable Rates
599 Shunpike Road, Williston, VT 05495
(802) 862-1924 • Fax (802) 860-9457 • Email: eacw@together.net
Web: www.vermontlimo.com • Contact: Mike Rooney/Tim Camisa

Types of Vehicles Available
New luxurious Ford Excursion SUV Limousines, seating 10–14. New Lincoln Super Stretch Limonsines seating up to 10. Lincoln Town Car sedans, passenger vans available, 47–55 passenger luxury coaches and a 26 passenger shuttle bus.

Special Wedding Packages
Wedding Packages are based on a **three** hour rental. Discounts offered for either overtime use or for multiple vehicles. Other vehicle types available to accommodate the small wedding party or larger group transports, include: luxury sedans and passenger vans for guest and family members. Experienced Chauffeur driven vehicles. All equipped with cellular phones to enhance communication for a timely professional performance.

Reservation Policy
A signed reservation outlining services is required with advance deposit or valid credit card number to secure the reservation. E-mail address and cell phone number recommended for confirmation. Reservations are confirmed 48 hours prior to actual date of service via E-mail, fax or phone. All reservations subject to availability.

Other Services Available
Passenger shuttle bus seating up to 26 passengers along with passenger vans for **shuttle service** are available throughout the reception to safely transport wedding guests as directed. Sedan, SUV or van service provided to all major airports throughout New England and Canada. Our office is located adjacent to Burlington International Airport. **Providing service coverage throughout Vermont.**

Financing and Guarantees
Each reservation is assigned a confirmation number. Recommended gratuities are stated with prices. Payment must be made by cash, check, money order, American Express, Visa, MasterCard or Discover Card, **at time of service**.

Reservations 802-862-1924

LIMOUSINE

Hanover Limousine

P.O. Box 571, Hanover, NH 03755 · Phone: 603-298-8880 · 800-528-0888
Web: www.hanoverlimousine.com

We have late model Lincoln stretch limousines up to ten passenger capacity. You may choose white or black properly maintained fully insured state, federal, and D.O.T. licensed vehicles.

Reservations

Most weddings occur on a Saturday. To ensure availability, please reserve your limousine as far ahead as possible. When making your reservation, please allow the maximum time for your needs, so that your limousine is scheduled accordingly. Last minute changes may not be possible as the limousine may be committed elsewhere. A $100.00 deposit and a four hour minimum rental is required, along with the date, times and location to hold your reservation. Deposits are refundable 90 days prior to the wedding day only! Mileage is charged for travel twenty miles beyond our Hanover Location.

Services

Limousines for weddings or airport services are provided with ice, soda water, and napkins. Alcohol is not provided. Customers may bring their own champagne/alcohol. Red carpet and "Just married" sign are available upon request. Service is available to and from all regional airports or other destinations.

Congratulations in advance for your happiest day!!!
We look forward to serving you...

Karen J. Munson Horse & Buggy

1342 Old Stage Rd., Westford, VT 05494 • 802-878-7715
www.kjmunsonhorseandbuggy.com

Types of Vehicles Available

Enjoy a magical ride in an elegant carriage drawn by a Vermont Morgan Horse or a team of Percheron Draft horses. I also have hay wagons and sleigh rides.

New in 2007

Newly and personally designed, **one-of-a-kind** custom, 12 passenger white vis-a-vis limo drawn by 4 horse hitch.

Special Wedding Packages

♥ Transportation of horse and carriage to and from site ♥
♥ Chauffeur in tuxedo and top hat ♥
♥ Spectacular floral spray in wedding colors ♥
♥ Bottle of champagne or non-alcoholic beverage ♥
♥ Just married sign ♥
♥ Bride and groom ride to reception ♥
♥ Rides for guests at reception includes two hours of total carriage time ♥

Reservation Policy

Cancellations within six months receive gift certificate. Please call for details. I have a selection of elegant carriages.

Other Services Available

Fall foliage, romantic rides, birthday parties, caisson/hearse for funerals, hay wagons and sleighs (with or without wheels), scenic picnics, use your imagination!

Stealing Away for a Quiet Moment

On your wedding day take an imaginative ride through centuries of royal tradition. Steal away for a few minutes after the ceremony and before the reception in an elegant carriage drawn by a Morgan Horse or a team of Percheron Draft Horses. Enjoy the romance of the jingling bells and harnesses and quiet hoof beats as you are taken on a fairy tale-like ride before you greet your guests.

PORTRAIT GALLERY

White Mountain Limousine Service, LLC

Make A Memory

1-802-328-2800 | TOLL FREE: 1-866-824-LIMO (5466) |
24 Fellows Road | Guildhall, Vermont 05905
www.whitemountainlimo.com | email: WhiteMtLimo@aol.com

A Family Owned and Operated Business

No two weddings or civil unions are the same. Yet every wedding employs many of the same elements. At White Mountain Limousine we understand how special this day is for you. We want it to be perfect. Let us tailor our wedding package to meet your individual needs. Our package is designed to be flexible and accommodating. For instance, we can transport the Groom, Best Man, and Ushers to the church, and then return to transport the Bride, Maid of Honor, and Bridesmaids. After the ceremony we will whisk the Bride and Groom and possibly the wedding party, off for pictures, to the reception, or whatever your destination, all in a timely, courteous, professional manner.

You can be assured that White Mountain Limousine employs only professional chauffeurs who are fully uniformed, complete with caps and white gloves. Our luxurious limousine is fully equipped with bar, ice, lighting, CD player, TV, VCR, leather seats, privacy glass, and more! A red carpet will be rolled out at the church for the Bride. After the ceremony, the newlyweds and bridal party will receive a complimentary champagne toast at your desired place and time, coordinated with your photographer so that nothing is missed. And don't forget the "Just Married" sign on the rear of the limousine!

Active Military receive discounts on all wedding packages

MEMBER
NEW ENGLAND LIVERY ASSOCIATION AND LIMOS.COM

www.whitemountainlimo.com   *Human Rights Campaign Member*

NOTES

NOTES

Photo courtesy of Portrait Gallery

The Ultimate Check List

How to Use the Check List

All weddings require careful planning whether you have an intimate gathering or a large traditional ceremony with a reception. The following check list and the services listed in this book will provide everything you need to organize a beautiful wedding in Vermont. Planning a wedding can be fun; don't let all the details overwhelm you. Take one item at a time, work with the individuals who provide that service and it will all come together.

Use this check list as a guideline, cross out what you don't want and add special touches and family traditions that you will need to plan. Our check list system makes it easy to see what has been done, what needs to be done and who needs to do it.

Important: Special Check Marks and Spaces

The "Person" space is for the person who has responsibility for that particular item (it will usually be the bride, groom, wedding coordinator, an attendant or a family member). The "Date" space is for when the arrangements were first secured. The "Done" space requires a check mark when you have finished working with the providers on the arrangement. The "Overseen By" space is very important. This is the place where you put a person's name who makes sure it happens the day of the wedding. Once you have completed the "Overseen By" list, make a separate list of all responsibilities for each person. Give them a copy of their duties and go over it with them. Find a person who will be responsible for overseeing the whole list so if there are wedding day questions the bride and groom will not be burdened.

Example

The "Date" for a florist is when you have chosen one, check the "Done" space when all the flowers are picked out and you have coordinated all the delivery and set up information. The name in the "Overseen By" space might be the wedding coordinator or the person in charge at the reception site. If it is an outdoor wedding and your sister is the florist, put her name in the space. When people see their duties, as well as hear them, they are more apt to remember them.

The Ultimate Check List

The Engagement

PERSON	DATE	DONE	OVERSEEN BY	
____	____	____	_____	Make announcement to your families.
____	____	____	_____	Have engagement ring fitted.
____	____	____	_____	Organize engagement party.
____	____	____	_____	Make a formal announcement.
____	____	____	_____	Send announcement to all appropriate newspapers.
____	____	____	_____	Arrange for families to meet each other.
____	____	____	_____	Other

Six to Twelve Months before the Wedding

____	____	____	_____	Set a date.
____	____	____	_____	Check marriage requirements.
____	____	____	_____	Determine your budget.
____	____	____	_____	Make a list of most important things to include.
____	____	____	_____	Decide the formality, number of people and location of your wedding.
____	____	____	_____	Reserve ceremony site.
____	____	____	_____	If outside, reserve a tent.
____	____	____	_____	Reserve reception facility.
____	____	____	_____	Start your guest list. Ask your parents to start theirs.
____	____	____	_____	Look into hiring a wedding consultant.
____	____	____	_____	Decide on your wedding attendants, flower girl, ring bearer.

PERSON	DATE	DONE	OVERSEEN BY	
——	——	——	————	Shop for your wedding gown and headpiece.
——	——	——	————	Other

Five to Eight Months before the Wedding

——	——	——	————	Meet with the clergy or officiant for your wedding.
——	——	——	————	Select musicians for the ceremony.
——	——	——	————	Select musicians for the reception.
——	——	——	————	Select photographer.
——	——	——	————	Select video person.
——	——	——	————	Ask your attendants to be in the wedding.
——	——	——	————	Select dresses for the bridesmaids.
——	——	——	————	Select formal wear for the groom and attendants.
——	——	——	————	Choose a florist and decide on your arrangements.
——	——	——	————	Select and order your invitations.
——	——	——	————	Choose a caterer and select your menu.
——	——	——	————	Choose bartender and liquor selection.
——	——	——	————	Reserve any rental equipment. (tents, tables, linens, chairs, bathroom facilities, lights, heaters, etc.)
——	——	——	————	Choose baker for your cake.
——	——	——	————	Choose favors.
——	——	——	————	Book room for your wedding night.
——	——	——	————	Discuss honeymoon destinations.
——	——	——	————	Choose wedding bands together.

PERSON	DATE	DONE	OVERSEEN BY	
———	———	———	——————	Book transportation for the wedding.
———	———	———	——————	Send list of area accommodations to out-of-town guests.
———	———	———	——————	Other

Four to Six Months before the Wedding

———	———	———	——————	Confirm ceremony details.
———	———	———	——————	Confirm your final guest list.
———	———	———	——————	Choose your cake style.
———	———	———	——————	Register for gifts: china, silver, etc.
———	———	———	——————	Complete honeymoon plans.
———	———	———	——————	Schedule fittings and delivery date for wedding dress.
———	———	———	——————	Reserve accommodations for special out-of-town guests.
———	———	———	——————	Reserve rehearsal dinner locations.
———	———	———	——————	Review all contracts to make sure they fit your needs.
———	———	———	——————	Make sure all deposits for services are paid.
———	———	———	——————	Have bridesmaids and attendants fitted for their formal wear.
———	———	———	——————	Order thank-you notes, imprinted napkins and wedding programs.
———	———	———	——————	Select balloonist, horse/carriage, doves, or other additions.
———	———	———	——————	Have mothers select their dresses.
———	———	———	——————	Take dance lessons.
———	———	———	——————	Other

Four Months before the Wedding

————— ————— ————— ———————— Purchase accessories to wedding attire.

————— ————— ————— ———————— Purchase accessories to ceremony and reception.

————— ————— ————— ———————— Book appointments with salon for skin and hair care to do trial run.

————— ————— ————— ———————— Book salon for make up and hair for the wedding day.

————— ————— ————— ———————— Address invitations and announcements.

————— ————— ————— ———————— Meet with caterer to firm up the menu details.

————— ————— ————— ———————— Finalize your flower arrangements.

————— ————— ————— ———————— Other

Two to Three Months before the Wedding

————— ————— ————— ———————— Arrange rehearsal and rehearsal dinner details.

————— ————— ————— ———————— Notify all appropriate guests of the rehearsal time and location.

————— ————— ————— ———————— The bride chooses gifts for the bridal party and the groom.

————— ————— ————— ———————— The groom chooses gifts for the attendants and the bride.

————— ————— ————— ———————— Discuss details of decor with the florist, the caterer and the reception site.

————— ————— ————— ———————— Discuss ceremony with clergy or officiant.

————— ————— ————— ———————— Choose readings and individuals to read them.

————— ————— ————— ———————— Dress fittings.

————— ————— ————— ———————— If you are writing your own vows, do them now.

—— —— —— ———— Complete wedding invitations, map and additional information.

—— —— —— ———— Mail your invitations. (Closer to two months than three.)

—— —— —— ———— Shop for stockings and lingerie for your dress.

—— —— —— ———— Shop for your going-away outfit.

—— —— —— ———— Give an attendant party.

—— —— —— ———— Send thank-you cards for gifts received early.

—— —— —— ———— Other

One to Two Months before the Wedding

—— —— —— ———— Make a list of songs you want the musician to play at the ceremony.

—— —— —— ———— Choose your wedding song and the songs you will dance to with parents.

—— —— —— ———— Make a list of songs you want the musicians to play at the reception.

—— —— —— ———— Make an outline of how the wedding will unfold.

—— —— —— ———— Give the outline to all the people who will be helping with the wedding.

—— —— —— ———— Record all your wedding gifts and who gave them to you.

—— —— —— ———— Buy a guest book.

—— —— —— ———— Have ceremony programs printed.

—— —— —— ———— Final dress fittings.

—— —— —— ———— Collect the proper documents if you will change your name.

—— —— —— ———— If you have a change of address, inform the post office.

—— —— —— ———— Confirm accommodations for out-of-town guests.

———— ———— ———— ———————— Confirm all details at the
ceremony site.

———— ———— ———— ———————— Confirm all details at the
reception site.

One Month before the Wedding

———— ———— ———— ———————— Make list of photographs you want
for the photographer.

———— ———— ———— ———————— Ask a responsible person to
oversee the ceremony.

———— ———— ———— ———————— Ask a responsible person to
oversee the reception.

———— ———— ———— ———————— Pick up your wedding rings and
try them on right there!

———— ———— ———— ———————— Make sure bridesmaids' dresses fit.

———— ———— ———— ———————— Continue to send out thank-you
cards for gifts received.

———— ———— ———— ———————— Spend an afternoon at a spa.

———— ———— ———— ———————— Confirm wedding cake delivery
and display.

———— ———— ———— ———————— Final fit for groom and
attendants.

———— ———— ———— ———————— Other

Two Weeks before the Wedding

———— ———— ———— ———————— Get your marriage license.

———— ———— ———— ———————— Arrange seating plan and write
place cards.

———— ———— ———— ———————— Delegate last-minute errands.

———— ———— ———— ———————— Write toasts for rehearsal dinner
and reception.

———— ———— ———— ———————— Ask individuals (best man, father)
to give toasts at the reception.

———— ———— ———— ———————— Send out wedding announcements
to the paper.

PERSON	DATE	DONE	OVERSEEN BY	
———	———	———	———————	Begin your honeymoon packing.
———	———	———	———————	Confirm all honeymoon details.
———	———	———	———————	Get tickets and travelers' checks for honeymoon.
———	———	———	———————	Confirm time flowers will be delivered and decorations will be completed.
———	———	———	———————	Confirm arrival time of musicians and set-up locations.
———	———	———	———————	Keep gift record and thank-you notes up to date.
———	———	———	———————	Have a gift table and a person who will oversee it.
———	———	———	———————	Go over procedure for the ceremony and the receiving line.
———	———	———	———————	Go over procedure for the dances at the reception, the dinner and cake cutting ceremony.
———	———	———	———————	Be sure all wedding attire is in order for the bride, groom and attendants.
———	———	———	———————	Complete all name change documents.
———	———	———	———————	Create seating chart.
———	———	———	———————	Other

One Week before the Wedding

———	———	———	———————	Finalize your rehearsal dinner arrangements, including out-of-town guests and transportation.
———	———	———	———————	Wrap gifts for attendees. Present them after the rehearsal dinner.
———	———	———	———————	Arrange to have the gifts you receive at the wedding transported to a designated place.

Person Date	Done	Overseen By	

Call guests who have not responded and ask if they will be attending.

Call caterer with final arrangements.

Confirm your final check with the florist, photographer, reception site, ceremony site, sexton, clergy or officiant, musicians, video professional, transportation and caterer.

Complete your honeymoon packing. Make sure your suitcases are safely stored.

Pack overnight bags (bride and groom) for your wedding night.

Arrange bags of bird, wildflower seeds for the ceremony.

Finalize party favors for the guests.

Create seating cards for guests.

Get a massage.

Other

Day before Your Wedding

Have a manicure and pedicure to pamper yourself.

Attend the rehearsal. Review all duties with clergy, attendees and parents.

Inform ushers where the bridal parties and reserved seating is.

Pick up wedding dress or have it delivered.

Pick up or have all formal wear delivered.

Person	Date	Done	Overseen By	
————	————	————	————————	Eat healthy, drink lots of water and get a good night's sleep.
————	————	————	————————	Assign last-minute responsibilities to people.
————	————	————	————————	Finalize seating chart.
————	————	————	————————	Organize accessories for the wedding day.
————	————	————	————————	Other

Your Wedding Day

————			————————	Have a healthy and hearty breakfast.
————			————————	Relax in a luxury bath or shower.
————			————————	Keep appointment with hairdresser and makeup artist.
————			————————	Allow plenty of time to get ready, at least two hours.
————			————————	Mail wedding announcements.
————			————————	Mail gift or thank-you to your parents for their help and support.
————			————————	Bring wedding rings.
————			————————	Bring your travel kits to ceremony and reception site.
————			————————	Bring marriage license (if not coordinated at rehearsal).
————			————————	Bring money that is due to all services.
————			————————	Other

Additional Plans

————	————	————	————————	Other
————	————	————	————————	Other
————	————	————	————————	Other

Have a wonderful day—enjoy every moment!

NOTES

Photo courtesy of Emma Dodge Hanson Photography

Your Budget

Wedding Costs

It is now time to combine your wedding vision with the amount you have budgeted for your wedding. Many couples are surprised by how much weddings truly cost. Today, the average wedding cost for 200 guests is $18,000. It is important that you understand your budget and how much you and your family can afford.

Each particular item's cost, such as attire and food, will be determined by your style, the location of your wedding and what you can spend on your wedding. It depends on what is most important to you, what you can live without and what is a "must". You may have to change your style slightly to fit your budget, but you can still have the same overall effect with just slight modifications.

There are many hidden costs associated with a wedding; be diligent and identify them. If your family is helping with the wedding, be sensitive to their financial situation. Although money may not be an issue for your families, they will still appreciate your courtesy about this matter.

Who Pays For What?

The traditional protocol of who pays for what has become less clear in recent years. It depends on the individual and families' financial situations. The fact that many people are waiting until later in life to get married also complicates the issue. The budget lists who traditionally pays for each particular item, but it has become more of a matter of who can help financially, whether it's the bride's or groom's family, not what is traditional.

Percentages

On average, weddings costs are as such:

50% Reception

15% Photography

10% Music

10% Flowers

7% Bride's attire

5% Invitations

3% Other Items

Traditional Breakdown of Costs

Below is the traditional separation of costs. As mentioned previously, this is just a guideline and not a rule. Weddings can be expensive and the financial weight has become less and less solely a bride's family responsibility. Many couples, along with both sets of parents, are sharing the expense of the wedding. This is a personal decision and only you can determine what will work for you and your families.

Bride

Groom's wedding ring

Gift for groom

Gifts for bride's attendants

Bride's Family

Engagement party

Consultant

Gown and accessories

Invitations and announcements

All flowers except bride's bouquet
and corsages for the mothers

Total cost of ceremony except the
clergy fee

Total cost of reception

Photography

Transportation for bridal party

Accommodations for attendants

Wedding gift for bride and groom

Attendants luncheon

Groom

Bride's wedding and engagement
rings

Bride's gift

Marriage license

All honeymoon expenses

Gift for groom's attendants

Clergy's fee

Groom's Family

Groom's attire

Groom's attendants' accessories
for their attire

Boutonnieres for the men of
the wedding party

Bride's bouquet and mothers'
corsages

Rehearsal dinner

Accommodations for groom's
attendants

Groom's family travel and hotel
expenses

Wedding gift for the bride and
groom

Wedding Attendants

Wedding attire

Travel expenses

Gift for bride and groom

Parties for the bride and groom

The Budget Spreadsheet

Like the "Check List" in this book, you will also use the Budget Spreadsheet as a guideline. Cross out what you do not need and add what you do. Be sure to include the tips, taxes and other additional expenses when necessary.

Special Check Marks and Spaces

The "Paid By" is to mark who will pay for that item. Be sure to plan ahead for who will be paying for what. The "First Draft" is so you can estimate how much you think it will cost and what you are willing to pay. Unfortunately, not all estimates will be on target, that is why we have included a second "Final Budget" column. This will allow you to have a better idea of actual costs and where your priorities are. "Actual" is just that, the actual cost of the item. You will probably know this amount once you confirm with a service and contract with them. If you prefer to use an electronic version, please visit our website for a link to a great Microsoft wedding budget template.

Your Budget Spreadsheet

Costs	Paid By	Draft Budget	Final Budget	Actual
Wedding Consultant				
Stationery				
Announcements				
Invitations				
Reply cards				
Reception cards				
Ceremony cards				
Pew cards				
Seating place cards				
Programs for ceremony				
Wedding announcements				
Maps, accommodations list				
Thank-you notes				
Calligraphy				

Costs	Paid By	Draft Budget	Final Budget	Actual
Napkins and matchbooks				
Postage				
The Ceremony				
Ceremony site				
Ceremony officiant				
Ceremony musicians				
Ring bearer pillow				
Flower girl basket				
Birdseed or flower packages				
Guest book, pen				
Alter candelabra				
Aisle runner				
The Wedding Attire				
Bride's gown				
Alterations				
Headpiece and veil				
Undergarments				
Jewelry				
Shoes				
Groom's formal wear				
Alterations				
Groom's accessories				
Beauty				
Massages				
Hairdresser				
Facial/makeup artist				
Manicure/pedicure				
Groom's haircut				

Costs	Paid By	Draft Budget	Final Budget	Actual
Photography and Video				
Bride and groom's album				
Parents' album				
Formal portraits				
Extra prints				
Proofs/previews				
Negatives				
Extra hours				
Extra film				
Video production				
Copies of video				
Costs for Attendants				
Bridal luncheon				
Attendants' accommodations				
Gifts for groom's attendants				
Gifts for bride's attendants				
Flowers				
Ceremony flowers				
Bride's flowers				
Tossing flowers				
All attendants flowers				
Floral hairpieces				
Mothers' flowers				
Other relatives and friends				
Reception flowers				
Cake flowers				
Flower set up & delivery				

Costs	Paid By	Draft Budget	Final Budget	Actual
Reception				
Location fee				
Hors d'oeuvres				
Main meal				
Bartending				
Beverages				
Cake cutting				
Champagne toast				
Toast glasses				
Valet and parking				
Coat and bathroom attendant				
Security				
Other _____				
Other _____				
Reception Rental Items and Decorations				
Tent				
Tables and chairs				
Tableware and linens				
Candles and lanterns				
Heaters				
Centerpieces				
Balloons				
Other _____				
Other _____				
Entertainment				
Reception music				
Soloist				
Dance lessons				
Other_____				

Costs	Paid By	Draft Budget	Final Budget	Actual
Cakes				
Wedding cake				
Groom's cake				
Wedding cake knife				
Cake delivery and set-up				
Cake top wrapping				
Candy gifts for guests				
Transportation				
Limousines				
Car rental				
Horse and buggy				
Other_____				
Rehearsal Dinner				
Additional Costs				
Newspaper announcements				
Marriage license				
Gown preservation				
Bouquet preservation				
Guest gift baskets				
Wedding bands				
Engagement ring				
Groom's gift				
Bride's gift				
Honeymoon				
Transportation				
Accommodations				
Attire				
Spending money				
Other_____				

NOTES

NOTES

Photo courtesy of Emma Dodge Hanson Photography

Worksheets

Appointment Calendar
January

Date & Time _____   Date & Time _____

Service _____   Service _____

Phone _____   Phone _____

Contact _____   Contact _____

Date & Time _____   Date & Time _____

Service _____   Service _____

Phone _____   Phone _____

Contact _____   Contact _____

Date & Time _____   Date & Time _____

Service _____   Service _____

Phone _____   Phone _____

Contact _____   Contact _____

Date & Time _____   Date & Time _____

Service _____   Service _____

Phone _____   Phone _____

Contact _____   Contact _____

Date & Time _____   Date & Time _____

Service _____   Service _____

Phone _____   Phone _____

Contact _____   Contact _____

Appointment Calendar
February

Date & Time _____

Service _____

Phone _____

Contact _____

Date & Time _____

Service _____

Phone _____

Contact _____

Date & Time _____

Service _____

Phone _____

Contact _____

Date & Time _____

Service _____

Phone _____

Contact _____

Date & Time _____

Service _____

Phone _____

Contact _____

Date & Time _____

Service _____

Phone _____

Contact _____

Date & Time _____

Service _____

Phone _____

Contact _____

Date & Time _____

Service _____

Phone _____

Contact _____

Date & Time _____

Service _____

Phone _____

Contact _____

Date & Time _____

Service _____

Phone _____

Contact _____

Date & Time _____

Service _____

Phone _____

Contact _____

Date & Time _____

Service _____

Phone _____

Contact _____

Date & Time _____

Service _____

Phone _____

Contact _____

Date & Time _____

Service _____

Phone _____

Contact _____

Appointment Calendar
March

Date & Time _____

Service _____

Phone _____

Contact _____

Date & Time _____

Service _____

Phone _____

Contact _____

Date & Time _____

Service _____

Phone _____

Contact _____

Date & Time _____

Service _____

Phone _____

Contact _____

Date & Time _____

Service _____

Phone _____

Contact _____

Date & Time _____

Service _____

Phone _____

Contact _____

Date & Time _____

Service _____

Phone _____

Contact _____

Date & Time _____

Service _____

Phone _____

Contact _____

Date & Time _____

Service _____

Phone _____

Contact _____

Date & Time _____

Service _____

Phone _____

Contact _____

Date & Time _____

Service _____

Phone _____

Contact _____

Date & Time _____

Service _____

Phone _____

Contact _____

Appointment Calendar
April

Date & Time _____   Date & Time _____

Service _____   Service _____

Phone _____   Phone _____

Contact _____   Contact _____

Date & Time _____   Date & Time _____

Service _____   Service _____

Phone _____   Phone _____

Contact _____   Contact _____

Date & Time _____   Date & Time _____

Service _____   Service _____

Phone _____   Phone _____

Contact _____   Contact _____

Date & Time _____   Date & Time _____

Service _____   Service _____

Phone _____   Phone _____

Contact _____   Contact _____

Date & Time _____   Date & Time _____

Service _____   Service _____

Phone _____   Phone _____

Contact _____   Contact _____

Date & Time _____   Date & Time _____

Service _____   Service _____

Phone _____   Phone _____

Contact _____   Contact _____

Appointment Calendar
May

Date & Time _____   Date & Time _____

Service _____   Service _____

Phone _____   Phone _____

Contact _____   Contact _____

Date & Time _____   Date & Time _____

Service _____   Service _____

Phone _____   Phone _____

Contact _____   Contact _____

Date & Time _____   Date & Time _____

Service _____   Service _____

Phone _____   Phone _____

Contact _____   Contact _____

Date & Time _____   Date & Time _____

Service _____   Service _____

Phone _____   Phone _____

Contact _____   Contact _____

Date & Time _____   Date & Time _____

Service _____   Service _____

Phone _____   Phone _____

Contact _____   Contact _____

Date & Time _____   Date & Time _____

Service _____   Service _____

Phone _____   Phone _____

Contact _____   Contact _____

Appointment Calendar
June

Date & Time _____   Date & Time _____

Service _____   Service _____

Phone _____   Phone _____

Contact _____   Contact _____

Date & Time _____   Date & Time _____

Service _____   Service _____

Phone _____   Phone _____

Contact _____   Contact _____

Date & Time _____   Date & Time _____

Service _____   Service _____

Phone _____   Phone _____

Contact _____   Contact _____

Date & Time _____   Date & Time _____

Service _____   Service _____

Phone _____   Phone _____

Contact _____   Contact _____

Date & Time _____   Date & Time _____

Service _____   Service _____

Phone _____   Phone _____

Contact _____   Contact _____

Date & Time _____   Date & Time _____

Service _____   Service _____

Phone _____   Phone _____

Contact _____   Contact _____

Appointment Calendar
July

Date & Time _____   Date & Time _____

Service _____   Service _____

Phone _____   Phone _____

Contact _____   Contact _____

Date & Time _____   Date & Time _____

Service _____   Service _____

Phone _____   Phone _____

Contact _____   Contact _____

Date & Time _____   Date & Time _____

Service _____   Service _____

Phone _____   Phone _____

Contact _____   Contact _____

Date & Time _____   Date & Time _____

Service _____   Service _____

Phone _____   Phone _____

Contact _____   Contact _____

Date & Time _____   Date & Time _____

Service _____   Service _____

Phone _____   Phone _____

Contact _____   Contact _____

Date & Time _____   Date & Time _____

Service _____   Service _____

Phone _____   Phone _____

Contact _____   Contact _____

Appointment Calendar
August

Date & Time _____

Service _____

Phone _____

Contact _____

Date & Time _____

Service _____

Phone _____

Contact _____

Date & Time _____

Service _____

Phone _____

Contact _____

Date & Time _____

Service _____

Phone _____

Contact _____

Date & Time _____

Service _____

Phone _____

Contact _____

Date & Time _____

Service _____

Phone _____

Contact _____

Date & Time _____

Service _____

Phone _____

Contact _____

Date & Time _____

Service _____

Phone _____

Contact _____

Date & Time _____

Service _____

Phone _____

Contact _____

Date & Time _____

Service _____

Phone _____

Contact _____

Date & Time _____

Service _____

Phone _____

Contact _____

Date & Time _____

Service _____

Phone _____

Contact _____

Appointment Calendar
September

Date & Time _____ Date & Time _____

Service _____ Service _____

Phone _____ Phone _____

Contact _____ Contact _____

Date & Time _____ Date & Time _____

Service _____ Service _____

Phone _____ Phone _____

Contact _____ Contact _____

Date & Time _____ Date & Time _____

Service _____ Service _____

Phone _____ Phone _____

Contact _____ Contact _____

Date & Time _____ Date & Time _____

Service _____ Service _____

Phone _____ Phone _____

Contact _____ Contact _____

Date & Time _____ Date & Time _____

Service _____ Service _____

Phone _____ Phone _____

Contact _____ Contact _____

Date & Time _____ Date & Time _____

Service _____ Service _____

Phone _____ Phone _____

Contact _____ Contact _____

Appointment Calendar
October

Date & Time _____

Service _____

Phone _____

Contact _____

Date & Time _____

Service _____

Phone _____

Contact _____

Date & Time _____

Service _____

Phone _____

Contact _____

Date & Time _____

Service _____

Phone _____

Contact _____

Date & Time _____

Service _____

Phone _____

Contact _____

Date & Time _____

Service _____

Phone _____

Contact _____

Date & Time _____

Service _____

Phone _____

Contact _____

Date & Time _____

Service _____

Phone _____

Contact _____

Date & Time _____

Service _____

Phone _____

Contact _____

Date & Time _____

Service _____

Phone _____

Contact _____

Date & Time _____

Service _____

Phone _____

Contact _____

Date & Time _____

Service _____

Phone _____

Contact _____

Appointment Calendar
November

Date & Time _____

Service _____

Phone _____

Contact _____

Date & Time _____

Service _____

Phone _____

Contact _____

Date & Time _____

Service _____

Phone _____

Contact _____

Date & Time _____

Service _____

Phone _____

Contact _____

Date & Time _____

Service _____

Phone _____

Contact _____

Date & Time _____

Service _____

Phone _____

Contact _____

Date & Time _____

Service _____

Phone _____

Contact _____

Date & Time _____

Service _____

Phone _____

Contact _____

Date & Time _____

Service _____

Phone _____

Contact _____

Date & Time _____

Service _____

Phone _____

Contact _____

Date & Time _____

Service _____

Phone _____

Contact _____

Date & Time _____

Service _____

Phone _____

Contact _____

Appointment Calendar
December

Date & Time _____

Service _____

Phone _____

Contact _____

Date & Time _____

Service _____

Phone _____

Contact _____

Date & Time _____

Service _____

Phone _____

Contact _____

Date & Time _____

Service _____

Phone _____

Contact _____

Date & Time _____

Service _____

Phone _____

Contact _____

Date & Time _____

Service _____

Phone _____

Contact _____

Date & Time _____

Service _____

Phone _____

Contact _____

Date & Time _____

Service _____

Phone _____

Contact _____

Date & Time _____

Service _____

Phone _____

Contact _____

Date & Time _____

Service _____

Phone _____

Contact _____

Date & Time _____

Service _____

Phone _____

Contact _____

Date & Time _____

Service _____

Phone _____

Contact _____

Important Names and Numbers

Association _____   Association _____
Name _____   Name _____
Phone _____   Phone _____
Fax _____   Fax _____
Email _____   Email _____

Association _____   Association _____
Name _____   Name _____
Phone _____   Phone _____
Fax _____   Fax _____
Email _____   Email _____

Association _____   Association _____
Name _____   Name _____
Phone _____   Phone _____
Fax _____   Fax _____
Email _____   Email _____

Association _____   Association _____
Name _____   Name _____
Phone _____   Phone _____
Fax _____   Fax _____
Email _____   Email _____

Association _____   Association _____
Name _____   Name _____
Phone _____   Phone _____
Fax _____   Fax _____
Email _____   Email _____

Important Names and Numbers

Association _____

Name _____

Phone _____

Fax _____

Email _____

Association _____

Name _____

Phone _____

Fax _____

Email _____

Association _____

Name _____

Phone _____

Fax _____

Email _____

Association _____

Name _____

Phone _____

Fax _____

Email _____

Association _____

Name _____

Phone _____

Fax _____

Email _____

Association _____

Name _____

Phone _____

Fax _____

Email _____

Association _____

Name _____

Phone _____

Fax _____

Email _____

Association _____

Name _____

Phone _____

Fax _____

Email _____

Association _____

Name _____

Phone _____

Fax _____

Email _____

Association _____

Name _____

Phone _____

Fax _____

Email _____

Important Names and Numbers

Association _____

Name _____

Phone _____

Fax _____

Email _____

Association _____

Name _____

Phone _____

Fax _____

Email _____

Association _____

Name _____

Phone _____

Fax _____

Email _____

Association _____

Name _____

Phone _____

Fax _____

Email _____

Association _____

Name _____

Phone _____

Fax _____

Email _____

Association _____

Name _____

Phone _____

Fax _____

Email _____

Association _____

Name _____

Phone _____

Fax _____

Email _____

Association _____

Name _____

Phone _____

Fax _____

Email _____

Association _____

Name _____

Phone _____

Fax _____

Email _____

Association _____

Name _____

Phone _____

Fax _____

Email _____

Important Names and Numbers

Association _____

Name _____

Phone _____

Fax _____

Email _____

Association _____

Name _____

Phone _____

Fax _____

Email _____

Association _____

Name _____

Phone _____

Fax _____

Email _____

Association _____

Name _____

Phone _____

Fax _____

Email _____

Association _____

Name _____

Phone _____

Fax _____

Email _____

Association _____

Name _____

Phone _____

Fax _____

Email _____

Association _____

Name _____

Phone _____

Fax _____

Email _____

Association _____

Name _____

Phone _____

Fax _____

Email _____

Association _____

Name _____

Phone _____

Fax _____

Email _____

Association _____

Name _____

Phone _____

Fax _____

Email _____

The Wedding Party

Name _____   Work Phone _____

Address _____   Home Phone _____

Position _____   Size _____

Transportation _____   Lodging _____

Name _____   Work Phone _____

Address _____   Home Phone _____

Position _____   Size _____

Transportation _____   Lodging _____

Name _____   Work Phone _____

Address _____   Home Phone _____

Position _____   Size _____

Transportation _____   Lodging _____

Name _____   Work Phone _____

Address _____   Home Phone _____

Position _____   Size _____

Transportation _____   Lodging _____

Name _____   Work Phone _____

Address _____   Home Phone _____

Position _____   Size _____

Transportation _____   Lodging _____

Name _____   Work Phone _____

Address _____   Home Phone _____

Position _____   Size _____

Transportation _____   Lodging _____

The Wedding Party

Name _____   Work Phone _____

Address _____   Home Phone _____

Position _____   Size _____

Transportation _____   Lodging _____

Name _____   Work Phone _____

Address _____   Home Phone _____

Position _____   Size _____

Transportation _____   Lodging _____

Name _____   Work Phone _____

Address _____   Home Phone _____

Position _____   Size _____

Transportation _____   Lodging _____

Name _____   Work Phone _____

Address _____   Home Phone _____

Position _____   Size _____

Transportation _____   Lodging _____

Name _____   Work Phone _____

Address _____   Home Phone _____

Position _____   Size _____

Transportation _____   Lodging _____

Name _____   Work Phone _____

Address _____   Home Phone _____

Position _____   Size _____

Transportation _____   Lodging _____

The Wedding Party

Name _____   Work Phone _____

Address _____   Home Phone _____

Position _____   Size _____

Transportation _____   Lodging _____

Name _____   Work Phone _____

Address _____   Home Phone _____

Position _____   Size _____

Transportation _____   Lodging _____

Name _____   Work Phone _____

Address _____   Home Phone _____

Position _____   Size _____

Transportation _____   Lodging _____

Name _____   Work Phone _____

Address _____   Home Phone _____

Position _____   Size _____

Transportation _____   Lodging _____

Name _____   Work Phone _____

Address _____   Home Phone _____

Position _____   Size _____

Transportation _____   Lodging _____

Name _____   Work Phone _____

Address _____   Home Phone _____

Position _____   Size _____

Transportation _____   Lodging _____

The Wedding Party

Name _____   Work Phone _____

Address _____   Home Phone _____

Position _____   Size _____

Transportation _____   Lodging _____

Name _____   Work Phone _____

Address _____   Home Phone _____

Position _____   Size _____

Transportation _____   Lodging _____

Name _____   Work Phone _____

Address _____   Home Phone _____

Position _____   Size _____

Transportation _____   Lodging _____

Name _____   Work Phone _____

Address _____   Home Phone _____

Position _____   Size _____

Transportation _____   Lodging _____

Name _____   Work Phone _____

Address _____   Home Phone _____

Position _____   Size _____

Transportation _____   Lodging _____

Name _____   Work Phone _____

Address _____   Home Phone _____

Position _____   Size _____

Transportation _____   Lodging _____

Guest Transportation and Travel

Guest

Arriving:

Airline_____ Date_____ Time_____ Flight#_____

Picked up by _____ Brought to _____

Departing:

Airline_____ Date_____ Time_____ Flight#_____

Dropped off by _____ Taken to _____

Guest

Arriving:

Airline_____ Date_____ Time_____ Flight#_____

Picked up by _____ Brought to _____

Departing:

Airline_____ Date_____ Time_____ Flight#_____

Dropped off by _____ Taken to _____

Guest

Arriving:

Airline_____ Date_____ Time_____ Flight#_____

Picked up by _____ Brought to _____

Departing:

Airline_____ Date_____ Time_____ Flight#_____

Dropped off by _____ Taken to _____

Guest

Arriving:

Airline_____ Date_____ Time_____ Flight#_____

Picked up by _____ Brought to _____

Departing:

Airline_____ Date_____ Time_____ Flight#_____

Dropped off by _____ Taken to _____

Guest Transportation and Travel

Guest

Arriving:

Airline_____ Date _____ Time_____ Flight# _____

Picked up by _____ Brought to _____

Departing:

Airline_____ Date _____ Time_____ Flight# _____

Dropped off by _____ Taken to _____

Guest

Arriving:

Airline_____ Date _____ Time_____ Flight# _____

Picked up by _____ Brought to _____

Departing:

Airline_____ Date _____ Time_____ Flight# _____

Dropped off by _____ Taken to _____

Guest

Arriving:

Airline_____ Date _____ Time_____ Flight# _____

Picked up by _____ Brought to _____

Departing:

Airline_____ Date _____ Time_____ Flight# _____

Dropped off by _____ Taken to _____

Guest

Arriving:

Airline_____ Date _____ Time_____ Flight# _____

Picked up by _____ Brought to _____

Departing:

Airline_____ Date _____ Time_____ Flight# _____

Dropped off by _____ Taken to _____

Guest Transportation and Travel

Guest

Arriving:

Airline_____ Date _____ Time_____ Flight# _____

Picked up by _____ Brought to _____

Departing:

Airline_____ Date _____ Time_____ Flight# _____

Dropped off by _____ Taken to_____

Guest

Arriving:

Airline_____ Date _____ Time_____ Flight# _____

Picked up by _____ Brought to _____

Departing:

Airline_____ Date _____ Time_____ Flight# _____

Dropped off by _____ Taken to_____

Guest

Arriving:

Airline_____ Date _____ Time_____ Flight# _____

Picked up by _____ Brought to _____

Departing:

Airline_____ Date _____ Time_____ Flight# _____

Dropped off by _____ Taken to_____

Guest

Arriving:

Airline_____ Date _____ Time_____ Flight# _____

Picked up by _____ Brought to _____

Departing:

Airline_____ Date _____ Time_____ Flight# _____

Dropped off by _____ Taken to_____

Guest Transportation and Travel

Guest

Arriving:

Airline_____ Date _____ Time_____ Flight# _____

Picked up by _____ Brought to _____

Departing:

Airline_____ Date _____ Time_____ Flight# _____

Dropped off by_____ Taken to_____

Guest

Arriving:

Airline_____ Date _____ Time_____ Flight# _____

Picked up by _____ Brought to _____

Departing:

Airline_____ Date _____ Time_____ Flight# _____

Dropped off by_____ Taken to_____

Guest

Arriving:

Airline_____ Date _____ Time_____ Flight# _____

Picked up by _____ Brought to _____

Departing:

Airline_____ Date _____ Time_____ Flight# _____

Dropped off by_____ Taken to_____

Guest

Arriving:

Airline_____ Date _____ Time_____ Flight# _____

Picked up by _____ Brought to _____

Departing:

Airline_____ Date _____ Time_____ Flight# _____

Dropped off by_____ Taken to_____

Guest Transportation and Travel

Guest

Arriving:

Airline_____ Date _____ Time_____ Flight#_____

Picked up by _____ Brought to _____

Departing:

Airline_____ Date _____ Time_____ Flight#_____

Dropped off by _____ Taken to _____

Guest

Arriving:

Airline_____ Date _____ Time_____ Flight#_____

Picked up by _____ Brought to _____

Departing:

Airline_____ Date _____ Time_____ Flight#_____

Dropped off by _____ Taken to _____

Guest

Arriving:

Airline_____ Date _____ Time_____ Flight#_____

Picked up by _____ Brought to _____

Departing:

Airline_____ Date _____ Time_____ Flight#_____

Dropped off by _____ Taken to _____

Guest

Arriving:

Airline_____ Date _____ Time_____ Flight#_____

Picked up by _____ Brought to _____

Departing:

Airline_____ Date _____ Time_____ Flight#_____

Dropped off by _____ Taken to _____

Guest Transportation and Travel

Guest

Arriving:

Airline_____ Date _____ Time_____ Flight# _____

Picked up by _____ Brought to _____

Departing:

Airline_____ Date _____ Time_____ Flight# _____

Dropped off by _____ Taken to_____

Guest

Arriving:

Airline_____ Date _____ Time_____ Flight# _____

Picked up by _____ Brought to _____

Departing:

Airline_____ Date _____ Time_____ Flight# _____

Dropped off by _____ Taken to_____

Guest

Arriving:

Airline_____ Date _____ Time_____ Flight# _____

Picked up by _____ Brought to _____

Departing:

Airline_____ Date _____ Time_____ Flight# _____

Dropped off by _____ Taken to_____

Guest

Arriving:

Airline_____ Date _____ Time_____ Flight# _____

Picked up by _____ Brought to _____

Departing:

Airline_____ Date _____ Time_____ Flight# _____

Dropped off by _____ Taken to_____

Thank-You Lists

Reason for Thank-You	Person To Thank	Address	Date	Thanked By Whom

Thank-You Lists

Reason for Thank-You	Person To Thank	Address	Date	Thanked By Whom

Thank-You Lists

Reason for Thank-You	Person To Thank	Address	Date	Thanked By Whom

Thank-You Lists

Reason for Thank-You	Person To Thank	Address	Date	Thanked By Whom

NOTES

Photo courtesy of Portrait Gallery

NOTES

Bride's Blue Pages

Professional Services Directory

All About Vermont

Vermont Convention Bureau
Burlington, VT
(802) 863-3489
www.vermontmeetings.org

Banquets & Reception Sites

1066 Ye Olde England Inne
Stowe, VT
(802) 253-5320
www.stoweromance.com

Barn at Boyden Farm
Cambridge, VT
(802) 644-6363
www.boydenfarm.com

Burke Mountain
East Burke, VT
(802) 626-7394
www.skiburke.com

Burlington Country Club
Burlington, VT
(802) 864-6646
www.burlingtoncountryclub.org

Dreaming Mountain
Johnson, VT
(802) 279-8947
www.dreamingmountain.com

Echo Lake Aquarium & Science Center
Burlington, VT
(802) 864-1848
www.echovermont.org

Edson Hill Manor
Stowe, VT
(802) 253-7371
www.edsonhillmanor.com

English Rose Inn
Montgomery Center, VT
(802) 326-3232
www.englishroseinn.com

The Essex
Vermont's Culinary Resort and Spa
Essex Junction, VT
(802) 878-1100
www.vtculinaryresort.com

Grand Isle Lake House
Grand Isle, VT
(802) 372-5024
www.grandislelakehouse.com

Green Mountain Inn
Stowe, VT
(802) 253-7301
www.greenmountaininn.com

Hampton Inn Burlington
Burlington, VT
(802) 654-7646
www.hamptoninnburlington.com

Hilton Burlington
Burlington, VT
(802) 658-6501
www.burlington.hilton.com

Inn at Mountain View Farm
East Burke, VT
(802) 626-9924
www.innmtnview.com

Old Stone House Museum
Orleans, VT
(802) 754-2022
www.oldstonehousemuseum.org

The Ponds at Bolton Valley
Bolton Valley, VT
(802) 434-6848
www.thepondsvt.com

Quarry Hill Club
South Burlington, VT
(802) 233-2563
www.quarryhillclub.com

Stowe Mountain Lodge
Stowe, VT
(802) 253-3560
www.stowemountainlodge.com

Stowe Mountain Resort
Stowe, VT
(802) 253-3558
www.stowe.com

Stoweflake Mountain Resort & Spa
Stowe, VT
(802) 253-7355
www.stoweflake.com

Stowehof Inn & Resort
Stowe, VT
(800) 932-7136
www.stowehofinn.com

Tabor House Inn
West Swanton, VT
(802) 868-7575
www.taborhouseinn.com

Trapp Family Lodge
Stowe, VT
(802) 253-8512
www.trappfamily.com

Beauty & Spa Services

The Essex
Vermont's Culinary Resort and Spa
Essex Junction, VT
(802) 878-1100
www.vtculinaryresort.com

Makeup Artist, ect.
Williston, VT
(802) 878-1236
www.makeupartistect.com

Catering & Bartending

**Blood's Seafood, Catering & Party
Rentals**
White River Junction, VT
(802) 295-5393
www.bloodsseafood.com

Tasty Persuasions
Grand Isle, VT
(802) 372-3123
www.tastypersuasions.com

Ceremony Sites & Officiants

Dreaming Mountain
Johnson, VT
(802) 279-8945
www.dreamingmountain.com

First Unitarian Universalist Society
Burlington, VT
(802) 862-5630
www.uusociety.org

Consultants & Planners

VT Weddings by Kim
North Troy, VT
(802) 988-4730
www.vtweddingsbykim.com

Decorations & Rental Items

**Blood's Seafood, Catering & Party
Rentals**
White River Junction, VT
(802) 295-5393
www.bloodsseafood.com

Florists

Creative Muse Floral Design
Enosburg Falls, VT
(802) 933-4403
www.creativemusevt.com

From Maria's Garden
Stowe, VT
(802) 345-3698
www.frommariasgarden.com

Maplehurst Florist
Essex Junction, VT
(802) 878-8113
www.maplehurstflorist.com

Gifts & Favors

Vermont Art Store
Averil, VT
(802) 822-5500
www.vermontartstore.com

Creative Chocolates of Vermont, Inc.
Essex Junction, VT
(802) 891-6048
www.creativechocolatesofvt.com

Music & Entertainment

Peak Entertainment
Stowe, VT
(802) 888-6978
www.peakdj.com

Best Bands
Hinesburg, VT
(800) 639-6380
www.bestbands.com

Evergreen Erb, Celtic Harp Music
Jericho, VT
(802) 899-3231
www.heartslonging.com

Full Circle
Burlington, VT
(802) 658-0832

Photography & Video

Cyndi Freeman Photography
Burlington, VT
(802) 658-3733
www.cyndifreeman.com

Jeff Schneiderman Photography
Williston, VT
(802) 878-0769
www.jsphotos.com

Landwerhle Photography
Stowe, VT
(802) 253-8831
www.llphoto.com

Lauren Stagnitti Photography
Stowe, VT
(802) 888-5433
www.laurenstagnitti.com

Saint Phalle Photography
Johnson, VT
(802) 635-2262
www.saintphallephoto.com

Rehearsal Dinners

Echo Lake Aquarium & Science Center
Burlington, VT
(802) 864-1848
www.echovermont.org

Transportation

White Mountain Limousine Service
Lyman, NH
(866) 824-5466
www.whitemountainlimo.com

Travel & Honeymoon

Dream Escapes Travel
Milton, VT
(888) 802-7364
www.honeymoon-travel-ideas.com

All About Vermont

Vermont Chamber of Commerce
Montpelier, VT
(802) 229-2294
www.vtchamber.com

Banquets & Reception Sites

Basin Harbor Club
Vergennes, VT
(802) 475-2311
www.basinharbor.com

Blueberry Hill Inn
Goshen, VT
(800) 448-0707
www.blueberryhillinn.com

Common Ground Center
Starksboro, VT
(802) 453-2592
www.cgcvt.org

Hawk Inn & Mountain Resort
Plymouth, VT
(802) 672-2101
www.hawkresort.com

The Inn at Baldwin Creek & Mary's Restaurant
Bristol, VT
(802) 453-2432
www.innatbaldwincreek.com

Inn at the Round Barn Farm
Waitsfield, VT
(802) 496-2276
www.theroundbarn.com

Inn at Lareau Farm
Waitsfield, VT
(802) 496-4949
www.laureaufarminn.com

Middlebury Inn
Middlebury, VT
(800) 842-4666
www.middleburyinn.com

The Old Lantern
Charlotte, VT
(802) 355-4396
www.oldlantern.com

Quechee Inn
Quechee, VT
(802) 295-3133
www.quecheeinn.com

Skinner Barn
Waitsfield, VT
(802) 496-4422
www.theskinnerbarn.com

Sugarbush Resort
Warren, VT
(802) 583-6804
www.sugarbush.com

Vergennes Opera House
Vergennes, VT
(802) 877-6737
www.vergennesoperahouse.com

Vermont State Parks
Waterbury, VT
(802) 241-3683
www.vtstateparks.com

Woodstock Inn & Resort
Woodstock, VT
(802) 457-1100
www.woodstockinn.com

Beauty & Spa Services

Makeup Artist, ect.
Williston, VT
(802) 878-1236
www.makeupartistect.com

Bridal & Formal Attire

College Formals of West Lebanon
West Lebanon, NH
(603) 298-7868
www.collegeformals.com

Lubiana's Bridal
Barre, VT
(802) 479-1966
www.lubianasbridal.com

Catering & Bartending

Blood's Seafood, Catering & Party Rentals
White River Junction, VT
(802) 295-5393
www.bloodsseafood.com

The Linen Shop at Occasions Catering
Rochester, VT
(802) 767-3272
www.occasionsvt.com

Ceremony Sites & Officiants

Greg Trulson & Stephanie Koonz
Waterbury, VT
(802) 244-5378

Vermont State Parks
Waterbury, VT
(802) 241-3683
www.vtstateparks.com

Consultants & Planners

Central Reservations of Vermont
Waitsfield, VT
(800) 451-4574
www.vtvacation.com

Megan Schultz Events & Designs
Moretown, VT
(802) 496-6466
www.meganschultz.com

Woodstock Productions
Woodstock, VT
(802) 356-5060
www.WoodstockProductions.com

Decorations & Rental Items

Abbott Rental
Littleton, NH
(800) 287-6557
www.abbottrental.com

Blood's Seafood, Catering & Party Rentals
White River Junction, VT
(802) 295-5393
www.bloodsseafood.com

Dimmick Wastewater Service
Randolph, VT
(802) 728-3805
www.dimmickseptic.com

Rain or Shine Tent & Events
Randolph Center, VT
(802) 728-3630
www.rainorshinevt.com

Weddings Tents & Events
Waitsfield, VT
(802) 496-3545
www.weddingstentsevents.com

Gifts & Favors

Comfort Cookies
North Ferrisburgh, VT
(802) 377-2873
www.comfortcookiesinc.com

Creative Chocolates of Vermont, Inc.
Essex Junction, VT
(802) 891-6048
www.creativechocolatesofvt.com

Invitations & Addressing

Robin Lindsay Fine Art & Design
Concord, NH
(603) 727-8581
www.robinlindsay.net

Music & Entertainment

Best Bands
Hinesburg, VT
(800) 639-6380
www.bestbands.com

Evergreen Erb, Celtic Harp Music
Jericho, VT
(802) 899-3231
www.heartslonging.com

Full Circle
Burlington, VT
(802) 658-0832

Lisa Carlson
Middlesex, VT
(802) 229-9901
www.lisaflute.com

Peak Entertainment
Stowe, VT
(802) 888-6978
www.peakdj.com

Tony's Mobil Sound Show
Bridport, VT
(888) 821-3511
www.tonysmobilesoundshow.com

Photography & Video

Barrie Fisher Photography
Waitsfield, VT
(802) 496-5215
www.bfisherphoto.com

Charlie Brown Productions
Waitsfield, VT
(802) 583-2410
www.charliebrownspage.com

Donna Lee Cook Photography
East Thetford, VT
(802) 333-9812
www.donnaleecookphotography.com

Jeff Schneiderman Photography
Williston, VT
(802) 878-0769
www.jsphotos.com

Transportation

Burlington Limousine & Car Service
Middlebury, VT
(802) 288-9810
www.burlingtonvtlimo.com

Hanover Limousine
Hanover, NH
(603) 298-8880
www.hanoverlimousine.com

Munson Horse & Buggy
Westford, VT
(802) 878-7715
www.kjmunsonhorseandbuggy.com

Travel & Honeymoon

Dream Escapes Travel
Milton, VT
(888) 802-7364
www.honeymoon-travel-ideas.co

All About Vermont

Okemo Valley Region Chamber of Commerce
Ludlow, VT
(802) 228-5830
www.yourplaceinvermont.com

Banquets & Reception Sites

1768 Hubbell Homestead at Colgate Park
Bennington, VT
(802) 447-3900
www.hubbellhomestead.com

The Arlington Inn
Arlington, VT
(802) 375-6532
www.arlingtoninn.com

The Brandon Inn
Brandon, VT
(802) 247-5766
www.historicbrandoninn.com

Castle Hill Resort & Spa
Ludlow, VT
(802) 226-7361
www.castlehillresort.com

Cooper Hill Inn
East Dover, VT
(802) 348-6333
www.cooperhillinn.com

Echo Lake Inn
Ludlow, VT
(802) 228-8602
www.echolakeinn.com

Equinox Resort & Spa
Manchester Village, VT
(802) 362-4700
www.equinoxresort.com

Honora Winery & Vineyard
West Halifax, VT
(802) 368-2930
www.honorawinery.com

Inn at Quail Run
Wilmington, VT
(802) 464-0942
www.theinnatquailrun.com

Inn at Westin
Weston, VT
(802) 824-6789
www.innwestin.com

Inn of the Six Mountains
Killington, VT
(802) 422-4302
www.sixmountains.com

Killington Grand Resort Hotel
Killington, VT
(888) 644-7263
www.killington.com

Landgrove Inn
Landgrove, VT
(802) 824-6673
www.landgroveinn.com

Lilac Inn
Brandon, VT
(800) 221-0720
www.lilacinn.com

Mountain Meadows Lodge
Killington, VT
(802) 775-1010
www.mountainmeadowslodge.com

Mountain Top Inn & Resort
Chittenden, VT
(802) 483-2311
www.mountaintopinn.com

Okemo Mountain Resort
Ludlow, VT
(802) 228-4041
www.functions.okemo.com

Old Tavern at Grafton
Grafton, VT
(802) 843-2211
www.oldtavern.com

Park McCullough House
North Bennington, VT
(802) 442-5441
www.parkmccullough.org

Riverside Farm
Pittsfield, VT
(802) 746-8822
www.riversidefarmweddings.com

Shelburne Musuem
Shelburne, VT
(802) 985-3346
www.shelburnemuseum.org

Vermont Inn
Killington, VT
(802) 775-0708
www.vermontinn.com

Beauty & Spa Services

Castle Hill Resort & Spa
Ludlow, VT
(802) 226-7361
www.castlehillresort.com

Hair Retreat
Manchester, VT
(802) 362-5199

Cakes

Hindinger Cakes
Perkinsville, VT
(802) 263-5924

Sharon Myers Fine Catering
Brattleboro,VT
(802) 254-2480
www.sharonmyers.com

Catering & Bartending

Bistro Henry
Manchester Ctr, VT
(802) 362-4982
www.bistrohenry.com

Blood's Seafood, Catering & Party Rentals
White River Junction, VT
(802) 295-5393
www.bloodsseafood.com

Sharon Myers Fine Catering
Brattleboro,VT
(802) 254-2480
www.sharonmyers.com

Ceremony Sites & Officiants

Dorset Church
Dorset, VT
(802) 867-2260
www.dorsetchurch.org

Consultants & Planners

Annellie Vallone Events, llc
South Burlington, VT
(802) 859-0110
www.annellieevents.com

The Wedding Wizard
South Burlington, VT
(802) 865-8989
www.weddingwizardusa.com

Decorations & Rental Items

Blood's Seafood, Catering & Party Rentals
White River Junction, VT
(802) 295-5393
www.bloodsseafood.com

Celebration Rentals
Brandon, VT
(802) 247-0002
www.celebrateinvermont.com

Green Mountain Tent Rental
Townshend, VT
(802) 365-7839
www.greenmtntents.com

Florists

Hawley's Florist
Rutland, VT
(802) 775-2573
www.hawleysflorist.com

Gifts & Favors

Klinger's Edible Art
South Burlington, VT
(802) 860-6322
www.klingersbread.com

The Party Store
Rutland, VT
(802) 773-3155
www.thepartystores.com

Vermont by the Bushel
Proctor, VT
(802) 459-2897
www.vermontbythebushel.com

Guest Accommodations

Best Western Windjammer Inn
South Burlington, VT
(802) 651-0635
www.bestwestern.com/windjammerinn

Holiday Inn Express Springfield
Springfield, VT
(802) 885-4516
www.vermonthi.com

Invitations & Addressing

The Party Store
Rutland, VT
(802) 773-3155
www.thepartystores.com

Music & Entertainment

Marina Carter
Manchester, VT
(802) 362-8124
www.vermontpianomusic.com

Peak Entertainment
Stowe, VT
(802) 888-6978
www.peakdj.com

Top Hat Entertainment
South Burlington, VT
(802) 862-2011
www.tophatdj.com

Photography & Video

Emma Dodge Hanson
Saratoga Springs, NY
(518) 587-4282
www.emmadodgehanson.com

Portrait Gallery
South Burlington, VT
(802) 864-4411
www.portraitgallery-vt.com

Transportation

Classic Limo Service
Shelburne, VT
(802) 363-5511
www.classiclimos.org

Travel & Honeymoon

Dreaming Mountain
Johnson, VT
(802) 279-8946
www.dreamingmountain.com

NOTES

NOTES

NOTES

NOTES

NOTES

Photo courtesy of Jeff Schneiderman Photography

Additional Resource Suggestions

Resource List

Below is an additional list of resources regarding a variety of specific wedding issues. The resource list has a few of my favorite magazines and books related to the wedding industry and beyond. These resources go into greater detail about topics such as style, budgets, family issues and beauty.

Small Budget

How to Have a Big Wedding on a Small Budget
by Diane Warner

Style

Martha Stewart Weddings
by Martha Stewart Magazines

Non-Traditional Wedding

Weddings for Grown Ups
by Carroll Stone

Etiquette Planning

Your Complete Wedding Planner
by Marjabelle Young Stewart

Religion

Interfaith Wedding Ceremonies
by Dovetail Publishing

Exercise and Relaxation

101 Essential Yoga Tips
by Sivananda Yoga Veendanta Centre

Beauty

Cindy Crawford's Basic Face
by Cindy Crawford

Ultimate Makeup Beauty
by Mary Quant

Ordering Information

Web Site Free Book Promotions

This year on our website you can receive one of our free promotional copies. Go to www.vermontweddingbook.com for more details.

Otherwise the book can be purchased for only $9.95:
Ordering Locations:

On the Web:

www.vermontweddingbook.com
www.amazon.com
www.bn.com

Bookstores:

Borders
Barnes and Noble
And many independent bookstores throughout Vermont

Special Promotions:

You will see our book throughout the year at special promotions. See our website order page for locations near you to get a copy of the book.

Mail Order:

For your convenience we have placed an order form on the next page.

A PERFECT GIFT!

Order Form

always get the latest edition

The Vermont, New Hampshire or South Carolina Wedding & Event Resource Guide

Wedding Resource Publishing
63 Red Chimney Road, Warner, New Hampshire 03278
Tel: 603-456-2255 • Fax: 603-368-0404
www.theweddingbook.net

GIFT FOR:

Name: _____

Address: _____

City: _____ State: _____ Zip: _____

Telephone: _____

FROM:

Name: _____

Address: _____

City: _____ State: _____ Zip: _____

Telephone: _____

_____ **Vermont Edition**　　_____ **New Hampshire Edition**

_____ **South Carolina Edition**

Book: $9.95 each (specify quantity of each above)

Sales Tax: Please add 5% sales tax for books shipped outside NH

Shipping: $3.20 for the first book and $2.00 for each additional book

Payment: Check or Money Order payable to:

Wedding Resource Publishing

No. of Book(s) _____

Sales Tax _____

Shipping _____

Total Payment _____

Quick and Easy Survey

Fax it back to 802-910-1005. Or use it as a self mailer and mail it back to us.

Please help us continue to make this book an important wedding tool for couples getting married in Vermont. Take a minute to fill out the survey completely and send it back to us.

Your name will be entered in a drawing to win a $100 gift certificate to your favorite Vermont business.

Name _____

City _____ State _____ Phone _____

Wedding Date _____ Wedding Location _____

Budget (approx.) $ _____

Number of Guests _____ Percentage of those from out-of-state _____

Are you honeymooning in Vermont? _____ Where? _____

Reason You Choose Vermont to Get Married?

_____

How did you hear about this book? _____

How did you receive this book? _____

Did you use our website (www.vermontweddingbook.com) to help you plan your wedding or event?

_____

Please list the businesses you contacted or used as a result of seeing them in our book or on our website:

_____

_____

_____

What additional information would be helpful for us to provide in the book?

_____

Would you recommend this book to a friend? _____

I give *Vermont Wedding Resource Guide* permission to quote me from this survey.

Signature _____ Date _____

Wedding Resource Publishing
P.O. Box 519
Woodstock, VT 05091

Photo courtesy of Lauren Stagnitti Wedding Photography

"This book is so well organized, it helped me relax about all the things that need to get done. It's also a good size book for keeping in my bag everywhere I go, so I can make notes of phone calls when I think of it."
Krista Hasert

"Concise, organized and full of creative ideas."
Jennifer Dumas

"The VWERG helped me to see the great variety of services out there and to choose the ones that best matched my budget."
Amy Laflam

"It was so great to have everything I need at my fingertips."
Elizabeth Dwinell

"After I got this book, I had a reception site reserved within one week!"
Jada Barton

"I am planning a long distance wedding and couldn't have done it without this book!"
Jodi Harris

"All in one book; It's great!"
Donna Goodman

"The most comprehensive single source of information about planning a wedding in Vermont…"
Vermont Life Explorer